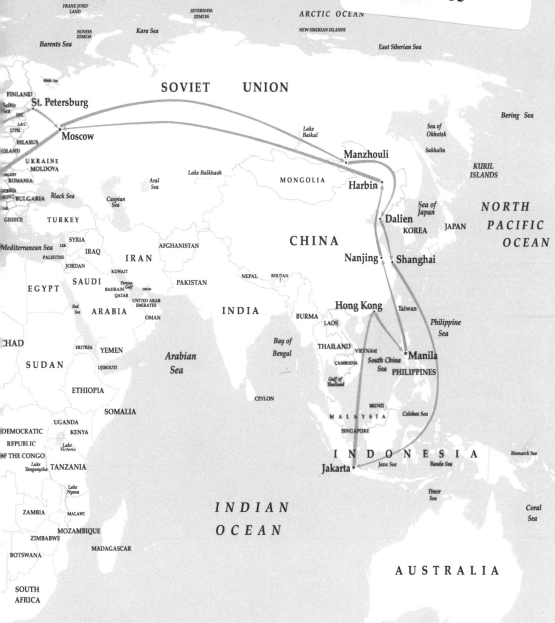

A Spy's Journey
1899-1935

KITTY HARRIS

The Spy with Seventeen Names

by

Igor Damaskin
with
Geoffrey Elliott

ST ERMIN'S
PRESS

A *St Ermin's Press* Book

First published in this form in Great Britain 2001
by *St Ermin's Press*
In association with Little, Brown and Company

A CIP catalogue record for this book is available from the British Library

ISBN: 1 903608 01 5

Typeset in Goudy by Palimpsest Book Production Limited,
Polmont, Stirlingshire
Printed and bound in Great Britain by
Clays Ltd, St Ives plc

St Ermin's Press
in association with
Little, Brown and Company (UK)
Brettenham House
Lancaster Place
London WC2E 7EN

Contents

Illustrations   vii
Preface   1
Acknowledgments   9

Prologue   13
 1 Gypsy   15
 2 Not a Care in the World   24
 3 The Windy City   31
 4 East Is East   44
 5 A Friend of a Friend   77
 6 The Spying Game   89
 7 Nazi Dances   110
 8 Back to School   132
 9 The Three Musketeers   143
10 London by Night   161
11 Night Flight   182
12 In the Shadow of the Aztec Eagle   200
13 Through Hell and Back   221
Postscript   232

Select Bibliography   244
Index   246

Illustrations

Whitechapel c. 1900, Kitty's birthplace (courtesy Guildhall Library).

Kitty Harris, a photograph taken for a false US passport.

The two loves of Kitty's life: Earl Browder photographed after his arrest in 1919, and Donald Maclean, the Foreign Office diplomat who spied for the Russians.

The leading figures of the American Communist movement in the 1920s: Jay Lovestone, William Foster, Charles Ruthenberg, Anna Damon and Max Bedacht.

Earl Browder with Tom Mann in China, late 1920s (courtesy *People's Weekly World*).

Liza and Vassily Zarubin, Kitty's long-time NKVD controllers.

The Bund, Shanghai's famous waterfront, in 1937.

The KGB headquarters, Moscow (courtesy SVR Archives).

Moscow Centre, as the actors in this story knew it – a rare view of the OGPU's headquarters in the early 1930s (courtesy SVR Archives).

Artur Artuzov, head of the INO, the OGPU's foreign department (courtesy SVR Archives).

Kitty with a hairstyle and glasses deliberately designed to create a forgettable appearance (courtesy SVR Archives).

Theodore Mally, the illegal *rezident* who ran the Cambridge Five.

Alexander Orlov, who trained and developed the Cambridge Five.

Arnold Deutsch, illegal *rezident* in London from 1933 and recruiter of the Cambridge Five.

Kitty in a rare moment of relaxation (courtesy the Harris family).

Karl Gursky, *rezident* in London 1941–3.

Grigory Grafpen, Kitty's last controller in London.

Itzhak Akhmerov, Soviet illegal and husband of Browder's niece Helen Lowry.

Naum Eitingon, a key Soviet illegals who masterminded the assassination of Trotsky in Mexico City.

A portrait of Vicente Lombardo Toledano, Kitty's contact in Mexico.

End-paper maps © Scott Lockheed, Carta-Graphics.

(The Russian text was unillustrated. While every effort has been made to credit the source of the above photographs in this expanded English version, any errors or omissions will be gratefully acknowledged and corrected in subsequent editions.)

Preface

by Geoffrey Elliott

I first glimpsed Kitty, or rather Kitty's name, across the crowded pages of a Moscow publisher's list of forthcoming titles at the back of a rather grey volume of reminiscences by a senior KGB officer. It took a year or more actually to get hold of Igor Damaskin's book, which I then translated into English to form the cornerstone of this extraordinary and very human insight into some key chapters of Cold War intelligence history.

Born in London at the turn of the century to a Russian Jewish émigré family, Kitty, alias Katherine Harrison, Elizabeth Dreyfus, Alice Read, Mrs Morris, Elizaveta Stein, and codenamed GYPSY, NORMA and ADA, and with at least ten other identities in her handbag, played many key roles from the 1930s to the late 1940s in support of the clandestine apparatus operated by the great illegals of Soviet intelligence to run their agent networks across the world from Shanghai and Berlin to Mexico, Los Alamos and London.

A petite, dark-eyed brunette, she can now be revealed to be the lover as well as the NKVD's front-line contact with Donald MacLean in the crucial first phase of his work as a Soviet agent.

1

But far from being 'the perfect spy', she was headstrong, naïve, undisciplined, moody, wore her heart on her sleeve and at times could be a little gullible. She was an indifferent radio operator, despite having been trained by the illegal Vilyam Fisher (later known as Rudolf Abel), was a less than proficient photographer of purloined documents, and had little or no formal education. Nor was her identity much of a secret for she had been through a form of marriage with Earl Browder, later leader of the American Communist Party (CPUSA), and had worked with him on a secret Comintern mission to China, where she had attracted the attention of US intelligence and the FBI.

Furthermore, she had been identified as a Soviet agent in 1939 by the high-level Soviet defector Walter Krivitsky, and her sisters had close ties with official Soviet trade and press agencies in the US. Browder's sister Margaret, who was Kitty's close friend, was a fully fledged NKVD agent in Europe, and his niece Helen actually married Itzhak Akhmerov, the Soviet illegal *rezident* in the United States, and became an illegal herself. Kitty's vulnerability increased when the painstakingly decrypted VENONA intercepts, plucked by American counter-intelligence from NKVD and GRU cipher traffic flowing in and out of Moscow from the *rezidenturas* in America and Mexico City during the 1940s, began to throw up references to an agent codenamed ADA, who was quickly identified by FBI analysts as Kitty Harris.

Despite having been compromised, she continued successfully on her clandestine path and although there are tantalising glimpses of her in a few now fading reports from the Shanghai Police, the US Office of Naval Intelligence and Department of Justice, she was never caught. Various researchers have sought in vain to track her down, and only now has Igor Damaskin's access to recently declassified files in Moscow's intelligence archives allowed the full story of her colourful and dangerous life to be told. He also reveals for the first time her role in London in support of the famous Cambridge Five as photographer, courier, controller and keeper of a safe-house, and eventually, far beyond the call of duty and in flagrant violation of every elementary rule of tradecraft, as Donald Maclean's lover in London and Paris.

Igor Damaskin's research in the KGB's archives uncovered four large volumes of files on Kitty. They provide a fascinating insight into hitherto undisclosed Soviet illegal operations and show how reliant they were on a risky and inefficient system of couriers criss-crossing the world, sometimes literally on the slow boat to China, carrying letters in invisible ink and microfilmed documents.

Because individual *rezidents* were obliged to seek Moscow Centre's permission for any initiative, action and response was sometimes very slow, and the intelligence gathered, often in considerable quantities and of very high quality, had to be channelled to Moscow in a form carefully calculated to pander to the prejudices and paranoia of 'one little old reader', as the late Lord Beaverbrook was jokingly termed in the heyday of his hands-on proprietorship of the London *Daily Express*. In this case the reader was Stalin.

It is a tribute to those who organised Kitty's cover that until now most researchers agreed that her trail went cold when she went back to Canada in the 1930s. Her family seems to have backed this fiction, for fiction it was and almost certainly part of a Centre-scripted legend, by claiming that she had disappeared while on a secret Soviet mission. Interviewed by the FBI in the 1950s, her sisters stoutly maintained that they had not seen or heard from her for decades, although she had visited them in 1942 and had conducted a sporadic secret correspondence with them via the KGB throughout the 1940s and 1950s. Though there may be other family photographs of her somewhere, the albums of one of her sisters have produced only one shot of Kitty, and the Soviet files have only the one picture for which she was probably 'made over' so as to leave a totally unmemorable impression. Considerable technical ingenuity, of which Kitty and her controllers would surely have approved, had to be applied to rebuild an image from a photocopy of a fading

US Department of Justice file to show Kitty as she was when she started down her lonely road.

In his pioneering trawl, or rather guided tour, through the KGB files in the early 1990s, the late John Costello was allowed to see brief references to a woman who had helped run Maclean and had fallen in love with him, but he was never able to get beyond her codename to her true identity or even her nationality.

We can now trace her life to its sad ending and understand her quirky, talented personality. The VENONA decrypts highlight her capacity for being wilful. 'Tell her we require our orders to be carried out without any discussion,' the Centre growled in frustration at the *rezident* in Mexico City, adding in a later message, 'we absolutely forbid ADA to . . .'

Quite what this was we will never know since the cipher groups which followed have never given up their secret, but she was clearly again attempting to use her own initiative, a quality intelligence services the world over have always regarded with suspicion.

'The behaviour of ADA . . .' ran another tantalising but incomplete fragment, reminiscent of a prep-school report. The Centre also spotted that her lack of education and social background gave her an inferiority complex that sometimes pushed her to emphasise her own importance; her accounts to her controllers of her early brush with the Mob and her sighting of Dr Goebbels in Berlin may reflect this.

Given the NKVD's obsession with what it termed *konspiratsia* – security, cover, 'need to know' and tradecraft – Kitty Harris was an improbable agent, but she must have had something special. As Damaskin's fascinating account shows, she was above all totally, even fanatically, committed to the cause of Communism and the Soviet Union. She spoke several languages well and was demonstrably resourceful and energetic. She had a retentive memory, invaluable when it came to listening carefully to what an asset like Donald Maclean was reporting, and passing it back verbatim to her controllers. Without ever losing her nerve, she travelled in and out of Nazi Germany carrying top-secret papers and money past surly and suspicious border guards, successfully juggling multiple identities.

The men (and one woman, the hard-as-nails Elizaveta [Liza] Zarubina) who ran her were not people who suffered fools gladly, or indeed at all, for their security and lives were on the line. Since 1927, when the controversial Agnes Smedley first nudged Kitty across the line into giving active support to the Soviets, she had worked with so many senior GRU, OGPU and NKVD officers that if she had ever decided to 'turn', or had been caught and compelled to talk, she could have provided her interrogators with an extraordinary insight into Soviet espionage. However, her handlers trusted her and were convinced her strengths and her loyalty outweighed her weaknesses.

It is a sad irony that while the lives of the pre-war Soviet spymasters and illegals, of whom so many were Jewish, were indeed at risk, savvy and street-smart as they were, only a few spotted before it was too late that their biggest risk lurked in Stalin's paranoid obsession with rooting out traitors and plotters and his visceral anti-Semitism. Thus as the grim recital in the Postscript – not published in Russia – underscores, many of them ended their lives not in Leavenworth or Wormwood Scrubs, but in Siberia, if they were lucky; or if they were not, slumped against the tiled wall of a cell in the Lubyanka, a bullet in their brain. In the case of the defector Walter Krivitsky, he died on the rumpled bed of a Washington hotel, an alleged suicide. Nor in the end was Kitty herself immune to the brutal injustice of the Soviet system.

Kim Philby is the only known spy to have made it into the *Oxford Dictionary of Quotations* with his self-serving dictum that 'to betray you must first belong'. As a British subject bound by the Official Secrets Act, Philby was clearly a traitor, whatever his Jesuitical justification. Kitty's position was more ambiguous. Though born in Britain, she also held Canadian and Soviet citizenship at various points, and while she spent many years in Chicago and New York, and at one time had American travel documents, she was never an American. Like so many others, she and her family had come to the West less in pursuit of the Holy Grail of democracy and capitalism than to flee a despotic, despised Tsarist Russia, which had cast them out from society and converted many of them in the process into ardent socialists, if not revolutionaries. Even when settled in the West, it would not follow that they automatically rejected their socialist views and their conviction, however misplaced, that a reborn, revolutionary Russia was worth fighting for. The crash, the Slump and the powder-keg political landscape of 1930s' Europe must have made many of them susceptible listeners when clandestine Soviet recruiters, sent in their direction by the Party's talent-spotters, sidled up asking them to help Russia and the anti-Fascist cause. Much has been written in recent years about the exact nature of the links between the CPUSA and the Soviet intelligence apparatus, but while this book is no part of that polemic it serves to underscore that the CPUSA's leadership aided and abetted the Soviet intelligence services by identifying potential agent recruits, as an invaluable source of moral and practical support, and, in some key cases, of crucial top-secret military, political and atomic intelligence.

Kitty's story should not be confused with another long-running debate, namely just how, and even when, the VENONA traffic was laboriously decoded. Mysteriously, the cryptanalysts attached real identities to so many of the obscure and otherwise clueless code names, among them Kitty's, that some suggest this may have been the fruit of an even more secret operation, perhaps an FBI 'black bag' raid on a Soviet mission in the USA. But this remains to be proved.

At the height of Stalin's witch-hunts, the Soviet press was fond of sneering at Jews as 'rootless cosmopolitans', a phrase which seems to fit Kitty well. She belonged first and foremost not to a country but to her family. The one feature of her underground life she found very heard to bear was loneliness and especially the *konspiratsia*-induced need to cut herself off from her parents and brothers and sisters, a matter on which the flinty-hearted Centre, as the VENONA decrypts show, temporarily relented during her Mexico years. She felt just as passionately part of the great family represented by the Party. She treasured the image of the Soviet Union but, like Philby and others after her, found its realities hard to take. Soviet intelligence, in its various acronymic manifestations of Cheka, OGPU, MGB, NKVD and KGB, was another family: a hard core of officers and support staff, moving from one trouble spot to another, marrying, betraying, helping each other, with the same personalities popping up in Harbin, Shanghai, Berlin, London, Paris, New York and Mexico City.

It has been claimed that the root of the rot which afflicted the British establishment in the 1930s, and brought the Cambridge Five into being, was the public school 'old boy' network: who you knew rather than what you knew. In its early years the CIA recruited from the same small football-helmeted, tweed-jacketed Ivy League gene pool. It is fascinating therefore to see the Soviets also using the same people over and again. They were people who could be trusted; they were 'one of us'.

It was standard Soviet practice, dating from the days of the Cheka, for all agents to write detailed personal biographies at the time of their recruitment. These insights were then constantly refreshed and cross-checked by an agent's case officer, who took every opportunity on routine contacts or mission debriefings to probe an agent's life, loves, friends and daily round. Agents were also encouraged, as we see, to write to their handlers in detailed, personal terms about what they saw, felt and did. The files thus contain an episodic 'diary' full of insights and confessions on matters both trivial and important, enabling us to know what Kitty felt about almost everything, from Moscow to how she spent her time on vacation, how every mission went, even down to the detail of Donald Maclean's sexual appetite, and allowing Damaskin the opportunity to use his imagination to translate some of Kitty's thoughts, feelings and descriptions of events into dialogue. Each file, in a grey, light green or light blue cover, depending on its date, contains some 300–350 pages. Some of it is duplicated, with handwritten letters or notes in English painstakingly translated and retyped in Russian. Quite often the documents turn out to be summaries of many preceding pages, perhaps with some new facts added. Damaskin describes his hunt for nuggets in the mass of paper as like one of the Labours of Hercules. Following the *konspiratsia* rules of the time, coded telegrams are filed only in the unscrambled version actually received by the desk officer, to guard against attempts to break the code by backtracking to the clear text.

It is tempting to speculate what a woman of Kitty's formidable character would find to believe in and commit to today. In another era she might have even taken the veil as a nun in some globe-trotting missionary order. A cynic might say that part of the price we pay for peace and prosperity is a dearth of bright shining causes to risk our lives for, other than famine, pestilence and plague. The reformatted and smartly retailored Russian intelligence services spy just as actively today as they ever did, but since the currency of Communist ideology has been totally debased, they have been forced to resort to hard cash, often in large amounts, to get what they need. Such a motive would never have appealed to Kitty, and she would not even have made it to a selection board for any of today's Western services, although a shrewd talent-spotter might have earmarked her as an asset for possible future use 'off the books'. Who knows? What we do know is that hers is a story worth telling.

Acknowledgments

Since Igor Damaskin first opened the Russian archives, much additional information has emerged, for instance on Kitty's relationship with Earl Browder, their time in Shanghai, and the real context of the VENONA intercepts, and this has been incorporated into the text, as has information published in the past year or two under the auspices of the Russian intelligence service, the SVR.

In the process I have been deeply indebted personally to Professor James G. Ryan, author of the definitive biography of Earl Browder, for so generously sharing key archival material on Kitty he had worked hard to obtain for his own book, and for his enthusiastic encouragement. Harvey Klehr provided the key to a new dimension of background information via an introduction to Kitty's family, and read this book in draft. Members of the Harris family whose privacy I respect, and whom I will therefore not thank by name, have allowed me to intrude on their lives with questions, and have provided me with invaluable anecdotal information as well as allowing me access to, and copies of, family photographs and letters. I thank them most warmly and hope that they will feel Kitty's memory has been properly served.

Harold Shukman and Oleg Tsaryev are an unlikely pair of midwives but both made considerable efforts to track down copies of the original book in Moscow and thus get the project started. Others to whom much is owed in many different ways include Robert Louis Benson, Morton Sobell, Nigel West, Hayden B. Peake, the *Jewish Chronicle*, Richard Cooper of the Jewish Genealogical Society, Professor Archie Brown, Robert Service, Mark Gamsa, whose guidance on China and Harbin was essential, Joseph Zehavi of the Pierpont Morgan Library who summoned Kitty back from a copy of a copy of a faded seventy-year-old photograph, the Lennox Hill Bookstore, G. Heywood Hill Ltd, St Antony's College, Oxford, Manon and Natalie Nightingale, Hannah Dyson, Professor Glen Dudbridge, Tom Whitaker, Carta-Graphics Inc., the Imperial War Museum, and the *New York Times* CyberTimesNavigator internet search programmes.

Thomas and James Sleep provided a sense of perspective throughout, while Fay Elliott put up with Kitty as a 'lodger' for far too long and input much of the text into the computer.

When there are no more Don Quixotes
Let's close the Book of History
There will be nothing in it worth reading
Turgenyev

Prologue

Their little town had sniffed the first rancid breath of another pogrom. True, the mob wasn't swarming down the street yet, waving clubs and yelling, 'Bash the Yids'. As yet there were no clouds of feathers flying as they gleefully ripped open treasured goose-down mattresses in search of hidden trinkets. The Jewish peddlers' market stalls, far too tawdry to be called 'shops', were not yet burning. The muddy central street was not yet paved with a mosaic of glass shards from smashed windows. The wailing of anguished mothers had still to make itself heard. The time would come, but for now there was little more than vague rumours, old men whispering in the synagogue: shifty characters had been spotted around town, ruddy-faced men in long, tight-belted coats, with the pudding basin haircuts favoured by the Cossacks. Everyone in Biyalistok knew everyone else. These men were outsiders.

When Josef came home from the synagogue, his wife met him, tearful and upset: 'Mrs Santsevich's maid was here. Told me her mistress wanted me to give her the boots straightaway, and if they weren't ready she wants her money back. Now.'

'But she doesn't need the boots till the autumn,' he replied. 'She never said there was any hurry.'

'I don't know anything about that. But I'll tell you something else. Petrochenko down at the shop says not a kopeck more on the slate. Strictly cash. And another . . .'

'Okay, Eva, okay. That's enough. You're a smart girl. You know what it all means. We've got to think what we do. Thank God at least we haven't got any money for them to steal. We'll stick the leather and my tools down in the cellar in the chest. Bring the mattresses and the kids' stuff downstairs. The kids can sleep in the cellar. Eight of them, for God's sake. Where are we going to find room for them all?'

'And what about the young couple?'

'Nathan and Esfir? Oh, God, I'm terrified when I think what they'll do to her. She's so young. So pretty. Isaac had the right idea. They should go to him. Smart fellow, Isaac. Dad was right when he said he was more brain than brawn. Remember how feeble he was as a kid? Always sickening for something. In London now, got his own factory. No pogroms there. They even had a prime minister over there, next most important man after their Queen, who was a Jew. Disraeli. Don't you remember me telling you what Isaac wrote? A Jew as prime minister already.'

This time there was no pogrom. Someone decided they didn't need it. Maybe someone in the provincial government, maybe in Warsaw, maybe even in St Petersburg itself. Maybe higher up still, in Heaven, the big shots – Orthodox, Catholic, Jewish – and God himself got together and maybe God told them, 'Enough of your quarrelling. Leave Biyalistok in peace. Leave Joseph to tap away at his boots. Leave Eva to stir the stewpot for her brood, and let Nathan and Esfir get their things together and set off on the long road to the unknown, to London, where it's all nice and peaceful and there aren't any pogroms.'

CHAPTER 1

Gypsy

The closest we can get is the late 1880s, but no month or date. The tramp steamer *Sanit* left Gdynia for Harwich with its usual mix of freight and passengers. For those like Nathan and Esfir, jammed into the single steerage-class dormitory overflowing with suitcases, bulky steamer trunks and sacks, the stale air, the crying children, the ceaseless rolling of the ship, the sea-sickness, a hundred people sharing just two toilets, all blurred into eighteen days of blind hope and acute discomfort known as 'emigration'.

The deck was out of bounds to steerage passengers, and the port-holes were their only windows on the stormy grey seascape and the seemingly never-ending itinerary of little Baltic and North Sea ports, where the *Sanit* called to load or unload freight. But for the young couple, handsome, healthy, on their own and with not much more than the clothes they stood up in, the voyage was more like a romantic adventure.

Uncle Isaac met them at Harwich, and after three hours in a smoke-filled Eastern Railways carriage thundering at what seemed to them breakneck speed through an alien landscape, they clambered out into the echoing caverns of London's Liverpool Street

Station. A horse-drawn cab clattered them off to Isaac's house at 23 Darling Row, on the corner of Whitechapel Road and Cambridge Heath Road, then as now the centre of gravity for Britain's most recent immigrants.

Isaac, his wife and their five children lived on the second floor and he worked downstairs. But 'the factory' he had proudly described in his letters home turned out to be a small shoemaker's workshop with benches for five people, Isaac included. Isaac gave the young couple a small room on the second floor and handed Nathan a hammer, a pair of pliers and a heavy needle. But although Isaac kept a beady eye on him, Nathan, who had been helping his father out at the cobbler's last since he was a kid, proved a fast learner; it was not long before Isaac was letting him take over parts of the process, and he soon graduated to handling bespoke orders from start to finish. But this was still not the stuff of Nathan's and Esther's (she had now anglicised her name) dreams. At the weekends, in their Sunday best, they liked to 'go up West' and stroll through the amazing, bewildering panorama of London: huge buildings, traffic going in six directions at once, people bustling along the elegant, clean and well-lit streets, some intent on their business, others just out for what the English, who believed in the efficacy of fresh air despite the fog and pollution, called a 'constitutional'. Victorian Britain wallowed in wealth. Money, manufactured goods and raw materials poured in from the colonies. Splendid new buildings were going up, fine ladies rode fine horses through Hyde Park, where up by the corner with Oxford Street cranks, wild-eyed zealots and tub-thumping firebrands roared at passers-by from makeshift lecterns. But it was not a world to which they could ever belong.

A year later Esther gave birth to her first daughter Jennie; then came Kitty, Alice, Lil, Abe, Harry, Nancy, Jessie, Tilly (who was handicapped from birth) and Bessie, who is thought to have died at the age of seventeen. The Russian files show two versions of Kitty's birth year, 24 May 1899 and 1900. Cross-checking the other facts in the files, Igor Damaskin is '99.9 per cent certain' that the latter is correct, but this is one aspect of her life in which, even after all the attention that has been brought to bear on it, Kitty has left us a puzzle, since Harris family lore is adamant that she was in fact eight years older than her sister Jessie and may even have been born back in 1892. Though checks in the UK Registry of Births for 1892–3 and 1899–1901 have found one or two entries for Kitty or Katherine Harris, the parents' names and addresses rule out any possibility of these being 'the real Kitty', so we are left to wonder, as we are about the original family name.

The absence of records might reflect efforts by the Soviet intelligence service to obliterate all trace of her, but it is also possible that her birth simply went unregistered. While there is no trace of her, Darling Row by contrast is still there, but unrecognisably so, the brick tenements long since swept away by the Luftwaffe and a wave of urban renewal, replaced by a supermarket and apartment buildings bearing the names of famous British seafarers.

Nathan worked all the hours God sent; and in what little time she had free from looking after her children, Esther, a skilled furrier, took in work at home. But however hard they worked, making ends meet became steadily more difficult. They had long since moved out of Isaac's house and were renting rooms in Montague Place, about three quarters of a mile to the north, and today the teeming heart of the Bengali immigrant community. Their rent, however, ate up almost half of what they managed to scrape together each week. Esther thought more and more often of Biyalistok, where, although for Jews danger always lurked in the air, at least they never went hungry.

Their lives were to change when, walking through Hyde Park one day on his own, Nathan stopped to listen to the speakers.

'Comrades,' it was the first time he had heard the word. 'Look around you. The rich are getting richer. Living in the lap of luxury. They even started a war with the Boers to protect their profits. But the poor are getting poorer. Prices are going up, your rent and your gas bill are sky-high, and we're still working the same long hours. They complain we work badly and have too many kids. Perhaps they will soon be complaining that we are still actually eating and using up their fresh air,' the speaker bellowed, waving at the banks of fog rolling across the Park. 'We socialists are the only ones who can unite the working men and fight for their rights, for the right to a decent life.'

Nathan went home a changed man, if not yet totally sold on all the speaker's ideas then at least nursing the first germs of a feeling of social protest. He began to go to meetings in Hyde Park in his time off and even joined a socialist group. Meanwhile, life became steadily harder, and it was depressing to be forced to depend on Isaac's workshop for a livelihood, all the more since his uncle was growing daily more crabby and mean. Something had to change. Out of the blue, when Nathan was back in the park one day, the speakers sounding off about everything from cat-breeding to world revolution, he heard a man making a pitch for emigration to Canada; everyone was welcome, especially anyone with a trade, he boomed. The sea passage across the Atlantic was free, and they'd get help settling in, a mortgage to buy or build a house, and a stack of other tempting offers.

Nathan and Esther lay awake all night whispering. It would be a huge decision, throwing away what little they had managed to make of their lives in eighteen years of hard work, giving up a job that, though not that well paid, was at least regular, and launching themselves off into the unknown.

But Nathan had seen the light. 'We're going,' he declared flatly, so in the spring of 1908, ignoring token objections from Uncle Isaac, the Harris family pulled its modest trappings together and set off across the Atlantic, the first of Kitty's many crossings, on the SS *Winnipeg*. Since this was their destination, Esther was convinced that the coincidence was a lucky sign.

After what for city-dwellers must have been an eye-popping trip up the St Lawrence River, lined with red maples, clapboard farms and herds of dairy cows, they disembarked in Montreal and boarded the train that in two days and three nights brought them across hundreds of miles of rolling prairie to Winnipeg, where they found that the Canadian pitchman had delivered pretty well what he promised. They were put up temporarily in a vacant house and given a loan to buy their own. The interest rate was higher than he had expected but Nathan shrugged it off as one of those things. He had brought over his tools, having bought them from Isaac, and soon set up a tiny workshop. And for the first time he hung out a shingle of his own, with a space for Esther to advertise 'A Selection of Furs. Your Own Furs Tailored'. The harsh Canadian climate meant that Esther was not short of customers.

Harris family lore has it that in fact Nathan's first venture was as a prairie homestead farmer, which would have fitted more with what the Canadian authorities were seeking to encourage, and that he resorted to his old trade only after failing, hardly surprisingly, to make a go of things. As the children reached school age, Nathan and Esther made an effort to give them a grounding in languages by speaking English, Russian and Yiddish at home, while the kids spoke French and German as well when they played with children from neighbouring émigré families. Thus from an early age Kitty could make herself understood quite easily in five languages, though she could only write well in English and she soon lost her fluency in Russian through disuse. She did well in subjects like history, literature and geography, but collapsed when faced with anything where she had to be accurate and precise, and even simple arithmetic was a real struggle. Homework she regarded as a waste of time, preferring to run off into the garden or clamber up to the loft to read *Tom Sawyer*. When it came time to hand her work in, she would quickly copy the answers from her brothers or friends and give it to the teacher with an innocent look. But the school soon had her measure, and after fourth grade her parents were called in and faced with the stark choice of having her tutored privately or simply giving up her schooling altogether. When he got back from the school, her father, by now feeling ever more ground down by the difficulty of making a living, told Kitty that it was time she helped the family

– her mother was losing customers through ill-health – and got a job.

So, at the age of twelve Kitty became a paid-up member of the working class. She got a job in a cigarette factory first as an apprentice and then on the shop floor, for a wage that was no more than a pittance. She had barely enough to buy lunch and dinner in the canteen, but at least it meant one less mouth to be fed at the family table. At first, ten hours a day at a repetitive, mind-numbing job left her totally lethargic and she didn't even feel like eating, just crawling into her bed, but she gradually got used to it and found time for other things, including making friends. Going off with them into the country for weekend picnics was a special treat, and one Saturday they had spread themselves out in a rolling meadow outside the city when a bunch of smart young things on horseback trotted up yelling, 'Hey you, clear out. This is our field.'

'We were here first. You'd better find yourselves somewhere else,' objected Kitty's friend Peter Skonetsky, a calm and sensible boy who was three years older than her.

'Oh yeah. My Granddad's owned this field for a zillion years and it's our private property,' someone shot back from the saddle.

'Okay, you get down and we'll see whose property it is,' said Joe, the strongest and most obstinate of Kitty's mates. The rider got down and strutted towards him, but at that moment one of the girls in the group, whom Kitty recognised as the daughter of the owner of the factory where she worked, nudged her horse closer.

'Guys,' she said, 'we didn't come out here to watch a fight! We'll just go and get the Sheriff and he'll clear you off, fine you and maybe put a couple of you inside for the night.'

'Okay,' Kitty replied. 'No need for an argument, let's find somewhere else,' adding under her breath in German and sticking out her tongue, 'I'll remember this, you little shit.' Her opportunity for revenge came a week later when the factory owner was celebrating some holiday or other. Kitty led her young friends into his garden and, in her first, semi-childish protest against unfairness, they hurled a volley of stones at his windows before slipping away into the night; the Sheriff never figured out who was responsible.

Time passed. Viewed from the factory floor, the rich seemed to be getting richer and the poor poorer, a process that the speeches and pamphlets of the labour activists claimed was accentuated by the absence of any laws to protect workers against holdovers from the Victorian era such as sweated labour, unfair fines and wage-docking. Peter had started to go to meetings of one of the working-men's groups which already existed in Winnipeg and had become much taken with socialist ideas; he talked about them to Kitty at great length. Though not a joiner by temperament, her father was also sympathetic to the socialists and encouraged his children to think the same way. Halfway around the world in Europe the Great War had started. Cut off in Winnipeg, isolated behind thousands of miles of wheat, it was hard to understand who was fighting whom and for what, but her father told Kitty that 'the imperialists were at war with each other to carve up the world' and that the workers would end up getting short-changed. It was from Nathan she first heard the idea that the conflict had to be transformed into a civil war in which workers would not be fighting their fellows but would unite against their common enemy, the 'oppressors and capitalists'.

Eventually that faraway war reached even Winnipeg and a Canadian Expeditionary Force, Peter and Joe among them, set off to fight for the British Crown. Joe died in the first wave of fighting. Peter came home wounded.

Rumours spread that there had been a workers' revolution in Russia. For some the news was a profound shock, for others it heralded a glorious future. Most working-class people who gave the matter any thought probably shrugged off the Terror, the civil war, the starvation, the suppression of personal liberties, even the murder of the Tsar, as the inevitable price that had to be paid if the revolution was to succeed. Seen through trades union eyes, the workers' only source of information, the 'capitalist press', was hardly an objec-

21

tive source of news. While the workers heard a distant call to arms, the owners of capital heard more alarming noises and concluded that they needed, to make some concessions on the basis that it was better to lose a little than to lose everything. The net result , union history would later claim, was a major boost to the workers' movement in the West, and in the East as well, in the 1920s, which extracted a range of workers' rights and material concessions by the employers.

The Revolution was maybe the key influence on Kitty's life. She had worked in the cigarette factory for five years, but as her health began to let her down, she took up a less arduous job as a seamstress and joined the garment workers' own trade union. As her eighteenth birthday approached, Kitty had grown into a tall, slender, dark-eyed brunette, whom the boys eyed appreciatively, though she took little notice of them. In fact, her interest in the revolutionary movement was all the keener because its leader in Winnipeg was her old friend Peter Skonetsky, whom all the war veterans respected and on whom, without anyone being aware of it or even admitting it too often to herself, she had a serious crush.

Peter's life was not wholly consumed by politics; he was an omnivorous reader, and when a touring opera company came to Winnipeg he took Kitty to see *Carmen*. With a young man's passion for detail and for going right back to the primary source of anything that interested him, he also read Mérimée's original novel and told Kitty, 'You know, you look like Carmen, and you carry on the same way.'

He began to read aloud: 'Her eyes were slanted, wonderfully outlined, her lips rather full but beautifully shaped, showing teeth whiter than shelled almonds . . . I was struck above all by a look in her eyes that was both sensual and fierce. The Spaniards say, and they're quite right, that "the eye of a gypsy girl is the eye of a wolf". If you don't have time to go to the zoo to see for yourself what a wolf's eye looks like, check out your cat next time she's lying in wait for a sparrow . . .'

Kitty snorted and flashed her nails like a cat's claws.

'Yup, that's it,' Peter laughed. 'The Gypsy Girl. You worked in a cigarette factory like she did and you're like her in everything else too. From now on we'll call you Gypsy.'

'Call me what you like,' Kitty shrugged. It could never have crossed her mind for a moment that, many years later, it would be used as her work name and form part of the historical record in the top-secret archives of the Soviet Foreign Intelligence Service.

CHAPTER 2

Not a Care in the World

By 1919 revolutionary fever had even reached Winnipeg and Peter was in the thick of it, preaching the gospel of the 'Wobblies', or Industrial Workers of the World (IWW), a fiery amalgam of socialists, left-wing unionists and a ragtag of radicals, all hell-bent on the destruction of capitalism and what he called 'expropriating the expropriators'. Kitty went to their interminable meetings, trying hard to decide who was right – Peter or his more conservative union colleagues – and fretting about what was going on in Russia; she was also finding herself still more than half in love with Peter.

As events continued to unfold, intellectual fervour had been overtaken by real labour unrest. After several months a metalworkers' stoppage developed into a general strike, involving 30,000 people, including the city police. The normally bustling Canadian Pacific Railroad station was silent, no factory sirens wailed, only the hospitals had electricity, mains water was turned on only twice a day and the schools were deserted. Peter joined the strike committee though he was kept firmly in the background because of worries about his extremist views. Convinced that they had a real revolution on their hands, the terrified Winnipeg authorities sent in troops to break up a peaceful street demonstration. Two demonstrators were killed, thirty were seriously injured and the members of the strike committee were jailed.

The trades union leadership in Canada and America not only failed to protest the killings, the use of force to suppress the strikes and the jailing of the activists, but, in what was seen by their more radical elements as a betrayal of their members' interests, urged them to settle the strike on the employers' terms. In the resulting backlash several unions, led by the International Ladies Garment Workers (ILGWU), which had a long history of militancy, walked out of the American Federation of Labour (AFL) to form a new grouping called OBU, or One Big Union. A few months later Kitty was elected Secretary of the local OBU committee and her first task, which she tackled with a twenty-year-old's limitless enthusiasm, was to raise money for the defence of those in jail and to help support their families. She went at it in American style, beginning with an amateur concert, the takings from which were donated to the defence fund. Then she persuaded her brothers and sisters (who were becoming steadily more embroiled in her activities), as well as some of their friends, to parade at the busiest downtown intersections with sandwich-boards urging passers-by to help the prisoners. This was followed by a 'bring and buy' sale and a raffle, all orchestrated with the lightest of touches, as if the money was being raised for the next 'Miss Winnipeg' beauty contest rather than to help a bunch of left-wingers behind bars.

In her spare time Kitty toured the apartment blocks collecting money door to door. As she told her chairman, 'I'm doing three things at once. I'm raising money, testing public opinion and spreading the word.'

'Whose word are you spreading?' enquired the OBU chairman Stanley Roberts, a garment factory engineer, a thick-set man in his forties with a talent for persuading the perennially squabbling activist factions to work together.

'Whose do you think? Our union, of course,' Kitty replied.

'If it's just the union, that's okay, but as regards any other good causes, just keep your mouth shut,' he warned. 'Otherwise you'll find yourself joining your chums in jail.'

Kitty relied on instinct to decide which doors to knock on, and more than once she was almost slung out on her ear amid a volley of insults directed at her, her jailbird pals and the 'Red sons of bitches' who had brought the Bolshevik plague to North America. She usually gave as good as she got, using the very rough edge of her tongue; and if she was lost for words, she would sometimes just burst into tears, stick her tongue out and stomp off, swearing revenge under her breath, though quite what form this would take she had no idea. After episodes like that, the best antidote was her family – her father, her mother and, of course, her brothers and sisters – who would proudly place the dollar bills and coins they had collected on the table to be carefully totted up by Kitty, who would then dole out titles depending on how much they had brought in: President, Adviser, Sheriff, or, for those who came up short, simply Trainee. It did not take long to raise the money needed to pay the fines and obtain the release of the jailed committee members.

Her father did not belong to a political party though socialism had permeated the family fabric as the children grew up. However busy he was, he still found time to read, even articles by Marx, Bakunin and Plekhanov. He and Kitty's mother would often reminisce nostalgically about their long-lost younger days, which, as they looked back now, seemed to have been a blissful, tranquil time. Kitty and the other children listened in fascination and began to want to know more about their roots.

According to Harris family anecdote, Nathan may have been something of a wanderer and absentee father, sometimes leaving home for months on end and reappearing out of the blue expecting home life simply to pick up again where he had left off as though nothing had happened.

When the Third International was formed in Moscow in 1919,

the Socialist Party of America had already been in existence for some time, and later argued, because one of its former members had been present, that it had been unofficially represented at the First Congress of the Comintern, but did not get a seat on the Executive Committee. A little while later left-wing members of the Socialist Party formed the Workers' Party, which in due course became active in Canada as well. When the Workers' Party in turn transformed itself into the Communist Party of Canada, Peter and Kitty automatically became members.

'Automatically' is an understatement, for they had fallen utterly and completely under the spell of its slogans; 'Workers of the World Unite', 'The Dictatorship of the Proletariat', even the name of Lenin himself were clarion calls. Lenin' s claim that 'the bourgeoisie stand in terror of the growing revolutionary movement of the proletariat' sent the blood racing through their veins. When he went on to say that, 'even if it costs thousands more lives, victory for us, victory for the worldwide Communist revolution, is assured,' they were mesmerised. Naïve children of their troubled and unique times, they saw themselves as brave young people striding forward arm in arm, heads lowered against the cold wind and pouring rain, towards a glorious future when the shining ideals of the first proletarian revolution and of the revolution's first home would prevail worldwide. Sadly, they had so much to learn, but Kitty kept that adolescent flame burning for most of her life, and it goes a long way to explain much of her later life.

In 1923 the Comintern and the recently formed Trades Union International, the Profintern, announced a new union policy based on the principle that divisions in the union movement only served the interest of the employers and weakened the position of the working class; it was therefore decided that the unions which had earlier broken ranks with the AFL should now be brought back into the fold. But having tasted power, the OBU's leadership did not like the idea of giving it up, which would have been the immediate price of reaffiliation.

One day, Kitty's old friend Daniel, an AFL stalwart, invited her to dinner, and since he rarely made this sort of approach a somewhat flustered Kitty mused to herself about what might be on his mind. 'I don't fancy him at all,' she said to herself. Actually, what Daniel had in mind was very different, soliciting Kitty's backstairs help in making sure that the OBU leaders, 'a pompous bunch who've lined their pockets from their union work', did not, as he put it, 'create a roadblock' to the reintegration. 'If you're going to fight, you need to know where the enemy is vulnerable. We need inside information, we need to know how they see things.'

Kitty had been given her first intelligence assignment and typically she went at it full tilt. She talked around, dug through files and sat innocently listening to indiscreet conversations. Two young AFL men provided by Daniel helped her, and they jokingly called themselves 'Kitty Harris & Co, Private Investigators'. The story they laid out for Daniel, which Kitty told him she could support with witnesses and documents, was like the plot of an Elmore Leonard novel: a treasurer who had lost union money at the racetrack; a senior official having an affair with the wife of a colleague; two of the leadership closet homosexuals; links to bootleggers. Daniel decided to arm Roberts, the outgoing President of the OBU, with the information, betting that he was honest enough to want to expose the whole can of worms. He also got Kitty to brief the *Labour Daily*, and the twin-track tactic achieved what he wanted: the Congress dissolved in mutual recrimination, the discredited leadership resigned and the OBU collapsed, its members meekly rejoining their former unions.

Kitty continued to work for the ILGWU and her relationship with Daniel remained strictly professional, but Peter was a different matter.

Soon after the court hearing for his release, he said to her gravely that he'd like to take her on a trip to the country as a way of saying 'Thank you'.

'You mean like a sort of fee for services rendered,' she bridled.

'What on earth do you mean?' Peter asked in confusion. 'I just wanted to do something nice for you. And myself, of course.'

Kitty and Peter had corresponded when he was serving overseas but always on a light note, never mentioning anything serious, and when he came home they had continued to see each other as friends, quite often quarrelling but always steering clear of any emotional undercurrents. And now this idea of a trip. She could play hard to get, but if she did maybe he would think that she didn't want to go with him. Why risk wasting the opportunity? She therefore agreed, and they set off on a Saturday on Peter's Harley Davidson, with Kitty riding pillion, her arms tight around his waist. They roared along a tree-lined riverbank, across miles of prairie dotted with distant homesteads, and along a winding dirt track through deep maple woods to an isolated lake. Swimming in the nude, the romantic glow of a bonfire, the intimacy of a small tent and the lonely hooting of an owl, Kitty remembered it as the happiest night of her life.

She and Peter became an item and she would often sleep over at his apartment, telling her mother, like girls the world over in similar circumstances, that it was her life and that she was old enough to do what she wanted.

Alongside her visions of world revolution Kitty dreamed about marriage and raising a family, but Peter was made of higher-minded stuff, parroting that marriage was like 'being in chains' and that 'the only lasting relationship, the one that in the end will prove to be mankind's salvation, is free love'.

Brought up in an Orthodox patriarchal family, this was more than Kitty could take, and eventually she told Peter that they had to go their separate ways, adding the trite epitaph handy for such occasions, 'but we can still be good friends'. She cried all night, blaming first herself and then Peter, and regretting the time she had wasted. From then on they were just Party friends and the subject of love, free or otherwise, never arose again. But the affair left a bitter taste in Kitty's mouth and every encounter with Peter was painful, making

29

her want to get out of Winnipeg so that she didn't have to see him again. Certainly life in Winnipeg was getting worse, not better, as the post-war boom seemed to have passed the city by and people started comparing life there unfavourably to the prosperity in the United States, where everything was on a roll, and although the rich were making bigger and bigger fortunes, even the workers were getting better wages. It was against this background that Nathan called the family together.

'A fish looks for food where the water is deepest, man goes wherever is best,' he began, never at a loss for a Russian proverb. 'You can see there's no future for us here, but my sister Riva in Chicago has written to say that things there are improving by the minute. Maybe we should swim down there, where the water's deeper. Let's go round the room and everyone can say what they think.'

Kitty spoke first. Nathan had been a little worried what she might say as she was the most militant of the children, yet at the same time seemed to have the deepest roots in Winnipeg, but to his surprise she was all in favour of moving. Once she had spoken there was not a lot more discussion. No one had any serious objections and they left in early 1923.

CHAPTER 3

The Windy City

The Harris family's move to Chicago brought them to a city that would be more familiar to a post-Soviet Russian than a contemporary American, for whom seventy-five years have passed since the Mob was all-powerful, corruption pervaded public life, there were street shoot-outs, contract killings, even the futile attempt at Prohibition and the riches of a few still contrasted with the poverty of so many. For some years the family lived in Franklin Avenue, near what is now Midway Airport, then an area of broad leafy streets that were a cut above working-class tenements, and now a burned-out, desolate slum.

Kitty started work in a garment factory, joined the ILGWU, and had her own passing brush with the Mob when a Winnipeg trades union activist named Lamberti turned up unexpectedly and gave her the Manitoba gossip. They chatted about friends they had in common and then he asked her if she would be interested in going back to Winnipeg for a couple of days. 'Nice idea,' she replied, 'but right now I really have to watch every cent. Besides I've got a job.'

'Don't worry,' he reassured her. 'I'll arrange for the union to pick up the tab for your fare and your expenses and see you okay for the wages you'll lose. But I need you to do me one little favour. I was supposed to be picking up a package before I left but it's not ready yet and I'm off tonight. Can I have it sent to you and then you can bring it with you?'

Kitty agreed, delighted at the deal. Lamberti had told her that someone named Johnny would be in touch, and a couple of days later a man with a nice, slightly accented voice on the telephone invited her to dinner in a half-empty downtown Italian restaurant. He recognised her straightaway, even though she hadn't given him her description, and put the small briefcase with Lamberti's package by her chair. He turned out to be good fun and they were having a great time when Johnny excused himself, saying that the group of Italian-looking men noisily celebrating around a big table by the rear wall were friends of his and he wanted to say 'Hello'.

Kitty sat spooning her Gelato, sipping espresso and gazing idly around. The place was full now, a pianist tinkled tunes from the old country at a battered piano, couples whispered sweet nothings over their spaghetti and the noise level at the big table grew steadily higher. A man sitting by himself at a side table put on his hat and left. A couple of minutes later the doors burst open and a group of masked men surged towards the big table, pulling out guns and spraying the noisy group with bullets. It was all over in a moment and Kitty watched horror-struck as the men slumped dead, among them Johnny. The sharp reek of cordite hung in the air and the killers vanished as quickly as they had appeared. For a moment there was a deathly hush, then women began screaming and men shouting. Everyone rushed for the doors in panic, sweeping Kitty, who had snatched up Johnny's briefcase almost as a reflex action, with them, jamming the exit with no nonsense about 'ladies first'. Once outside people suddenly seemed to worry that while the immediate danger had passed there might be more to fear from the police, whose sirens could already be heard in the distance and who were well known for taking a hard line with eyewitnesses to gang shootings.

Kitty decided not to tempt fate and slid away, shivering with fright, to a nearby bus stop. Once home she began to calm down and to wonder what she ought to do with Johnny's briefcase. Should she hide it or get rid of it? Perhaps there was something valuable in it. Someone was bound to come looking for it and her, but how would anyone know that Johnny had actually given it to her? she asked herself as she realized that she was mixed up in something shady and it would be tricky to extract herself. After a lot of thought, she decided to open the briefcase; inside she found a bundle wrapped in newspaper and tied with twine. She undid it, trying to keep the folds and knots in a way that if she had to put it back together, it would not look too obvious that she had fiddled with it. Inside were neat wads of $100 and $500 bills, $175,000 in all, more than she had ever seen let alone dreamed of; nine hundred months of pay-checks, seventy-five years of work. She was well aware that it was dirty money, and it was money no one could prove she had, but if she kept it, the mobsters didn't need proof; they had their own justice. Why had they picked on her as the mule? Probably because, as she now realised, unlike Lamberti she was not known to the police and would probably not attract any suspicion when she crossed the border.

It would have been wonderful simply to keep the money, buy a few small houses for her family, get a car and stick the rest in the bank, using the interest to help her mother in her old age; she would be able to give up her job, go to college to read literature or history, though certainly not maths. She dropped off to sleep with visions of sugarplums dancing in her head. The next morning brought the cold light of reality. 'He who steals what isn't his, must pay the price and go to prison,' to adapt one of her father's many pearls of Byalistok folk wisdom. Maybe, she thought as a final flight of fancy, she should hand the cash over to the Party, but she shuddered as she remembered all too well the brutal scene in the restaurant. These were people you messed with at your peril, so she duly took a week off work and left for Winnipeg.

She had crossed the Canadian border before, always without the slightest apprehension, but this time was different and the moment she took her seat she was panic-stricken. The briefcase full of cash was at the bottom of her case, nestled in her underwear and toiletries, and she felt that everyone else in the compartment was staring inquisitively at her and, more to the point, her suitcase, when they should have been admiring the industrial landscape of greater Chicago slipping past the windows. The simple explanation, that she was better looking, never occurred to her.

Closing her eyes to bring back happy childhood memories did not help her relax since the first vision that came to her mind was how scared and furtive she had felt when she and her brother Abe had shared a clandestine cigarette in the yard, and then had spent ages trying to hide the butt so that their parents would not find it. She began to fret about the imminent customs inspection and tied herself into ever-tighter knots. As night came she could not sleep; instead she sat staring and shivering with fright. It was not until nearly morning, with the other passengers dozing around her, that she finally dropped off, but had terrible nightmares about being chased over the train roof by police. Suddenly a torch flashed and two men loomed at the door, asking for identification. Kitty rubbed her eyes and the other passengers were awake too, yawning, stretching and fumbling for their papers. For a moment she was totally disoriented, but when she recovered she pulled out her driver's licence, the customs man gave it a cursory glance and, with a flood of relief, she heard him say, 'Thanks, Miss. Enjoy your stay.' He stepped back into the corridor and the train puffed across the border into Canada.

When Lamberti met her in Winnipeg, she spared him only one detail of the gruesome experience, that she had looked inside the case and knew about the money. He clucked sympathetically, if not that convincingly, about Johnny, gave her the money for her ticket and her lost time and work, and topped it up with a couple of hundred dollars for her restaurant ordeal. When he had the nerve to ask if she would help him out again, Kitty refused point-blank.

She took the chance to catch up with Peter, who was planning to move to New York, and Daniel, who was still working for the Party, and her trip back to Chicago the next day was uneventful. A little while later she was elected secretary of the ILGWU's local division, which was continuing to live up to its nick-name 'the Striking Amazons'. Busy as she was on union matters, Kitty still had time for the Party. Chicago, with its long revolutionary traditions, had by that time effectively become the CPUSA's centre of gravity, where the National Committee met frequently, and it was the Party's hub for the distribution of propaganda. One day the secretary of the Party's Chicago branch sat her down for a series of probing questions without at first saying what he was leading up to. Finally, after asking about her reading habits, he suggested that she read more political material because the Party wanted to give her the job of distributing it around the local trade unions.

Kitty duly started to read. She could just about cope with pamphlets and magazine articles, but found Marx a hard and indigestible slog. After a series of false starts, she did manage to wade through his essays on the position of the working class, but *Das Kapital* and his other weighty tomes were almost incomprehensible and frankly boring, and she made do with the summaries she found in some of the Party pamphlets. Kitty had always had a gift for organisation and she set about her new distributing job by enlisting a good team to help her. The Party leadership noticed her hard work and soon she was formally appointed head of the distribution division in Chicago.

Nineteen twenty-three was a far cry from the heady militant days of 1919. Prosperity had arrived, if only temporarily as things turned out, and the standard of living, wage rates and working conditions all began to improve. This encouraged workers to drift away from the unions, causing their influence to wane. Many of the more radical elements in the unions were attracted to the Communist Party, which was legalised in 1923; with 28,000 members (a claim thought by historians to be much exaggerated), it fielded candidates in the 1924 presidential election in thirty of the forty-eight states. However, the CPUSA was divided, with little influence, and the gains it had fought for so hard began to erode.

One day Kitty went into the Party Secretary's office and found him with a youngish, powerfully built man with piercing grey eyes, who was introduced as Earl Browder, a Secretary of the National Committee. Their formal handshake signalled the start of a long, dangerous and eventually sad adventure that would take Kitty across the world and back; she could have had no idea what she was getting into. Browder's devious life and his complex personality have been authoritatively portrayed in James G. Ryan's *Earl Browder: The Failure of American Communism.* Unlike so many of the American Communists, *shtetl*-bred to their fingertips, Browder was a good-looking, all-American prairie boy, born to a large Mid-Western hard-scrabble farming family united against a hostile world by a losing battle against failure, foreclosure and poverty. That he had served a jail term for incitement to draft avoidance in the First World War, and, more to the point, had left a long-suffering wife Gladys and son back in Kansas, seem to have been some of those eminently forgettable bourgeois details about which he never bothered to tell Kitty. Browder was renowned in the Party as a ladies' man, and it was even alleged that he had conducted an affair with the Party's matriarch Ella Reeve, known as 'Mother Bloor', who was twenty-eight years his senior. By the time he appeared in Kitty's life, he had tried his hand at broom-making and book-keeping, and had flirted with various left-wing movements before becoming a rising star in the Party.

More major economies with the truth were to dog the relationship over the years, some perhaps because the truth was embarrassing, others because of the CPUSA's obsession with security. After the Department of Justice had smashed the IWW, arresting or deporting hundreds of people, the Party had learned from its Soviet mentors to organise itself into an underground structure of small, watertight cells of trusted people who knew only what they strictly needed to know.

Surrounded by boxes crammed with Party publications, Kitty left the next morning for the AFL congress in Detroit, where she and her assistants set up a stall in the lobby. The proceedings were more of a fairground than a formal congress, complete with brass bands, banners, balloons and a noisy crowd of delegates hell-bent on having a good time, for whom the actual proceedings were rather a sideshow. At one of the intervals the AFL President William Green, an imposing man whom Kitty had met at the Montreal congress, came out of the hall to make a ceremonial tour of the lobby. Recognising Kitty, he came over to say 'Hello', but when he caught sight of the stall piled high with Party books and a poster proclaiming the Workers' (Communist) Party of America, his smile vanished. 'Why have you brought this filthy Red propaganda here?' he barked, losing his temper. 'This is some kind of put-up job by the Commies to undermine the AFL and the American way of life.'

Kitty, barely able to restrain herself, interrupted him. 'I am one hundred per cent within my constitutional rights,' she retorted, 'and I'm not going to stand here and let myself or my Party be insulted. The Party is totally legal and you can't stop citizens of this country from expressing their views.'

Green forced a smile and, muttering 'Okay, okay,' swung back into the congress hall, leaving Kitty the winner on points, although, not being a citizen, she was not on the firmest ground. By the time she returned to Chicago, her friends had already heard the story. 'Good for you, Kitty,' Browder told her. 'Doesn't *anything* scare you?'

'Mice,' she replied shyly.

Browder suggested having a drink to celebrate her victory, offering her a glass of Coke as the best 'cocktail' they could hope for in that era of Prohibition; he also asked her to have dinner with him that night. She accepted, but said that she still had a lot of work to clear up.

'Leave it,' Browder told her. 'Business can wait.'

She found it impossible to say 'No' to the serious, self-confident Browder. It was hard to say just what his attraction was. Perhaps it was that although he was not much older than Peter, Daniel and her other friends, compared to him they seemed like schoolboys. He took her to quite a smart restaurant, a place where she would usually have felt a little uncomfortable, but somehow his self-assurance was infectious.

'Well, tell me about yourself,' he said. 'Do you come from a big family?'

Kitty began to talk, shyly at first, then opening up, encouraged by Earl's responses. She told him about her parents, her father's socialist beliefs, and her brothers and sisters, adding that two of them had also joined the Party. She avoided telling him much about herself.

'You didn't manage to finish school?'

'No, I couldn't even remember the five times table,' Kitty laughed. Though she found it hard to understand why, she was not at all embarrassed to admit her lack of education.

'Look, Kitty,' Browder continued. 'You don't want to pedal a sewing-machine for the rest of your life. I reckon you've got a flair for organising. You need to work on that, and that means starting by learning some sort of skill.'

'But learn what, and where?' she replied. 'I'm not a teenager any more, in case you hadn't noticed, and I can't sponge off my parents.'

Earl thought for a moment. 'Well, the Party, or rather the Party administration, needs competent people. People who are "one of us", that we can trust completely. Secretaries, typists, all sorts. Why don't you do a shorthand-typing course? It's something that will always stand you in good stead. And there's no maths involved . . .' he smiled.

'Do you think I could cope with it?' she asked.

'What are you talking about? Hundreds and thousands of girls take those courses all the time and go on to get good jobs.'

'Okay, but courses cost money.'

'Sure, but if you go on the understanding that you come back to us when you finish, we'll pay for it and we'll also see if we can't run to a living allowance.'

'I'll think about it,' she replied.

'What's there to think about? If you don't say "Yes" right now, I'll change my mind,' Earl growled in mock severity.

'Fine, fine,' Kitty agreed hastily. Although she thought of herself as a feisty free spirit, Earl had overwhelmed her and she felt weak and defenceless, a feeling she actually rather liked.

She gave up work and enrolled on a shorthand-typing course, which was hard going at first, but she gradually got into it and found that she had time on her hands, even if she had no one to spend it with. She had left all her old friends behind in Winnipeg and had not made any new ones.

Kitty and Earl went out on a couple of dates that she later remembered vividly. On the first, he took her on a steamer trip round Lake Michigan. It was a calm evening with the setting sun lighting up the vast Chicago cityscape, already punctuated with its first few skyscrapers. The steamer's band played Strauss waltzes, and Kitty sheltered from the light breeze in the lee of Earl's powerful body and stared silently at the shoreline, where the first few lights of the evening were just beginning to twinkle. 'Aren't you cold?' Earl asked and, without waiting for an answer, slung his jacket around her shoulders. She shot him a silent smile of gratitude. Things went no further on that first trip but each of them went home quietly happy.

Their next date was a Sunday outing to a fair, where the crowd was having a great time and so did they. They rode the Ferris wheel into the sky, gazing at the city views, and Earl began to rock their chair. Like the girls in the chairs above and below them whose boyfriends were doing exactly the same, Kitty began to squeal. Earl grabbed at her as if he were going to tip her out and she began to scream in earnest; he recoiled with a pained shout of surprise, pressing his hands to his ears to drown the noise. 'You silly little thing. Do you *really* think I'd chuck you out?' he murmured. She remembered his affectionate tone for a long time.

When they left the fair, they went to a milk bar run by Morris Childs, a close friend of Browder's and also of Kitty's brother Harry (who was also known as Bucky), who combined an active role in the Party with a successful milk bar, whose business had been boosted by Prohibition. Nick-named, as a result, the 'Red Milkman', he had been born Moishe Chilovsky in Kiev in 1902 and had emigrated to America with his parents when he was thirteen. He had joined the Party in 1921 and later rose rapidly with Browder's backing.

Kitty and Earl had been there before and Childs greeted them warmly. He was a roly-poly, red-cheeked, good-natured man, who looked as though he had stepped straight out of a dairy farm advert. Kitty had never imagined how many things you could make out of milk: yoghurts in every conceivable flavour, sweet, heavy creams, dozens of different ice creams, more cheeses than she could count and milkshakes in every colour of the rainbow. Grown-ups and children gorged while Morris rushed from table to table with a friendly smile for everyone. In the future Kitty would visit Childs on her own several times, either to deliver Party pamphlets or to pick up envelopes for Earl.

Kitty and Earl did not see that much of each other, for he was either busy or travelling, but she had no other boyfriends. Though not unsociable, she usually found it difficult to get on with other women. She never had close girlfriends, or indeed any girlfriends at all other than her classmates or those she worked with in the factory, or the ILGWU. There had never been a friend with whom she could share her innermost thoughts, probably, she reflected, because even as a child she had preferred to hang out with boys; however, when she grew up, the boys she felt most comfortable with had tended to be old for their years. Having had to earn her own living from the age of twelve, she had matured much earlier than her contemporaries. The girls in the factory, on the other hand, already had their own lives, their own little secrets. She had no patience for their endless gossip, to the point where she would often lose her temper and flounce off, leaving them open-mouthed. With men it was different, for with them she could talk seriously about the revolutionary struggle, their dreams of a glorious future, about faraway Russia where the word of the Revolution was becoming flesh, and about secrets too. Not silly, girls' stuff about who they had slept with, when, and how often, but real Party secrets, the kind of thing that, handled carelessly, could land someone in a lot of trouble. Secrets were perhaps what first drew her, even seduced her, into the clandestine life, a life which no one who has not lived it can begin to understand. Kitty loved to talk politics but hated chitchat about dresses, boyfriends, or anything she regarded as trite. Having had practically zero education, she was attracted to educated people from whom she could learn new things. In effect, only men could play this role, since none of the girls she knew was much better educated than she was, or as mature. Men were also easier to get on with since they tended to be more patient and less impulsive, the latter a failing to which Kitty herself was prone.

One pleasant exception was her friendship with Margaret, a shorthand typist in another left-wing union office where Kitty sometimes called on Party business. Tall, thin, bespectacled, every inch an English schoolmarm, Margaret was in fact a cheerful, plain-speaking Mid-Westerner with whom Kitty found a lot in common even though Margaret was seven years older, a gap which can seem quite daunting to someone of twenty-three. They shared the same political convictions; they detested capitalism, took much pleasure from news reports of the emergence of a 'new Russia' and enjoyed working for the Party. Margaret had had a number of jobs, including four years as a shorthand typist, a nasty spell in a sweatshop in Kansas City, and running her own secretarial bureau before working for the Party full-time. She had been transferred to Chicago about a year before. It was only by chance, in a heart-to-heart talk about men some time after they had met, when Kitty admitted that she was much taken by one of the Party's National Secretaries, that she found out that Margaret was Earl's sister.

Margaret professed astonishment and delight though how much she already knew we can only surmise. She told Kitty that she herself had been married for a while to a Party activist, Thomas Sullivan, 'but he was too active in the Party and not active enough at home'. She was now about to try marriage again, with Harrison George, another of the Party's leading lights, and urged Kitty to get serious with Earl. Evidently Margaret did not mention the minor bourgeois impediment of Browder's wife Gladys and their son.

Soon afterwards Earl proposed and Kitty, who wasn't in the habit of taking advice, followed her instincts and accepted, telling her parents after the fact. Her mother had a token cry and her father had a brief, equally token grumble, and both then bowed to the inevitable. When in due course they met Earl, they were much taken by his country-boy's aw-shucks style and, in Nathan's case, by his political views. A very low-key wedding followed shortly thereafter, and Kitty moved in with Earl. In fact they were not together that much, since Earl was overwhelmed with work and came home late, worn out and sometimes irritated. He was constantly travelling at home and abroad, sometimes for months on end, fire-fighting the problems of a Party leadership riven by dissension. For good tradecraft reasons Earl rarely told Kitty where he was going and what he was doing, and if indeed her father had been something of a wanderer, she might not have thought Earl's long and frequent absences anything unusual. It is the period described by Browder's biographer as a dramatic and unexpected turning-point in his life as he shifted from mundane office routine to international intrigue: 'He travelled third class on third world passenger trains and crossed oceans on tramp steamers in the process of becoming a respected Comintern veteran.'

Though Kitty's archive file does not mention it, one of Browder's absences abroad must have been an exceptionally long one because in January 1926 he went to Moscow to attend a Comintern arbitration between the CPUSA's New York and Chicago branches, a dispute in which Stalin himself became involved at one point. Even that encounter was probably not the high point of the visit since Browder also found time to start an affair with Raisa Luganovskaya, an ambitious and nubile thirty-one-year-old Profintern bureaucrat. Raisa bore him a son, Felix, in 1927, but whether she was aware of Earl's first marriage and his two sons, or that he had been through some form of marriage ceremony with Kitty, is uncertain.

Kitty did her best to keep a nice home, but money was a problem as she earned next to nothing and the Party did not pay Earl much. In 1927 they moved to New York, where Kitty took a secretarial job with the International Workers Aid Organisation, a front organisation used by the Comintern to channel funds to overseas Parties. Other members of her family also moved to New York. Her two sisters and brother had married, and their father was now an invalid, his health deteriorating, though her mother was still going strong, having less to worry about with the children gone.

CHAPTER 4

East Is East

More and more often when Earl Browder did get home, he was in a foul mood and Kitty knew why, for he made no secret of the fact that things in the Party were going from bad to worse; it was steadily losing what little influence it had in American political life and its ties to the unions were eroding. Though it did its best to maintain an outward show of unity, the CPUSA was deeply split to the point where there were in fact two controlling centres and two Party lines, with a baleful finger pointing at both left- and right-wing 'opportunistic tendencies', as the Party jargon had it.

Each faction fought for its own platform. One was known factually, if unimaginatively, as the Ruthenberg-Pepper-Lovestone faction; the other had the even more unwieldy title of the Foster-Bittelman-Dana-Cannon group, whose titular head, William Z. Foster, was a highly effective trades union organizer and early backer of Browder, but no friend of his. Foster was perennially among those jostling for position towards the top of the Party's very greasy pole, but never quite made it to the pinnacle to hold the position of General Secretary in his own right.

Each faction was itself torn by disunity and disagreement. Cannon, a die-hard Trotskyite, preached ultra-revolutionary theories and advocated militancy, the creation of a Red Army and immediate revolution in the United States, while Lovestone advocated the theory of American Exceptionalism, arguing, based on the post-war boom, that the golden age of capitalism had dawned and that the United States was immune from economic crisis. The long arm of the Kremlin managed to prevent a public split when Charles Ruthenberg, the Party's General Secretary, suddenly died at the age of forty-five Though the Foster faction almost grabbed the reins, Comintern intervention saved the day and Lovestone took his position.

Earl grouched around with a face like thunder. For one thing, the shift in the balance of power within the Party could put a serious crimp in his career. All his friends were with him in the minority, while Lovestone and his closest associate Ben Gitlow made no secret of their hostility. But perhaps the most depressing reason was that, in his heart of hearts, he found himself coming around to Lovestone's point of view that America might be different. One day he told Kitty that he could simply not face any more squabbling and that he needed to get away and bone up on theory. He told her that he had been offered a job with the Profintern organising their work abroad for a year to eighteen months. Would she come with him?

'I'd even go to China if you wanted,' Kitty thrilled.

'You guessed,' Earl was taken aback. 'That's where the job is. In Shanghai.'

Kitty, who had always dreamed of travelling the world, clapped her hands in glee.

Earl then said that she would have a job to do as his assistant. She would also have some assignments of her own, which would be interesting but possibly a bit risky at times.

'I'm not scared of anything,' she replied.

'Just mice,' Earl interjected.

They had made up their minds and the Party leadership raised no objections. On the contrary, Browder was an active and dangerous opponent in their factional fights, he was popular and had quite a lot of support, so the opportunity to take him off the playing field for a while was too good to miss. His friends also supported his move, since a power base among the militant merchant seamen around the Pacific would be a worthwhile card in future Party tussles. A few days later Earl asked, 'Would you like a surprise?'

'Of course I would,' she replied. 'What is it?'

'Where would you like to go best of all besides China?'

'Well,' Kitty pondered, 'Miami, Yellowstone Park, San Francisco, Paris, Monte Carlo . . .'

'How about Moscow?'

'Whaaat, Moscow?' Kitty screamed. 'You're pulling my leg? I've never even dared dream of going there.' Moscow. Mysterious, magnificent Moscow. Revolutionary Moscow, fountainhead of all her cherished beliefs, her City on a Hill. 'You really mean it? Moscow?' she repeated.

He assured her that he wasn't joking and that they were going via Moscow partly because it was an easier way to get to Shanghai but mainly because he needed to agree their plans with their Comintern and Profintern colleagues, get their instructions and also pick up some propaganda literature.

'And you know what I'm going to do while you're busy with that?' she said. 'I'm going to explore every inch of the city, look at the people, breathe the Moscow air and lay my hands against the wall of Lenin's tomb; just touching it will give me strength.'

Earl told her to start packing as they were sailing in a week's time on the *Nordwyck* from New York to Hamburg via London. From Hamburg, they would take a Soviet ship to Leningrad, and from there go by train to Moscow.

The week dragged interminably and at night Kitty fell asleep dreaming about the trip, waking each morning terrified that something would happen to stop her going. She counted the days and the hours, and, harking back to her childhood, tied a yellow ribbon round a chair leg to help make her wish come true. The day before they were scheduled to leave, the Party Treasury gave Kitty $10,000 (nearly $150,000 in today's values) as seed money for their China work and to provide financial support for the Chinese trades unions.

It was later alleged that the money was in the form of one single $10,000 Treasury note, which is maybe why Kitty had little trouble hiding it from any inquisitive customs inspectors. Whether the note was genuine or a forgery is a matter of some speculation since, according to the defector Walter Krivitsky, Stalin had authorised a sophisticated currency counterfeiting operation with the specific aim of creating money to fund the Comintern's China initiatives, in the hope that banks that far away would be less alert and sophisticated. He records that the operation ran into trouble when its prime movers could not resist using some of their product in the US and tangled with gangsters in laundering it. Gitlow later claimed that an attempt by Browder to cash the note in the Philippines drew the attention of counter-intelligence authorities to his Shanghai activities.

Kitty's NKVD files are silent on how she contrived to get the passport she needed for the trip, but fortunately the US State Department's are not. Until the 1930s the Department refused to grant passports to known Communists, so those who needed papers to travel had to break the law and bend the truth. Kitty's application was a farrago of falsehood in almost every particular, save for her height of five foot three, and the colour of her eyes and hair. It took only three days from the application, dated 23 November 1927, for a crisp new passport to be issued to Katherine Harrison, who declared she had been born in San Francisco on 24 May 1899, clearly taking advantage of the Great San Francisco earthquake and fire of 1906, which had wiped out almost all of the city's official records. Describing herself as a student, she gave her address as 350 West 21st Street, New York, and claimed that her father Nathan had been born in Chicago and had died in 1920. Two people vouched for her, a totally fictitious uncle, Jack Harrison, in fact an alias for John W. Johnstone, subsequently described by the Department's investigators as 'an important Communist leader', and a witness named Vivian Wilkinson, whose aunt Grace Hutchins, as the assiduous investigators later pointed out, owned the building on New York's lower West Side which housed the CPUSA head-quarters. Kitty seems even to have fudged her travel plans, saying that she was sailing in the *Leviathan* rather than, as her file shows, the *Nordwyck*, and that she was going abroad to study.

The great day finally dawned and the couple were seen off by three of Earl's Party colleagues, his sister Margaret and her husband, his niece Helen Lowry and Kitty's brothers and sisters. Before the *Nordwyck* left, they managed to get through two bottles of cham-pagne, ships being outside the reach of Prohibition, and Margaret whispered to Kitty with a wink, 'Bring us back a baby Chinaman.' Kitty simply sighed sadly for she had always wanted a child, but for some reason she and Earl had never been lucky. This both worried and annoyed her, despite Earl's constant reassurance that 'this is no time to be bringing kids into the world anyway', an attempt at justi-fication which neatly skirted the issue of his son growing up in Kansas.

Their escorts said their farewells and disembarked to watch from the quayside as the ship was nudged out into the open sea by her tugs. Earl and Kitty stood on deck waving goodbye, watching Manhattan slide past in the dusk, like some huge ship itself with its towering, brightly lit superstructure.

A few hours after entering the Elbe estuary, the *Nordwyck* was gliding smoothly across Hamburg harbour. They could see scores of other ships, some ploughing slowly towards them, some moored alongside the wharves, while fast launches bustled importantly to and fro. Looming above the water, huge cranes loaded and unloaded cargo. The brightly painted terminal buildings of the famous ship-ping lines of Europe and the Americas were silhouetted against the skyline, each topped by their company logo in huge letters. Seeming to have shrunk somehow against this grandiose background, the *Nordwyck* found its berth and moored. The pilot went ashore clutching his traditional gift of a bottle of whisky and the customs and immigration officials came on board. Not that they presented any problems; their reaction to an American passport was the universal one, in those days, of a bow, a scrape and a wave of the hand, insulating the bearer from any tedious questioning or bag opening.

Earl and Kitty took a taxi to the Soviet consulate, clattering through Hamburg's cheerful and lively streets, bustling with the vitality of a busy port. Sailors roamed in packs in search of the seedier parts of town while on the main streets stolid burghers and their solid Fraus promenaded proudly with their children. Nothing, it seemed, could ever disrupt their placid, well-established way of life. Peace and prosperity would surely prevail for ever.

The consulate was clearly expecting them and gave them a gracious reception, at which they received their Soviet visas in a mere fifteen minutes. The Vice Consul told them that the *Komsomol* was sailing for Leningrad the day after next, so they had plenty of time to relax and see the sights. He recommended the Schlesienhof, an inexpensive, modest, but above all clean, little hotel. Kitty gazed at him in awe, for he was after all the first Russian (or Soviet) she had ever laid eyes on. As they chatted in German and English, his excellent grasp of both languages amazed her because she had gained the impression from the American press that the new breed of Russian diplomats were ex-miners or stable lads who could not even speak their own language properly. They unpacked their bags at the Schlesienhof and then set off to explore the city. The sense of ordered calm and the outgoing, friendly people struck them again. Kitty, as the German speaker, stopped a couple of times to ask the way and was impressed that the passers-by did not just go to great lengths to explain but even offered to guide them.

The next day she wanted to visit the Hagenbach Zoo and on the way back Earl fancied a beer, so they stepped down off the street into the next basement bierkeller they saw. Inside they found a bizarre scene, with rows of young men in brown uniforms bellowing a song and beating time on the tabletops with their mugs. Kitty went white with rage. 'What are they singing?' Earl, who spoke no German, asked, puzzled. Kitty translated angrily:

'Losing my Life,
Will be of some use,
If that's what it takes,
To get rid of the Jews.'

'Let's get the hell out of here,' muttered a shocked Earl. The mood had been broken and the image of a decent, well-run city shattered, so they walked back to their hotel in silence.

Early next morning, 15 October, they boarded the *Komsomol* for the voyage to Leningrad, back down the Elbe and through the bustling Kiel Canal. Its banks were lined with tiny hamlets, which merged into one another in an almost continuous ribbon, some of the houses so close to the bank that, helped by what seemed to be the local custom of leaving the curtains undrawn, you could see right inside. There were only a handful of passengers though, like the *Nordwyck*, the *Komsomol* also carried cargo. Kitty prowled the deck, keeping herself to herself, listening to the Russians talking and trying to make out at least the general drift of what they were saying.

Almost all the way across the Baltic they were wrapped in rain and mist, the foghorn blaring non-stop. The sun reappeared only as they were approaching Leningrad, where they moored alongside a cargo wharf and Kitty's fairy-tale began to come true. A well-dressed young man in a hat and a carefully knotted tie came on board and introduced himself as Michael, their Intourist guide. He gathered up their passports and escorted them to the exit, waving them through customs and immigration. Parked outside was an almost new Ford ('The 1925 model,' Earl whispered, much impressed), in which he drove them to the Astoria Hotel in the city centre.

Kitty was tremendously impressed by Leningrad. London aside, of which she had no real memories, she had lived in Winnipeg, Chicago and New York, and had made the brief stopover in Hamburg, but none of them could compare to this magnificent city. Whether Michael had chosen the route with care, or whether each street really was just more splendid than the last, she did not know, but Kitty sat transfixed. When they reached the Neva and she saw ahead of her the fantastic sight of the Winter Palace, the Isaakieyev Cathedral and the Admiralty, she rubbed her eyes in disbelief.

The hotel gave them a pleasant double room, and a splendid dinner in the downstairs restaurant left them almost unable to move. They spent the next day in a whirl of sightseeing at the Hermitage, Detskoe Selo and the Peterhof, before boarding the Red Arrow for Moscow. Preening herself in their neat and comfortable compartment in the international class carriage, Kitty declared, 'I could live in here for ever.'

'You might fancy it now, but I bet you'll be singing a different tune after nine days,' Earl laughed. 'That's how long it takes to get to China.'

'Nine days?' Kitty asked in astonishment. 'What a huge country this is.'

When their train arrived at the Oktyabrsky Station in Moscow, another Intourist guide, Yuri, met them and took them to the Hotel Savoy, one of the hotels reserved for foreign visitors and off-limits to Russians save for the omnipresent secret police watchers.

Moscow seemed drearier and poorer than Leningrad, with so many buildings with peeling stucco, their walls at odd angles, crowds of ill-dressed people on the streets, and beggars and homeless children everywhere. Even right in the centre, in Okhotny Ryad, there were more squalid little houses, a flea market and sad clusters of street kids huddled around the street-pavers' tar cauldrons trying to keep warm. 'All of this is the legacy of the Tsar's time made worse by the after-effects of the war,' Earl sought to explain.

'But the war's been over for six years,' Kitty objected.

'Yes, but we've been through two wars here, lasting from 1914 to 1921,' Earl explained. 'The country was in ruins for seven years. Sure, we're still lagging behind. Last year America produced six million cars while here we produced none. But we're going to catch them up and overtake them,' he enthused, parroting an early Soviet slogan.

Yet again they had a splendid room and an equally splendid dinner. Although Browder was in a hurry to reach Shanghai, he had first to be briefed by the Profintern and he went there every day, just like a full-time office job, taking Kitty with him for the last few meetings since she was officially his assistant.

Earl's apparently successful attempts to keep both Kitty and the pregnant Raisa (whose lobbying of her Profintern boss, Solomon Lozovsky, had produced the Shanghai assignment) happy and unwitting must have been a stiff test of his skill and stamina. Before he took Kitty to the Profintern headquarters for the first time, he explained the basic background, slightly as though he was reading the words off an invisible card: 'The Profintern also goes by the names of the Trade Union International or the Red International of Trades Unions, and is a sort of subsidiary of the Comintern, trying to unite the workers in the fight against capitalism. At least that's the long-term goal. Near term its job is simply to co-ordinate the fight wherever the need arises. But you and I have some very specific missions for the Profintern out East. The labour movement there is just beginning. The local and colonial authorities are on their necks all the time, and they've even murdered some of the activists.'

'One unfortunate aspect,' he continued, 'is the racial hostility between the white expat workers and the local people, a tension which the bosses encourage by giving the expats better pay and working conditions. The local nationalists are stirring things up but they have their own agenda. We're going there to help organise the union movement and recruit supporters. This is how the Profintern have described our mission' – Earl pulled some sheets of paper from his pocket – '"To use all means to assist the trades union move-ment in the colonies, liaising with them as closely as possible and deploying your propaganda, agitation and organisational resources to help them."'

Kitty nodded in blank agreement at this formalistic phrasing. She would do whatever she could, though just what that meant she had no idea. An invitation, coupled with an admonition to wrap up warmly, arrived for Earl and Kitty to watch the parade marking the tenth anniversary of the October Revolution from a stand in Red Square. On 7 November they rose earlier than usual, ate a hearty breakfast to insulate them against the cold and made their way through a series of militia cordons to Red Square. The troops were already drawn up on parade. More and more people crowded into their stand and a tense silence hung in the air broken only by the bark of drill commands in the Square. Kitty tried to make her dream come true and actually touch Lenin's tomb, but wasn't allowed anywhere near it so she went back to the stand.

Suddenly there was a roar of applause as a group of men appeared on the roof of the mausoleum, but Kitty did not recognise any of them. 'There's Stalin,' Earl said *sotto voce*, pointing out a rather short, mustachioed man in a grey greatcoat. The applause grew as he turned towards their stand. Caught up in the excitement Kitty also began to clap as hard as she could, and Stalin gave them a wave of greeting and took up position in the centre of the group.

The Kremlin clock chimed and a smartly uniformed officer emerged from the gates on a prancing white horse. 'Who's that?' Kitty asked.

'Voroshilov,' Earl replied. This was a name Kitty knew as a hero of the civil war, and she watched him with rapt attention as he bellowed a greeting to the troops on parade. After the troops had been inspected, the march-past began, led by the infantry followed by the cavalry and the artillery, with armoured units bringing up the rear. It was an extraordinary, inspiring sight. The people around them cheered and clapped as the loudspeakers boomed across the Square: 'The military might of the first Socialist country stands ready to defend peace worldwide.'

A wave of happy, orderly banner-carrying demonstrators, many with children on their shoulders, flooded into the Square, waving good-naturedly at the crowds in the stands. Kitty waved back, never having felt so elated and proud to be on the same side as them.

A few days after the holiday, she and Earl left for Shanghai in the international class carriage, which would be hitched from Moscow to Changchun on to the Trans-Siberian Express. The day they left was warm for November, and until night fell Kitty sat gazing out at the woods around Moscow, their foliage fast turning yellow, the broad fields long since stripped bare by the harvest, and the peaceful little villages. The next day it was still warm as they crossed the Volga and headed towards the Urals, but when Kitty awoke the third morning it was to a world turned white. Sverdlovsk, Omsk, Irkutsk, Lake Baikal and Chita were all deep in snow. Their train reached the Chinese border in the middle of the night and, evidently forewarned of their arrival, the Soviet officials gave them no trouble.

Damaskin's account of Kitty's time in Shanghai from November 1927 is based on her personal file, not Browder's, so it does not mention that Earl had been to China before. The fact that he had not told her that he had also previously visited Moscow suggests that, as far as she was concerned, she had stayed at home in New York knowing no more than that he was simply 'off on the road on Party business'. In fact, Browder had landed in Canton some eight months previously and had travelled north through Jianxhi Province, spending about a month in China as a member of a Profintern delegation to the Pan-Pacific Trades Union Conference in Hankow, accompanied by the veteran British trades unionist Tom Mann and the French Communist Jacques Doriot. An undated Shanghai Municipal Police summary of events in China during that period, probably compiled in 1929 or 1930, states that the

Conference decided to set up a secretariat headed by Browder through which 'Communist work in this part of the world would be conducted'.

At the end of the Conference Browder had addressed a meeting of local workers, an event remembered for a charming misunderstanding of Anglo-Saxon names and titles which produced a proudly waving banner proclaiming 'Welcome the Earl of Browder'. Apparently referring to his return with Kitty in November, the police report added that 'soon afterwards he became active in this work' assisted by Kitty alias Mrs Alice Read, who 'joined as his wife'.

Kitty and Browder had crossed the frontier into a China torn by almost twenty years of civil war, in which recent Soviet attempts to exert influence over the outcome had been resolutely rebuffed, with the result that Soviet officials or anyone suspected of being involved with them were at significant risk. Though not without straightforward geopolitical motives, Soviet interest in stirring up trouble in China and the Far East – via the Comintern, the union movement and its intelligence services – used as its intellectual justification Lenin's argument that, as the West relied heavily on the backward Asian nations and their low-paid workers as a source of profit and raw materials, and as an outlet for Western goods, labour agitation was warranted. Indeed, all the more if it led to nationalist revolutions, which would be an effective flank attack on capitalism and accelerate its demise. Stalin's strategy for China, which he was as yet not able to pursue as a dictator and was subject to criticism from Trotsky and others, was to force the fledgling Communist Party in a united front with Chiang Kai-Shek's Nationalist Kuomintang (KMT) movement, as it fought to stamp out the feudal warlords and robber barons who held sway over various large areas of the country. Never more than a temporary expedient, this alliance had, for the past three years, broken down several times into fierce fighting, in which the Japanese, British and Americans all backed their different factions at different times.

At the Manzhouli Station the Chinese border guards and customs officers stood waiting. As far back as March 1926 the NKVD's Harbin *rezidentura* had reported to the Centre that the Nationalist authorities had ordered all Soviet citizens crossing the frontier at Manzhouli to be thoroughly screened, as a result of which several Russians intending to work in the various Soviet missions in China had been detained. By the end of 1927 the situation had deteriorated to the point where almost every incoming Russian was given a lengthy interrogation and intrusively searched. Kitty and Earl watched the Chinese gendarmes giving a Soviet engineer and his family a hard time, with all their belongings strewn along a customs bench, and with even the children's toys and potties subjected to minute scrutiny.

Kitty and Earl had two suitcases of books and pamphlets, which they were worried would create difficulties, but yet again their American passports worked like a charm. The Chinese saluted and, with a 'Yes, yes,' and a smile, waved them through. At Changchun they changed to a local train to take them to the port of Dalien (known as Dal'nii in Russian and Dalian in Japanese), whence they had a 1,000-kilometre, two-day boat trip to Shanghai, after having come more than halfway round the world.

The military campaigns had brought civil strife and bloodshed across the country, and the Shanghai that awaited Earl and Kitty had experienced more than its fair share. Euphemistically known as the Paris of the East, and more bluntly as the 'city of sin', Shanghai while geographically Chinese was in fact totally cosmopolitan, half of it governed not by the Chinese but by foreign powers through their own territorial concessions; in fact, it was the epitome of an outpost of Empire, 'about as international as the Tower of London,' as one disillusioned American visitor huffed. The British dominated trade, investment and banking and held a firm grip on the key levers of power, such as the Municipal Council and the customs, which governed the two and a half million people. The principal instrument of control was the International Settlement Police, which was a tough and vigilant British-officered force that was the hub of a seamless web tying together the British Special Branch, the Secret Intelligence Service and various branches of military intelligence.

The city lived up, or down, to its reputation, with its public face being trade, commerce and finance, and the ornate magnificence of the Bund, an embankment glittering with brightly coloured shop signs, its frontage festooned with ribbons and lanterns, all permeated with the odours of strange foods. Its not-so-private underside was a gangland heaven of drugs and prostitution – involving many of the White Russian women and girls who had fled to Shanghai from the Revolution, and catering for every imaginable and many unimaginable tastes – murder, and kidnapping. It was the base for the tycoons and robber barons who backed the KMT, the underground headquarters of the Chinese Communist Party and a magnet for adventurers, racketeers, con-men, spies, refugees and the flotsam and jetsam of the world. With all that, it was also a haven for intellectuals, among them Agnes Smedley, who was then living at 185 Chingquing Road in the city's leafy and architecturally distinguished Luwan district. A self-taught radical American journalist and crusader, Smedley described Shanghai for the faraway readers of the *Frankfurter Zeitung* as follows:

Life follows its normal carefree path. There are opulent official receptions and balls, new banks opening, the establishment of great financial groupings and alliances, gambling on the Stock Exchange, opium smuggling and mutual insults by foreigners and the Chinese . . . and there are nightclubs, brothels, gambling clubs, and tennis courts and so on. And there are actually people who call this the beginning of a new era, the birth of a new nation. This may be true for a certain class of Chinese, for the merchants, bankers and racketeers. But for the Chinese peasantry, that is for 85% of the Chinese people, all this is like a life-destroying plague.

Earl and Kitty arrived in a city still reeling from the menace and bloodshed of the previous months. In March 1927 British and American gunboats had bombarded Nanjing to protect the evacuation of foreigners to Shanghai after a number of them had been killed by Nationalists. When the Nationalists applied pressure on Shanghai, the Western powers reverted to Palmerstonian gunboat diplomacy, sending twenty-eight warships to moor offshore and landing a sizeable force of troops as a warning that the International Settlements were not to be touched.

While the flotilla lurked on the horizon and the KMT forces surrounded the city waiting to take control, the Communist-led unions seized power, but Stalin, still pursuing his dream of a united front, ordered that the KMT troops should be allowed to enter the city. When they did so, their erstwhile Nationalist allies turned on them, assisted by the infamous Green Gangs, in a massacre that left 300 Communists and union activists dead, but the Concessions unscathed.

It was the poverty and squalor, rather than the wealth, that first struck Kitty. As their ship moored, junks swarmed around, crammed with beggars – some armless, some legless, some with holes where their noses should be – blind men and men with suppurating wounds, all beseeching the passengers for money. There were even more of them on shore, but the police maintained a semblance of order there by clubbing the beggars and cripples out of the passengers' way.

Waiting for Earl and Kitty was a tall, sinewy man with Chinese features that seemed slightly out of focus. He introduced himself as 'Joe Linxin, actually "Zhou" in Chinese, but I'm half American. My dad was in the US Navy and my mother Chinese, like Madame Butterfly. So I'm genuinely international,' he laughed. 'We could take a taxi, but I want to give you your first taste of the exotic side of Shanghai so we'll go by rickshaw.'

'You mean, we'll be hauled along the streets by *people?*' Kitty protested.

'Well, do you want to leave them without even a crust of bread?'

Joe replied. 'They need to work to survive. If we don't hire them, they and their kids will go hungry. There aren't any more ships due in today.' Joe whistled and a crowd of coolies rushed up, all of them thin, wiry and long-legged. He crooked his finger at three of them and the rest slunk away in disappointment. Feeling very awkward, Kitty scrambled aboard one of the rickshaws. Joe shouted something and they moved off, the coolies seeming to make light work of pulling the flimsy carriages on their large wheels smoothly through the streets. The harbour was almost at the heart of Shanghai, so they quickly emerged on to the Bund. There were almost no automobiles, but the streets were jammed with pedestrians and cyclists. Outside some of the shops and the less salubrious establishments barkers touted for business. It reminded Kitty of New York's Chinatown, but on a much larger scale.

They turned off the Bund on to a clean, quiet street lined with well-kept houses. On the corner a policeman standing by a raised barrier saluted as they passed and, at a signal from Joe, the rickshaws came to rest. As the coolies stood panting, with sweat running down their faces and their half-naked bodies, Kitty realised that their job was hardly as easy as it looked. Joe paid them off, though to judge from the grumbling that ensued they had not received what they had hoped for; he cut them short with an angry bellow and a meaningful look in the direction of the policeman, leaving them to turn away dejectedly. 'You mustn't overpay those guys or they just keep asking for more,' he declared.

At the house which they were to live in during their stay, the maid, a pretty young Chinese girl, curtsied to her new master and mistress. Kitty loved the house, which was small, on two floors and comfortably furnished in the European style. The previous inhabitant had been an English professor who had left a week before, Joe explained.

Using at this point the cover name Mr and Mrs Harrison, Kitty and Earl set to work. His cover was as a representative of a firm of ships' chandlers, owned by a reliable man named Perkins from a working-class background, a business that gave Earl a legitimate excuse to meet people from all over without arousing suspicion. Perkins raised absolutely no objection about Earl spending whatever time he had to on his Profintern mission and went out of his way to reinforce his cover. Kitty paid several visits, ostensibly on the firm's business, to the Soviet consulate, where she got to know the Vice Consul, Vasily Roshchin, and their paths would cross several times in the years ahead.

Their arrival in the small goldfish bowl of the international community in Shanghai did not go unnoticed. Community protocol required that they give a cocktail party quite quickly, and this was Kitty's first experience as a hostess. She had no idea what to wear or how to go about things, but realised that, as she was there as an illegal, it was best not to stand out in any way and simply to do what everyone else did. Her maid Din was a great help and, although young, she was experienced, observant and spoke quite good English. Evidently the professor and his wife had entertained a lot and Din knew just what to do; she therefore took charge of everything, even suggesting what Kitty should wear.

On the appointed evening the guests began to trickle in, some late, others very late. Earl had stressed that she must remember who they were supposed to be and avoid expressing any political opinions. Kitty, rather insulted, just snorted. Earl circulated among the men, while Kitty paid attention to the ladies, whom she regarded as very dull and boring. Even the girls back in the factory had been better company. These women were heavily made up, dressmakers' dummies who knew nothing and were interested in even less. They prattled on about bridge and greyhound races at the dog track, which lay conveniently close to where many of them lived, halfway between Avenue Joffre and Route Frelupt. They seemed preoccupied by the latest Hollywood movies and were constantly moaning about how boring Shanghai was. Only one of them made any sort of impression on Kitty, a woman whom most of the other ladies seemed to go out of their way to ignore.

This was Agnes Smedley. Three years older than Kitty, plainly dressed with fine chestnut hair and lively emerald eyes, Smedley had moved to Shanghai after many years in tireless support of radical causes ranging from birth control to Indian independence. She was to spend many years chronicling the Chinese revolution as a war correspondent and, rather less obviously, as a Soviet agent. Some three years after meeting Kitty, Smedley was to introduce another spy, Ruth Kuczynski (alias Sonia Beurton alias Mrs Paul Hamburger and later the Soviet contact of atom spy Klaus Fuchs), to Richard Sorge, the GRU illegal who was to achieve notoriety in wartime Tokyo. Sorge and Smedley were to have an affair, but when he tired of her he described her dismissively as 'not the marrying sort . . . a mannish woman'.

Kitty and Smedley were too alike to become close friends, both headstrong and volatile, and Smedley also suffered from bouts of deep depression, but their political views were almost identical and Kitty talked with her quite openly. As far as the tense situation in Shanghai allowed, Earl began to extend the scope of his activities, which required him to set up links with trade unions in Hong Kong, Singapore, Jakarta and all over South-East Asia, where there was no union organisation. The staff in the ships' chandlers was small, but only Perkins, Joe and another employee, Chen Yen Yuichen, knew what Earl's real tasks were. Chen was a gregarious, cheerful soul, quite untypical of an underground Party worker. Earl trusted both of them implicitly, and they were often with him when he met people arriving from other parts of China or from abroad, although, if he did not need an interpreter, Earl would conduct his meetings in private, relying on Kitty to maintain a secret card index of his agents.

As Kitty and Earl developed their network, the political situation continued to deteriorate, and on 14 December the KMT government closed the Soviet consulates in Shanghai, Hankow and other cities, and arrested Soviet officials. By the end of the year practically all the Soviet organisations in southern China had ceased to function and communications with Moscow had been cut.

It was in this atmosphere that one day Chen reported to Earl that the network had noted that some of the individuals who had visited Earl were under surveillance. This set off alarm bells, and Earl told Kitty that they could not ask their contact from Jakarta to risk coming to Shanghai. She would have to go there herself to deliver a letter from the Profintern, to give them instructions, some cash and some leaflets, to get to know the people and to report back on what they were up to. Joe warned her to be careful, for the Dutch colonial police were on the look-out for any chance to catch trade unionists red-handed with literature they deemed subversive.

'Think of yourself as a bored, Auntie Mame type, who's decided on a whim to go off on a trip and just enjoy herself,' suggested Earl, sketching Kitty's cover story for her voyage south. She left on 20 December on the cargo steamer *Pearl of the Southern Seas*. Four days later she was in the South China Sea enjoying, as a Christmas present to herself, a harmless shipboard fling with the first mate, Tung, a half-caste Douglas Fairbanks lookalike. When she reached Jakarta, she had three days to do her job, handing over documents to a trade unionist named Djarra at a back-alley rendezvous and picking up a report from him. She also had time to see the city's exotic sights, checking constantly for hostile surveillance.

Although Djarra had echoed Joe's warning that the Dutch police stopped at nothing, even murder, in their attempts to smash the unions, she was staggered to hear from a dejected Earl when she finally returned that, not long after she had left, Djarra himself had been beaten to death, though apparently he had managed to get rid of his incriminating documents first. Kitty burst into tears, for a man had died because of her, and she became convinced that she must have been careless and had failed to spot her tail. 'But I checked and double-checked,' she sobbed in justification. 'No one was following me.'

Earl reassured her that there might have been another reason altogether. Maybe the authorities were watching him already.

Kitty's next mission, to Hong Kong, was shorter, and Earl and Joe gave her another thorough briefing. When she arrived, she made an extra effort to check for surveillance. Once again, she was convinced that there was none and she reached her rendezvous, exchanged recognition phrases and was taken to a small house by a canal, where she met Li, a thick-set, stern Chinese, and a burly European named Harold, from the semi-legal Stevedores Union. Kitty handed over the documents and cash she had brought with her, and they sat for a long time chatting and sipping green tea. Suddenly they heard the clatter of boots and a loud knock at the door. 'Police. Open up,' a voice bellowed.

Harold jumped up, stuffed the papers in Li's hand, and told him urgently to run for it and to hide Kitty. He would delay them.

With the police hammering even harder at the front door, Li grabbed Kitty by the arm and scuttled out of a door at the rear of the house on to the canal bank. It was pitch dark, but Li kept a firm hold of her and pulled her along a narrow path at the water's edge, clambered over a fence and kept on running. Behind them they could hear pounding footsteps and someone yelling at them to stop, but they stumbled down some muddy steps into a moored junk where two men waited. They paddled frantically out into the stream while Kitty flattened herself on the wet deck as two pistol shots cracked across the water. Their junk soon merged indistinguishably into a fleet of other small, lantern-lit boats.

On the other side of the canal Li and Kitty vaulted out into the darkness and disappeared into the crowd. Li decided that she should not go back to her hotel or the ship, and hid her with a Chinese family for three days until he returned with a friend. 'Harold's fine,' he told her. 'He's back at work already. They would have needed to catch him with documents on him as evidence and they didn't.' He then introduced his friend Deh, who was going to take her to a boat which would take her home. It wouldn't be de luxe, but at least it would be safe.

After what seemed like an endless circular tour of the teeming streets, a small boat took them out to a large Shanghai-bound freighter moored in the harbour. Kitty spent three days in a dark closet well below the waterline, with a pungent and rudimentary toilet stall next door, doing her best to sleep in between visits from anonymous crewmen who brought her scraps of food. Finally back in Shanghai, she left the ship as surreptitiously as she had boarded it and took a rickshaw home, where she recounted the whole story to a horrified Earl. He sat quietly for some time reflecting on what she had said. 'I think I'm beginning to understand what's going wrong,' he said without explanation. Joe was against her being sent out on another assignment but Earl was firm. 'I need you to go to Manila in a couple of weeks, but I'm sure that this time there will be no problem,' he said, and that evening he had a long talk *à deux* with Chen.

When the time came for her departure, Earl and Joe briefed Kitty again in minute detail. But just before she left, and she was alone with Earl, he asked, 'Did you understand and remember all the things we told you?'

'Of course,' she replied.

'Well, now you can just forget them. Forget everything. I'm going to give you a new set of instructions and that's all you'll need to remember. It's simple. When you get to Manila, you're to stay at the Bagio Hotel. And that means *stay there*. Don't go out at all. After three days you turn around and come back here. Is that clear?'

'No, actually . . . But, whatever you say. What do you want me to do with the documents?'

'An errand boy will bring you flowers. Give the papers to him. And if he hands you something, take it.'

Kitty did as she was told and endured a boring week on a boat, followed by three days stuck in the hotel. Then she at last received the promised visit from a flower-laden errand boy, who discreetly produced an envelope from under his shirt. She took it, handed him the documents she had brought and tipped him a dollar. It all went like clockwork, but the day she was due to leave Kitty spotted a report in the local English-language daily about a raid by the police on the home of a colonial official. Whatever they were looking for, they had failed to find, and as the outraged official had considerable clout with the authorities, the police were seriously embarrassed and the Commissioner was under pressure to come up with a public explanation. The official's address, she saw with astonishment, was the one she had been given in her original briefing and which, despite Earl's admonition, she had not forgotten. When Kitty got back to Shanghai, Joe was not to be seen. When she asked where he was, Earl just shrugged. 'You could say he's moved on,' Chen told her expressionlessly but with a suggestive skywards jerk of his head. 'No, actually he's more likely to have gone that way,' he corrected himself, pointing even more meaningfully at the floor. 'Traitors don't go to heaven.'

Kitty subsequently made three more courier runs for Earl, all of them trouble-free, but elsewhere the Soviet network was under constant attack. One case in particular, which centred on a spy using the identity of a businessman calling himself Noulens, who claimed to be Swiss, brought the undercurrent of espionage to the surface. The dramatic events surrounding the episode can now be recounted in some detail, much having been revealed in the unpublished memoirs of a British intelligence officer, Major (later Brigadier) Leonard Field, who had been attached to the Shanghai Defence Force and played an active part in directing the operations of the Special Branch in 1926 and 1927. The Branch had become aware that a Comintern agent was operating a sizeable organisation from Shanghai involving the use of fourteen post-office boxes, six separate telegraphic addresses and three business offices. Surveillance revealed that much of the organisation's communications were addressed to Noulens, but were written in an unbreakable cipher, and it was only when an office cleaner, who was a police informer, found a scrap of paper that contained the title of a book lodged in the wickerwork of a wastepaper-basket that the police got the breakthrough they had been praying for.

The next day Field broke into Noulens's apartment and, in a classic example of life imitating art, found on the shelves an espionage novel by E. Phillips Oppenheim, part of the title of which matched the one on the scrap of paper. A hastily ordered copy enabled the authorities to establish from Noulens's cipher traffic that he was the Comintern's senior representative in the Far East and the main paymaster for the Chinese Red Army, channelling them as much as £3 million a year in gold, which, according to Field's investigation, came in by diplomatic bag to the Soviet consulate and was handed over to an American intermediary or 'cut-out'.

Noulens was arrested, thereby paralysing the Red Army's initiatives, but Field recorded that the mysterious American was 'too quick for us' and the local American authorities were 'unable to take effective action'. Various lawyers materialised to prepare Noulens's defence and attempted to demonstrate that he was, first of all, a Belgian, and when that failed a Swiss national, and that in any event he should be extradited rather than tried in China. With help from the British Secret Intelligence Service, Field was able to disprove the citizenship claims and Noulens was jailed for life. He was to confide to his diary that as the Chinese saw little purpose in feeding a prisoner for twenty or thirty years at state expense, Noulens probably did not survive very long.

The US Office of Naval Intelligence noted that after Noulens's arrest, the clearance of mail from the post-office box for the Oriental Literary Society, which had been rented by Kitty, ceased abruptly. When they eventually opened the box, police found it stuffed with material 'mainly of a Communist nature'.

Although apparently undaunted by the loss of Noulens, Browder did experience considerable difficulty with his link to Moscow, for he had arranged, while he was preparing for their China mission, to have his correspondence with the Profintern channelled via the Soviet consulate in Shanghai. Since Browder and Kitty both worked for Perkins's firm of ships' chandlers, it would be unlikely to arouse suspicion for them to call at the consulate, ostensibly to discuss supplies and repairs for Soviet vessels. However, the Chinese closure of the Soviet offices in December 1927 had served to cut that channel of communication and the Soviet intelligence services found themselves similarly handicapped. Conditions were to get considerably worse, even though as a precaution an illegal *rezidentura* had been set up in Shanghai. Mikhail A. Trilliser, the OGPU's deputy chairman and also head of its foreign department (INO), had instructed the Harbin *rezidentura* to cease all operations and communications via the Shanghai consulate and arrange for sensitive papers to be hand-carried by specially recruited couriers.

In the mid-summer of 1928 Earl prepared a report for the Profintern, a document which Kitty had to take to the consulate in Harbin. She had a watertight 'legend' for the trip since Earl was also the Shanghai representative of the Singer Sewing Machine Company, which had shops in Harbin, and Kitty's cover story was that she was going there for him on an inspection visit. She made no secret that she was planning the trip, talking about it to Agnes Smedley and several other friends.

Harbin was a predominantly Russian town, largely populated by White Russians, situated in the middle of Manchuria, astride the Songhua River, 350 miles north-west of Vladivostok. When Kitty was planning her visit, it was governed by a municipal administration caught in an uneasy Soviet-Chinese struggle for power. Originally the headquarters for the construction in 1898 of the Trans-Manchurian (or Chinese Eastern) Railway, it flourished as a major transport hub in the Russo-Japanese War and the First World War. It was home to the biggest Russian community ever to exist in the Far East, vastly swollen by the flood of refugees from the Bolshevik revolution, and the cosmopolitan atmosphere was enhanced by Japanese, Korean, Chinese Mongol and Jewish communities.

When Kitty was in the midst of getting organised, Agnes Smedley said that she wanted Earl to meet Harry Terras, a businessman from

New York. Kitty told Earl, who raised no objection, and Terras, a tall athletic young man with piercing dark eyes, came to see them the next day and announced that he knew exactly who they were and what Earl's mission was. He said that he was also on an assignment from the Comintern, but having arrived in Shanghai he found himself without a channel of communications. He added with engaging frankness that he had absolutely no proof of his Comintern connection, but that if Kitty would do what he was about to ask, his colleagues in Harbin would vouch for him.

'What do you want her to do?' Earl asked.

'One of our Chinese comrades is a delegate to the Comintern Congress coming up soon in Moscow,' he replied, 'and we need to help him get to Harbin. And for that we need to give him cover. I've also got a letter I'd be grateful if you could stick in your bag and take for me too.' Terras explained that with China torn by war, the only people who were still able to travel with relative freedom were foreigners and people accompanying them. His friend, whom he said was called Van, could not take the ferry to Dalien since there were strict embarkation controls in Shanghai and he might be recognised. Anyway, Terras grinned, poor Van suffered terribly from sea-sickness.

Together, Earl and Terras decided that Van should accompany Kitty as both a personal secretary and an assistant. Some time earlier, not knowing when he might come in useful, Earl had cultivated a friendship with Tao Siang, head of the Chinese administration of the International Settlement. Earl now invited him over to the house and explained that Kitty needed to go to Harbin on business and that, because he could not leave, he was reluctant to let her make such a long and dangerous journey on her own. He wanted her to take a personal secretary along as an escort, and he asked Tao to issue Van with the necessary travel document. Glad to be able to help his good friend Harrison, within a few days Tao produced the document, which bore a photo of Van over a false name.

With these precautions completed, Kitty and Van made their way through the milling crowds at the Central Station and reached their seats in the first-class train compartment. They had travelled only about a hundred kilometres before they began to see the first signs of war: bombed-out railway stations and derailed trains tilting crazily down the embankment. The train moved slowly, often stopping to be tucked away in sidings, sometimes in the middle of nowhere. Eventually it came to a complete halt at a deep gorge, where a trestle bridge had been blown up only very recently. The engine driver pulled on the whistle for a long time in a forlorn bid to get help, but eventually the guard came through the carriage telling the passengers that they would have to get out and walk a short distance to where a temporary wooden bridge had been constructed. Kitty, Van and the rest of the passengers shuffled off obediently; 'a short distance' turned out to be an hour's walk away, and the 'bridge' was nothing more than a few clumsily nailed planks and a rope for a handrail, with the whole contraption swaying dangerously over a roaring stream.

Kitty went first, trying not to look down into the ravine below, where the water smashed angrily against the rocks. Van followed close behind her, his hands stretched out to grab her if she slipped. She thought that maybe if she closed her eyes, it would be easier, but then she risked losing her footing. Somehow she edged her way across while the other passengers behind her waited patiently in a long line. 'I made it,' she squealed triumphantly. Van nodded with approval. He spoke almost no English but seemed to manage to get the drift of what was said if people spoke slowly.

Someone said that they would have to wait for another train to reach them from the next station down the line, and as night was falling the passengers huddled around several hastily improvised bonfires. Food, plain but very welcome, seemed to appear from nowhere, and children were tucked down to sleep. Kitty had often been surprised by the ability of the Chinese to adapt stoically to whatever came along, and she joined Van in a group around the largest fire. The Chinese chatted quietly for a while and then began to sing. Noticing that Kitty had been squeezed out of the gathering, a woman smiled at her and gestured to her to come in close to the fire. It grew colder and someone slipped a lumber jacket around her shoulders.

The next morning a train appeared but took them only as far as the next station, where they were told they had to change. The firm police grip on the crowds, so much in evidence at Shanghai Central, was conspicuously lacking and people pushed and shoved their way into the carriages, reminding Kitty of a movie she had seen about the civil war in Russia. Van, powerfully built and not a man to stand on ceremony, bullied his way through, pulling Kitty in his wake. There was no question of trying to find the first-class compartments; they were just relieved to be on the move again across the Great Chinese Plain, which began at Nanjing. Carefully cultivated fields stretched as far as the eye could see, tilled by entire families, the women with their babies strapped to their backs. There was almost no sign of war, but the train soon began to stop again to allow military trains to pass, carrying troops supporting Chiang Kai-Shek's attack in the north on Zhiang Zuolin, the warlord who had run Manchuria since 1917.

At the Xianan River they found themselves in a combat zone where Japanese troops had intervened on Zhiang's side in a bid to maintain Tokyo's own claims and influence. Shells began to burst near the train and the engine driver slammed on the brakes, allowing the passengers to rush for cover in the bushes until the shelling stopped. When they finally got back on to the train, it remained stationary and a group of soldiers appeared, pushing aggressively through the carriages and picking out the younger men, who trailed off after them, heads bowed in submission. 'What's going on?' Kitty asked in terror. Van managed to explain in pigeon English that the soldiers were press-ganging young men to serve in Chiang's army ahead of the big assault.

The soldiers came down the carriage towards them and a senior NCO looked appraisingly at Van, much like a plantation owner at a slave market, and gestured to him to get out. Realising what was about to happen, Kitty shrieked wildly that they had no right to take Van, that he was her secretary, that she was an American citizen, and much more besides. The soldiers obviously could not understand a word she said, but were clearly taken aback by her ferocity. One of them scurried off to fetch an officer, who strolled up self-importantly. Kitty turned her attack on him, waving Van's *laissez-passer*, and protectively tugging Van to her side by his sleeve. It was not clear whether the officer understood what she saying, except that the word 'American' appeared to have an impact. He probably reckoned that, since the United States was backing Chiang Kai-Shek against the Japanese, it would be best not to tangle with this hysterical Yankee. In any event, he waved his hand, indicating that they were to be left alone, and the soldiers sloped off, marching their press-gang with them.

The train eventually raised steam, but soon stopped again because of more fighting ahead, and the passengers had to disembark and trek for several hours around the town, with Van managing to hire a cart to take them to the banks of the Yellow River. The only way to cross was on a rickety ferry, and as twenty or more other refugees from the war zone also wrestled their way on board with everything they owned, the ferry sank lower and lower in the cloudy ochre water until it was lapping at the gunwales. The water was as choppy as the sea, and Kitty was petrified that the next wave would send them to their eternal rest on the river's muddy bottom. Fortunately, they made it across and reached the railway station after another long walk. Trains were running, but their Shanghai-issued tickets were not valid in Zhiang Zuolin's domain so they were obliged to buy new ones.

They chugged across China for another whole week, stopping, changing trains, having their papers checked incessantly. The only disturbance in an inconvenient but otherwise uneventful journey came near Tianjin, south of Beijing, when a gang of *Khunkhuz* (literally 'Red Beard') bandits from Manchuria stopped the train and swaggered through the carriages demanding gold and jewellery. Kitty was forced to hand over a little gold ring and $38 in cash, but the rest of her money was hidden in her clothes, and the macho pride of the bandits meant that they would not stoop to search a woman.

From Tianjin the railway ran north-east to the coast of the Gulf of Bohai at Qiningdao, and then to Shenyang, across the Liao River to Changchun, requiring a change of trains on their journey into China. At long last Kitty and Van reached Harbin, where they made straight for a safe-house whose address they had been given by Harry Terras. It was the first night that they were able to spend in more or less normal, even if modest, surroundings and to stuff themselves with hot food, allowing Kitty to show off her prowess with chopsticks.

The next morning Kitty went to the Soviet consulate and asked for someone who spoke either German or English. A woman who gave her name as Yunona Sosnovskaya appeared, and after talking to Kitty for a few minutes took her in to see Erich Tacke, whom Kitty guessed correctly, given his fluency in the language, was actually German. She was to discover only later that he and Sosnovskaya were man and wife. She handed over Earl's letter to the Profintern and told him about Van, whom Tacke confirmed they had been expecting for some time. He asked Kitty about the situation in Shanghai and made a careful note of her comments, which were based not just on her own observations but also on what she had been told by Earl, Agnes and others.

When she mentioned Harry Terras and handed over his letter, there was an awkward pause. Tacke took the letter but gave Kitty a puzzled look and said that he did not recognise Terras's name, although he added that he didn't know the names of 'all our people'. The next day Kitty moved into a hotel and validated her cover by visiting the Singer representative office. She also said a warm goodbye to Van, whom she never saw again. Some days later he and a number of other delegates to the Comintern's Sixth Congress crossed out of China illegally on their way to Moscow in a clandestine operation orchestrated on the Centre's orders by Vassily Roshchin, who had been transferred to Harbin from Shanghai.

Despite constant harassment from the Chinese and Japanese security apparatus, Roschin worked with Tacke and others to successfully intercept Japanese diplomatic mail in and out of Harbin; they also got a copy of the so-called Tanaka Memorial, a secret Japanese diplomatic paper which laid out a timetable for Japan to annex adjacent Mongolian, Chinese and Soviet territory as a step to establishing its hegemony in Asia. The memorandum had had a lot of play in the contemporary press and was seen as one of the factors behind a cooling in Japan's relations with the United States. In fact, the Japanese authorities believed that it was the Americans who had actually stolen it and some doubt was also cast on its authenticity.

After three days in Harbin Kitty returned home, uneventfully, via the more usual route, by the train to Dalien and then by ferry across the Yellow Sea to Shanghai, only to find that she and Earl must have passed each other halfway, for he had left her a note to say that he had received a telegram inviting him to attend the Comintern Congress. It may have been this journey which resulted in a brief entry on his police file, noting that he had been spotted arriving back in Shanghai on 11 October 1928 aboard the SS *President Cleveland* from Manila. This report, which was later passed to the US Office of Naval Intelligence, revealed that Kitty, using the name Mrs Morris, had moved from an unknown address to rented rooms at Flat 205, 1552 Avenue Joffre, a street which bisected the French Concession. Evidently Browder had joined her there, using papers identifying him as a journalist named George Morris, and had stayed until he left again for Dalien on 1 December on the *Dalien Maru*, claiming that he was en route to Berlin via Siberia.

According to the police file, Morris had rented a post-office box, but in doing so had given an address in the British Concession, where the police, armed with a photograph, swiftly got the servants to identify Morris as Browder. Calling herself Alice Read, Kitty also rented a post-office box in the rather grander name of the Oriental Literary Society.

After Browder's departure, his flat in the British Concession was taken over by 'W. A. Haskell, alias Shidlov, alias Lund, believed to be an American', and the police watchers saw Kitty calling there frequently with letters and papers. Perhaps coincidentally, in 1943 Moscow Centre informed the NKVD's New York *rezidentura* that an agent named LUND, a German national, was en route to the United States to operate as an illegal. Given the passage of time it is unlikely, though not impossible, that this was the same man.

When the peripatetic Earl got back from Moscow, he told Kitty that there had been yet another bitter and fruitless wrangle between the CPUSA's various factions and that being sidelined in China was not doing him any good. It was time to go home. Accordingly, Earl and Kitty left Shanghai in February 1929 (although her police file records her departure on 25 June). They sailed on the *Hoten Maru* to Dalien, where she told the Japanese immigration author-ities that she was en route to New York, and used her bogus San Francisco passport, which gave her birth date as 1879. Conceivably, this subterfuge was actually nothing more than a simple misreading of a scrawled '1899'.

The couple broke their journey in Moscow, where Earl spent most of his time at the Comintern Executive Committee, and where one afternoon he and Kitty were delighted to spot Morris Childs, the famous 'Red Milkman', in the cafeteria. On Browder's recommen-dation he had been offered a place at the Comintern's Lenin School, where candidates were taught the skills of spreading propaganda and fomenting subversion. Browder told Kitty that he thought Childs was honest and had a good head for business, hoping that he would take the post of Party Treasurer.

(Browder's complete confidence in Childs was sadly misplaced, for he was later to become a committed anti-Communist. Childs's first post after his return from Moscow was as the Party's district organiser in Wisconsin, and in 1935 he took a similar but more important job in Chicago. He later moved to New York and in 1946 was appointed editor of the Party's newspaper, the *Daily Worker*. In 1947 he lost his job, his health and his wife in one of the endless bouts of Party infighting and, disillusioned, he was induced by his brother Jack to become a covert informant for the FBI. Re-established in the Party's good graces in the late 1950s, and tasked to solicit financial support from the Soviet Union, over the next seventeen years Childs is said to have made fifty-two trips to Moscow and travelled extensively throughout the Communist Bloc, reporting every detail of his high-level contacts to the FBI, and in the process channelling to the CPUSA via Canada millions of dollars in Soviet covert funding, on which Jack is said to have taken a rake-off before he died at the age of eighty-nine in 1991. This sort of double life required quite a thick skin. In the 1950s, on the basis of their old family friendship, Morris was asked by a member of the Harris family for advice on how to respond to a subpoena from the House of Representatives UnAmerican Activities Committee. Whether or not scripted by the FBI, Childs's advice was to 'take the Fifth [Amendment]', advice which in the event was not followed, fortunately for the person concerned.)

Their last months in Shanghai were to prove to be the beginning of the end of the relationship between Kitty and Earl. He had become steadily more difficult to live with, more withdrawn and more impatient. Bizarrely, the cause of the first major row they had ever had, and the start of the cooling-off, was the 4,000-year-old, simple-looking but sophisticated and complex Chinese game of Go, in which the uneducated Kitty somehow always outwitted her clever husband. One win too many sent him into a tantrum that, looking back, was the first sign of trouble, although there may have been other contributors. He may have deliberately distanced himself from Kitty, having realised that the termination of his Shanghai mission would also curtail his ability to juggle wives and lives at each end of the Trans-Siberian railway. Alternatively, he may have had to choose, and may well have made the cool calculation, or been told by some shadowy figure in Moscow, that his personal future and Party career would be better served if he stood by Raisa and their child.

CHAPTER 5

A Friend of a Friend

In the middle of a freezing Moscow January in 1930 Artur Artuzov, then head of the OGPU's counter-intelligence section and designated as the next Chief of the INO, its foreign department, was summoned to a meeting with the OGPU Chairman Vyacheslav Menzhinsky. A brilliant linguist and by some accounts an extraordinary polymath, Menzhinsky had been born to a Polish family in St Petersburg and had come to intelligence work after many years in exile as a revolutionary. Artuzov, diminutive, music-loving, artistic and uxorious, and regarded as having been very effective in his counter-intelligence role, had unusual roots for a Soviet intelligence officer for he was the son of a Swiss-Italian cheesemaker named Frauchi, who had settled in Tsarist Russia.

'Artur Khristiyanovich,' Menzhinsky began. 'We have to make a presentation to the Politburo. You've been going through the INO files and you were personally involved in a number of the major cases. I want you to draft a paper to cover three main issues. First, what our Service has achieved in the past three years. Second, where we went wrong and why, plus the conclusions we've drawn, and third, how we plan to do a better job.'

'Who's actually going to present the paper, Vyacheslav Rudolfovich?' Artuzov enquired.

'You are. Trilliser's sick and I don't know if he'll be back on his feet in time. You really need to rehearse carefully. When they start in on questions, they can pick up on things you never expected and they can zero in very hard. The paper has to go to the Central Committee in ten days so you've got plenty of time to do your homework.'

Blessed with a steel-trap mind and total recall of all the cases involved, all the successes, the failures and the missed opportunities, Artuzov could have polished off most of the paper that same day. Having already given it a lot of thought in anticipation of his new job, he was also clear about his proposals for the future. But a Politburo presentation required more than ideas for it had to be backed up with precise facts and figures, make well-argued and succinct recommendations, and have a well-honed script. And even though they would have had the paper in advance, maybe with several bulky appendices, the Politburo only gave you fifteen minutes to actually state your case, which meant a good deal of meticulous rehearsal.

Artuzov briefed one of his subordinates to draft the first section, on results, confident that he could always expand or revise it himself later. He decided to tackle himself the second and most delicate section, on their failures, the reasons for them and the conclusions to be drawn. The paper had to be honest, but at the same time it had to avoid putting at risk officers who may have had a part in the cases in question but who had not been responsible for their failure. Nor should it reflect negatively on the Service as a whole, since several of the failures had been due to circumstances outside the Service's control.

Artuzov began to study the files of memoranda on failed or unsuccessful operations, on major penetrations by hostile services, and on traitors and defectors, and decided to start with 1927, which he recalled as being 'a very difficult year'. In March the Poles had rolled up the Soviet network in Warsaw, then the Turkish authorities had arrested Soviet agents in the trade mission in Istanbul, and in April the police in Beijing had raided the Soviet consulate and seized a number of operational documents. Shortly afterwards there had been similar raids in Shanghai, Tientsin and Canton, though there the police had gone away empty-handed. A little later the Swiss had arrested eight members of a local network run by a Communist Party member and in May a number of officials in the Austrian Foreign Ministry had been taken into custody for passing secret documents to the Soviets. Finally, there had been the British police raid on Arcos, in the wake of which Anglo-Soviet relations had gone into a steep decline. Furthermore, there had been the raid on the consulate in Harbin, when Tacke's wife Sosnovskaya had calmly walked out through the police cordon with secret files stuffed up her dress, pretending that she was pregnant.

Artuzov spent a long time distilling the essence of the file and reflecting on the lessons to be learned. His most depressing conclusion was that when things went wrong, it jeopardised the work of regular Soviet diplomatic missions and consulates. Anti-Soviet feelings were aggravated, even to the point where diplomatic relations were broken. Moreover, intelligence officers operating out of Soviet organisations were under constant surveillance, and failure had repercussions, not just for the diplomats but also for the local Communist Parties, and put the Soviet Union on the defensive by having to explain their conduct. If diplomatic relations were severed, contact with Soviet agents was lost and networks built at great cost in terms of time and effort became redundant overnight. As he contemplated the implications, Artuzov doodled, and in the middle of a blank page he drew a building to represent a diplomatic mission, with a tangle of little paths leading from the back door to squares that symbolised individual agents and networks. He then crossed out some of the paths and replaced others by broken lines, all the time thinking up alternative structures for running operations under cover.

The Politburo met on 30 January, and Menzhinsky, Artuzov and Trilliser were called in on schedule and the Chairman, Molotov, asked Artuzov to speak. 'The results of our work,' he began, but Stalin, who was padding restlessly around the room, interrupted him with a wave of his pipe.

'Comrade Artuzov,' he purred, 'we know what you've done. We've read the paper. So go on to your next point.'

'As regards failures . . .' Artuzov began again.

'Yes, yes, we know about those as well. As I said, we've read your paper. I find it hard to say this to men in whom we have so much trust but what I can't understand is why, when things go wrong in your work, it rebounds on the state itself, the Party and on other Communist Parties? Accepting that things do go wrong from time to time, how can we structure the work so that the damage is localised, so that our international interests aren't compromised? How do we set things up so that if one agent is blown, it doesn't bring the enemy's bloodhounds sniffing round our embassy door?'

'Comrade Stalin,' he replied. 'We've given this a lot of thought, and we've concluded that we have to close our legal *rezidenturas* in the diplomatic and trade missions and create a completely separate, illegal agent network. The agents would operate secretly, as foreign nationals and have their own lines of communication with the Centre.'

'An interesting thought,' Stalin said, 'but, you know, Comrade Lenin taught us that it's a question of finding the right balance between legal and illegal methods. Admittedly he was talking about the Party, but what he said is equally relevant for intelligence work. It comes down to a question of emphasis. By all means let's put more weight on illegal operations, but at the same time let's keep going with the legal *rezidenturas* in our overseas missions.' Stalin stopped talking but, as no one seemed to care to break the silence, he eventually continued. 'Comrade Lenin always stressed how important it was to have reliable communications. As you know he ran an extensive and reliable network of agents through his newspaper *Iskra*. That means we need reliable couriers. I repeat "reliable". If we don't, it'll ruin the whole effort.

'Finally we need to train our intelligence officers in special schools, where they can become totally fluent in the languages of the countries where they're to be posted, totally immersed in the way of life. So, I want you to let us have detailed plans for the creation of an illegal service. Carry on . . .'

When Artuzov had finished, Stalin summed up: 'Our intelligence service has acquired some useful experience. It has certainly been successful in operations against the White émigrés and in producing important political intelligence. But it's still not providing what the leadership needs. As the international situation gets more complex, we need to be fully informed on an even broader range of issues. Above all we need reliable intelligence on what the main capitalist states are planning against us. You have to focus on Britain, France, Germany, Japan and the countries around our borders. We need you to find out for us what plans the ruling circles in those countries have to blockade us financially and economically. You have to get hold of copies of the secret military and political treaties between them. Finally, Soviet industry needs intelligence on new technical developments, design and production drawings and plans, the sort of thing we can't get in the ordinary course of business.

'I believe Comrade Artuzov can handle these tasks. We can find another appropriately senior position for Comrade Trilliser,' concluded Stalin, and this was duly recorded in the Politburo minutes.

Soon afterwards Artuzov was confirmed as head of the INO and Trilliser was appointed Deputy People's Commissar of the Workers' and Peasants' Inspectorate. Trilliser, who had been born in Astrakhan in 1883, had spent time in jail and in exile in Siberia for revolutionary activity against the Tsar and it had been the legendary Felix Dzerzhinsky, the founder of the Cheka, who had brought him into the intelligence service. In 1935 after his spell with the Inspectorate, which may have been a temporary sidelining,

Trilliser was named head of the Comintern's OMS, or External Relations Section, a highly secret unit which worked hand in glove with the OGPU in financing foreign Communist Parties and supervising the activities of the Comintern abroad.

Back in the Lubyanka, Artuzov set about planning the new illegal service. Part of it did indeed include Stalin's suggestion of setting up a network of foreign nationals, men and women, to serve as couriers. Both illegal and legal *rezidents* would have a hand in their recruitment as would case officers visiting from the Centre.

For Kitty, of course, all of this was in the future, for in mid-February 1929 she and Earl returned to New York; the CPUSA's sixth congress opened the following month. Earl immersed himself in Party work, including negotiations between the majority and minority factions, while at the congress itself, which ran from 1 to 9 March, much time was taken up debating the Comintern's warning about the dangers of right-wing opportunism. This led to Lovestone's ousting as General Secretary and the so-called Foster-Browder group taking control. Earl was now consumed by a new and even more heated battle whose epicentre shifted between New York and Moscow, including a session of the Comintern's Executive Committee at which he represented the CPUSA, and in October 1929 Lovestone and Gitlow were expelled from the Party.

Almost simultaneously the Wall Street crash marked the start of the greatest economic crisis America and the world have ever seen. But slump or no slump, the internecine struggle into which Browder had flung himself continued to rage ferociously and absorb every minute of his day and much of his night.

When she got back to New York, Kitty took some time off and caught up with her family. She found that her father was seriously ill and fading fast, and her mother, a prematurely aged sixty-three year old, spent all her time at his bedside. Her elder sister Jenny, who had been married for some time and had several children, was totally absorbed in running her home. Both Jenny and her mother had kept up, and were proud of, their British citizenship, and in effect Kitty had kept hers too, since Canada was a British Dominion whose citizens were considered British subjects. Though on perfectly good terms, Kitty and Jenny were not especially close, their values and their interests being too far apart, although Harris family lore has it that Jenny was the first one to follow their parents into socialist and Communist beliefs and then converted her siblings.

Kitty enjoyed a very good relationship with her sister Nancy, who was also married with two children, and with her two sisters who still lived at home, Jessie, a cheerful girl of seventeen, and the handicapped Tilly, then aged twenty-one. Kitty spent most of the time she had taken off with them. Meanwhile, her brother Abe, aged twenty-five, had majored in sport at school and was a trainer, while twenty-two-year-old Harry worked in an office. Nancy's husband, Thomas Bell, a dour Glaswegian and committed Communist, was to graduate from the Comintern's Lenin School, to which he travelled using a false passport in the name of Milton Hathaway, which brought him later under the FBI's surveillance; whether the name was concocted by a Party passport fabricator with literary leanings, we shall never know.

Kitty also caught up with Margaret Browder, who was now back from a stint working in Moscow for the Profintern. She was saddened to hear that Margaret's second marriage was on the rocks, to be ended in divorce in 1929. Though Kitty confided to Margaret that things between her and Earl were not going well either, Margaret appears to have kept silent about her brother's relationship with Raisa, as she had done with the little matter of his first wife and family.

The Browders were far from financially well-off and, contrary to the myths about Moscow millions, Earl's Party salary was tiny and Kitty really needed to find a job. She found one eventually with the American Negro Workers' Congress, and worked there until March 1931, but as a charity they could not pay much and she left in search of a better post in March 1931. This was hardly easy, given the slump, so Nancy recommended that Kitty approach

Amtorg, the Soviet trade organisation. Armed with a recommendation from the Party, which Earl's position reinforced, she started work with Amtorg on 20 May 1931 and worked as a secretary until April 1932.

In 1931 Amtorg was one of a handful of Soviet organisations in the United States; and until formal diplomatic relations with the Soviet Union were established in 1933, there were no Soviet trade missions in America, leaving Amtorg as the sole channel for trade and commerce. As a result, Amtorg received a steady stream of American businessmen wanting to trade with the USSR, a flow which increased with the slump, since the Soviet Union was thought to be a reliable and credit worthy international trading partner. The visiting businessmen made every effort to cultivate the Amtorg staff from top to bottom, down to the humblest secretaries, and Kitty often found herself invited to have lunch or a cup of coffee, though her hosts usually went away disappointed by her determination not to talk business.

Towards the end of 1931 Kitty was delighted to recognise one of the visitors as Harry Terras, the same Harry who had asked her to take Van with her to Harbin. He had some business with one of the Amtorg engineering staff but when he returned he asked her, as visitors often did, all the more since she was attractive, to have dinner with him. They met on the corner of 58th Street and Lexington Avenue, and Harry guided her to what he said was his favourite Manhattan restaurant, the Henri Quatre. Coming off the street into a medieval castle was quite a surprise, and at the top of the stairs stood two knights in armour, swords in hand. The basement restaurant was fitted out in what Harry claimed was authentic twelfth-century style, with three portraits of Henri IV on the walls. In the first he was on his throne, wearing his crown and holding a sceptre. In the second he was prostrating himself, barefoot and humble, at the feet of Pope Gregory VII, while in the third he was shown in an angry and majestic pose expelling the Pope from his kingdom. The artificial medieval effect was spoiled by the brooding presence in one corner of the room of a sad man in a high-necked tunic singing plaintive Russian folksongs and playing the balalaika.

'How do you like it?' Harry asked.

'At least it's different,' Kitty nodded towards the singer. 'Maybe they couldn't find any troubadours in New York, though with so many people looking for work you'd have thought they could even find ancient Greeks if they wanted to.'

Harry laughed and they sat down; they began chatting, and hardly stopped. She told him about her adventures in China with Van, and could even see a funny side to having to scramble over the wooden bridge, saving Van from the press-gang and being held up by bandits. She also told him that when she had mentioned Harry's name at the Soviet consulate, they had claimed not to recognise it.

'I can understand that,' Harry said smoothly. 'They can't be expected to know everyone in the organisation.'

They talked about getting by and making ends meet in the Depression, and Kitty confided that she rarely saw her husband nowadays as he had moved himself to Party headquarters, claiming that he needed to be close to the action. She talked nostalgically about how full and exciting life had been in what everyone else thought of as boring Shanghai, and told Harry about her trips to Jakarta and Manila, how she had run from the police in Hong Kong and spent three days hidden below decks in the steamer.

'I can see you've had a lot of underground experience,' Harry said with apparent surprise. 'But I imagine you're fed up with all the travelling.'

'Not at all,' Kitty declared. 'I can't sit still, I get bored.'

'In that case I may have a proposition to put to you. But first I have to ask you a few questions and you have to give me absolutely straight answers.' In fact, he had a lot of questions, about her attitude to the Party, the Comintern and Communist Russia, and, among others, how she would feel about being away from her husband for long periods of time. She must have given the right answers because eventually Harry said, 'I'd like to offer you the opportunity to see the world and to do something else at the same time, to serve the cause you clearly believe in and I know from what you've said you want to help. In a nutshell, I'd like to send you to Europe for several years to work as a courier.'

'For the Comintern?' she asked.

'Well,' Harry hesitated. 'Sort of for the Comintern. But you've worked underground and you know not to ask questions. The less you know before you need to the better. I can tell you this though, you'll be working against war and against Fascism.'

'I saw the Fascists in Germany four years ago. It was terrible. Tell me,' Kitty asked excitedly, 'will what you want me to do help Russia?'

'Yes,' said Terras emphatically.

'Then I'll do it,' Kitty exclaimed. They chatted a little longer and then Terras confessed that their meeting hadn't been an accident. She had been the reason he had gone to Amtorg, and he already knew a great deal about her.

'We may not meet again,' he said, 'but people will get in touch with you on my behalf and when they do, they'll say . . .' He thought for a moment looking at the restaurant walls. 'They'll ask you, why did Henri the Fourth go to Canossa? And you'll answer, "To deceive Pope Gregory". Remember that. Not to repent, like the history books claim, but to deceive. Henri may not have been an intelligence officer but he knew that you have to deceive your opponent.'

When they said goodbye outside the restaurant, Harry raised his clenched fist in the Communist salute and murmured 'Red Front' before completely disappearing from her life for ever, as if he had never existed. The detail of this recruitment, a highly significant event, has even been almost completely expunged from Kitty's NKVD file, for on page 214 there is a note signed by Pavel Sudoplatov stating baldly: 'By whom, and when, recruited, unknown.' Later in the file, on a separate page, there is a single sentence: 'Recruited by Harry Terras, 1931. The latter's identity has not been established. No trace on operational records.'

This lack of detail, so uncharacteristic of the NKVD's files in which every apparently innocuous item is carefully recorded, may have an explanation in Stalin's purges. If, like so many others, Terras had been executed as 'an enemy of the people', someone may have sanitised the file to protect Kitty from being contaminated by his alleged crimes. The only surviving reference is in a separate file in which someone named 'Taras' was listed on a *rezidentura*'s expense claim mentioning him as a recruiter of couriers, in conjunction with GIN and GYPSY. Attached was a message addressed to the Centre from ARTYOM, the code name for Boris Berman, then the *rezident* in Berlin: 'Send urgently the biographies of GIN and GYPSY and advise by whom recruited or tasked.'

GYPSY, of course, was Kitty's code name, and GIN, later to be known as ANNA, was revealed in the file as Margaret Browder, who was recruited in 1931, at almost the same time as Kitty, by the same 'Taras'. Further research in the archives disclosed a single memorandum recording that TARAS, aka Terras, was in fact the work name of Abraham Einhorn, who had been arrested by the NKVD on charges of being a foreign spy and being involved in a plot, sentenced by the Military Collegium of the Supreme Court and shot. The memorandum also mentioned that GYPSY and GIN knew each other, adding further support to the identification of the two agents. As for their recruiter, Einhorn was recognised as having been an outstanding intelligence officer. According to Volume II of *Studies in the History of Russian Foreign Intelligence*, Abraham Osipovich Einhorn was one of the Service's more active intelligence officers in the scientific and technical line.

Born in Odessa in 1899, he became an officer of the State Security Organisation in 1919 and served in the Civil War. He travelled illegally to Turkey, Greece, Palestine, France and Germany. He commenced service in the INO in 1925 and was in Italy from 1926 to 1927 attached to the legal *rezidentura*; after this, he worked illegally in the United States. While working there Einhorn travelled to China and Japan to carry out orders from the Centre. In the US he set up a company (with an American businessman as its President) to orchestrate the shipment of military goods to the USSR via third countries.

Other information obtained by Igor Damaskin indicates that Einhorn had also recruited an agent codenamed POP (PRIEST) in the US, who was well connected with government and business, advised a number of firms and the Government itself on the Soviet market, and played a major role in organising wartime shipments to the USSR under the Lend-Lease programme. Whether PRIEST and the President of the US company were one and the same remains unknown. Einhorn and his networks also made an important contribution by obtaining blank US and Canadian passports (sometimes with Austrian and German visas already added) for use by illegals.

CHAPTER 6

The Spying Game

Kitty woke up, stretched like a cat and opened her eyes, to be greeted by a view of huge waves through the porthole. Even a large liner like the *Queen Mary* was buffeted by the rolling waves, rising and falling to an inexorable rhythm as its bows smashed through the storm. Most passengers had long since taken to their bunks, miserably sea-sick, and Kitty looked across sympathetically at her cabin mate who lay grey-green and sweating profusely, her eyes tight shut.

Kitty was impervious. On the contrary, whenever she had the chance she would head for the upper deck to peer out at the raging ocean, which was like a picture from a story book: stormy, low black clouds sliced by sheets of lightning, and thunder merging with the beat of the ocean into a terrifying continuous rumble. Kitty watched it all from behind the comforting shelter of a glass screen streaked with spume, imagining what it would be like to be out there in a fishing boat.

'Man is tossed about by Life like a frail barque on the billows,' she remembered from one of her childhood books of poems. 'Just like me, actually,' she laughed to herself, wondering just what she was sailing into, what storms lurked ahead and what was waiting at the end of the voyage. Her mind went back over those last months in New York, when she and Earl had become no more than friends. He had rarely been at home, spending his time locking horns in Party in-fighting, in the middle of which he went to Moscow for a meeting of the Comintern Executive Committee. He now had the top job, General Secretary, but though Lovestone, Gitlow and some of the other prominent members had been expelled, they were still stirring things up with volleys of complaints to the Central Committee and attempts to rally the rank and file to their support. Party membership had shrunk to derisory levels – a mere 9,000 – and its influence on American political life, marginal at best even in its heyday, was now zero. When Kitty told Earl that she was off to Europe for a while, his only reaction in the midst of his preoccupations was to nod, for their marriage was over. (A pen portrait of Earl at work at that time appeared in, of all unlikely places, the fledgling heavyweight US business journal *Fortune*. Its author too was unlikely – the essayist and photographer, Walker Evans. In a long and thoughtful piece on the CPUSA, he wrote of a visit to the Party's headquarters on Manhattan's lower West Side, where the General Secretary and the Central Committee occupied the top floor of a nine-storey building that stretched between 12th and 13th Streets. Its lower floors housed the *Daily Worker* offices and various Party operations. Browder, Evans wrote, sat in a large room with two desks, three chairs, a blue spittoon and a bust of Lenin three times life size.)

There were no rows and no recriminations. Kitty never lost her respect for Earl as a man and as a political leader, but love was gone for ever, if indeed it had ever been there. Maybe it had been no more than her need for submission to a domineering, macho man. Maybe her temperamental, active and restless nature hadn't been right for him. Maybe what he needed was a quiet, loving homebody to make a fuss of him and give him lots of children. Whatever the reason, they parted as friends. Earl knew why Kitty was going to Europe and made no objection. Margaret too vanished from her life, declaring that she was off to study in Moscow. Minus both husband and best friend, Kitty waited impatiently for whomever Harry Terras was going to send.

One day the messenger duly appeared, a self-effacing, dark-haired young man, who came into the Amtorg office and asked to see the President. 'Do you have an appointment?' Kitty asked. 'If you don't, it's going to be tricky because he's got back-to-back meetings.'

The visitor said that he would wait, but a little later, when the lobby was empty, he asked Kitty a question which would have sounded distinctly peculiar to anyone else who might have heard it. 'Do you happen to know why Henry the Fourth went to Canossa?'

'What do you mean? Why?' Kitty asked, taken by surprise. Then the drill came back to her and she answered with a nervous laugh, 'Well, everyone knows why. To deceive Pope Gregory the Seventh.'

They agreed to meet in midtown and she arrived on the dot. The man, who said his name was Leon, arrived a few minutes later, and they did not talk for long. Leon's first question was whether Kitty was ready to leave. She was, she confirmed. A businesslike man of few words, he pulled a transatlantic shipping timetable out of his pocket. 'The *Queen Mary* sails in exactly two weeks, on 25 April,' he informed her.

'The *Queen Mary*! How absolutely wonderful,' Kitty thrilled.

Leon seemed to go out of his way not to respond to her enthusiasm. 'Yes,' he said flatly. 'Someone will meet you when you get to Bremerhaven.'

'But how will we recognise each other?' she asked. 'There will be hundreds of passengers.'

'Don't worry,' Leon told her, smiling for the first time. 'The person meeting you knows you and you know them. Now, to business. There's enough cash in this envelope to buy a second-class ticket from New York to Bremerhaven, to cover your travel expenses and to keep you going for a while after you get to Germany. After that they'll pay your expenses and salary out there.' Lowering his voice to a conspiratorial whisper, but speaking with obvious sincerity, he added, 'Kitty, I want you to understand that we live in difficult times and that our country is still poor. All of us who work abroad have to share the hardships of the folks back home. So don't expect a big salary.'

Kitty interrupted him, 'The money wasn't why I agreed to work for you.'

'Well then, we're in business,' Leon said, reverting to his former crisp manner. 'I don't need to tell you to keep your mouth shut. You're not to tell anyone what you're going to do, or even that you're in contact with us.'

'So what do I tell my family?'

'Tell them you're going to study in Moscow.'

Kitty immediately thought of Margaret, who had just left 'to study in Moscow', and smiled to herself.

'One more thing,' he continued. 'In the interests of security we all use code names. Do you have one you'd prefer?'

Kitty thought for a moment and then said, 'One of my friends once nicknamed me "Gypsy". Let's use that.' Kitty now had the first of what was to be a long series of agents' work names.

'Unless there's anything else you want to ask,' Leon drew their talk to a brisk close, 'it only remains for me to wish you a good trip and success in your work.' With that they walked off in different directions.

Kitty quit Amtorg on 15 April 1932 and bid an emotional goodbye to her family, with a special hug for her father whom she was sure she was seeing for the last time. She gave Jessie, but no one else, a hint of her secret, telling her that she wouldn't just be studying but that she would have some other things to do as well. And now here she was on the deck of the *Queen Mary*, an elegant American girl off to seek adventure in Europe.

Kitty was lucky to get away. The State Department had issued a circular the previous month to American consular officers world-wide expressing doubts about Kitty's status and asking to be informed if she applied for a new US passport. Since they assumed she was still overseas, the circular seems not to have been drawn to the attention of passport-issuing offices in the US itself, and in those far-off pre-computer days it took weeks before her application filtered back to Washington. It had been processed and granted at Manhattan's City Hall on 12 April 1932 (again in the name of Katherine Harrison, but this time giving as her address 101 West 11th Street – a block away from CPUSA headquartrers.)

When eventually the alarm bells rang, investigators were dispatched to the scene, but the bird had flown and they could do no more than report in classic 'FBI-speak' that neighbourhood enquiries showed that Kitty was known to speak several languages and was 'an evil woman . . . whose apartment was the venue for meetings of foreign men of various races'.

Kitty was blissfully unaware that her passport had raised suspicions, and even less that the latest reports from Terras and Leon to the Centre were sewn into a mattress in the cramped stokers' quarters deep in the heart of the liner. Until the Soviet Union established diplomatic relations with Washington DC, all Soviet intelligence traffic was smuggled across the Atlantic by crewmen on the stately transatlantic liners. Unlike cargo ships, the liners ran to a fixed schedule so that mail could be sent and received regularly.

By evening the storm had died down and the next day brought sunshine and a clear blue sky. Kitty sunbathed in a steamer chair on the top deck, leafing idly through a book she had brought along for the voyage and casually brushing off an older man who was coming on to her. When the liner berthed at Bremerhaven alongside the fleet of historic ships belonging to the German Maritime Museum, Kitty scanned the waiting crowd for a familiar face and eventually spotted, a long way from her studies in Moscow, none other than Margaret Browder. They kissed and hugged, delighted to be together again and working for a common cause, work that would be interesting but dangerous. Margaret had already handled several missions and felt that she had earned her spying spurs. She briefed Kitty quickly, gave her an address and password for making contact in Berlin, and took her to the trolleycar stop, where they said goodbye. Margaret then strolled unobtrusively back to the dockside to meet the courier from the engine room.

In less than an hour Kitty was in the ancient heart of Bremen. The Berlin train was not scheduled to leave until the evening, so she had the day to herself, wandering round the market, the Gothic cathedral and the Baroque town hall, in front of which stood Roland's Column, a symbol of the city's freedom, with another monument nearby commemorating the intrepid quartet of donkey, dog, cockerel and cat immortalised by the Brothers Grimm as The Bremen Town Musicians. The next morning she was in Berlin, whose grey and sooty streets filled with edgy, scurrying pedestrians were a sad contrast to Bremen's beauty and charm. On the walls fluttered the last tattered scraps of the posters put up for the previous month's presidential elections, in which Hindenburg had received eighteen million votes, Hitler eleven million and Thälmann some five million. Competing for wall space were the screaming posters slapped up by the Communist Party exhorting the Social Democrats to join forces with them in resisting wage cuts. A united left-wing front might have offered some prospect of defeating the Nazis but unity was a pipe dream. The Communists denounced the Social Democrats as traitors, and the latter hit back by portraying the Communists as the devil incarnate, and swinging their support behind Hindenburg, rather than Thalmann, as the lesser of two evils compared to Hitler and as a bulwark against Fascism. Less than a year later, on 30 January 1933, Hindenburg would cede power to Hitler. Right now, however, Kitty's most important task was to find her way from the station to her hotel, weaving through a sullen crowd, some sporting the same brown shirts that she and Earl had seen in the Hamburg bierkeller four and a half years earlier.

Kitty could only afford a cheap hotel, but that was what she preferred anyway. It was, she thought, typically German, spotlessly clean and tidy. Though modest, it managed to provide a sumptuous breakfast, and she had several days to get the feel of Berlin, travelling practically every metre of the U-bahn, which was as uncomfortable as the New York subway but a whole lot cleaner. She walked down the Unter den Linden, past the Soviet embassy with its red hammer-and-sickle flag, mentally blowing it a kiss, past the Brandenburg Gate and the Reichstag, through the Tiergarten, past the Siegesäule, the triumphal column celebrating Germany's victory in the Franco-Prussian War, and along the bustling Kurfürstendamm. But though on the surface the people around her seemed to be having a good time, the atmosphere struck her as more strained, more edgy, than she remembered in Hamburg, to the point of being slightly scary. Though she was no longer a novice at the game, when the day came for her first rendezvous she was as nervous as a schoolgirl walking into an exam room.

'I'd like to buy my husband a Meerschaum pipe. What can you show me?' she asked the man behind the counter.

'We've got quite a good selection but I'd recommend one with an amber mouthpiece.'

'Meerschaum' and 'amber mouthpiece' were the key words in the recognition signal and response, and the tobacconist ushered Kitty into the shop's back room and asked her to wait. For no good reason she had visualised her future controller as a stout, balding man with a red face and powerful hands. In reality he turned out to be slim, and with the sharp features usually indicative of a sharp mind.

'Hello,' he said in German, 'or would you prefer English?'

'I don't mind,' Kitty responded. '*Guten Tag!*'

'Okay, German it is. You could use the practice. My name's Karl. How was the trip?' They relaxed, and Kitty told him all about the voyage over. Then, at Karl's urging, she shared with him her first impressions of Berlin.

'You're right. Everyone here's pretty nervous,' he confirmed. 'The Fascists are hungry for power. If it suits them, they'll use legal means like elections as the way to get it. But if it's to their advantage, they'll have no compunction about seizing power illegally. There's no one to stand in their way. The Left is split. The Social Democrats have betrayed the workers' movement and hope that when Hitler comes to power he'll include them in the Government. Some chance. He wrings anyone's neck if he thinks he can get away with it. And once he's seized power, there's no way he won't plunge the country into war, maybe even a world war, but he'll go for Russia first. He said as much in *Mein Kampf*. He says he needs *Lebensraum* in the east. That means Russia. Our job is to stay right on top of everything that's going on here. There are other tasks too, but I'll tell you about them in due course. Now let's talk about finding you something to do. What are you planning to do? For cover, I mean.'

'I haven't thought about it yet.'

'You need to legitimise your being here. A woman who does nothing, living off income from unknown sources, is bound to arouse some suspicion among the people you run into as well as the police. I reckon the best thing would be for you to enrol in Berlin University's German for Foreigners course. You'll have to pay but we'll help with that, of course, and attendance isn't compulsory, which suits us nicely.'

'But don't you think I'm too old to be a student?'

'Don't worry about that,' Karl laughed. 'Some of the students there are in their sixties. Find yourself a decent apartment that doesn't cost too much, in a nice part of town, we'll show you where to look. Try to make friends with the landlady and make the best impression you can on your neighbours, the local shopkeepers, the postman, the doorman, really on everyone you meet. It's very important, because if the police ever do take an interest in you for whatever reason, you need people to say nice things about you. Another thing, not a word about politics. No contact with left-wingers, no meetings and demonstrations. It's too easy to come to the attention of the police that way. So avoid them like the plague!

'As far as what you'll be doing for us, although it isn't all that complicated, it is vitally important. You'll be holding in your hands not just documents but the fate, and it wouldn't be overdoing it to say the freedom and the lives, of many people. If you're careless, if you get sloppy, if you don't pay constant attention, they may be uncovered, they may be arrested and they could even die.' He stopped and looked sympathetically at an evidently distressed Kitty. 'Have I scared you?'

'Yes,' she admitted nervously, 'a bit.'

'Don't worry,' Karl reassured her. 'I'm sure you'll be just fine.'

There was a knock at the door and a woman came in with a pot of steaming coffee and a plate of biscuits. Karl introduced her to Kitty as Gerdy, the tobacconist's wife, and said that they would be working together. The two women took to each other straightaway. After they had chatted for a while Gerdy left, and Karl asked Kitty to tell him about herself. When she mentioned meeting Tacke in Harbin, Karl blurted out, 'You know Erich!', and then stopped abruptly, since he was not cleared to tell Kitty that back then in Harbin and now here in Berlin Tacke had been his, and now her, controller. If Erich thought she needed to know, he would tell her himself. They talked for an hour or more about their assignment, settled their emergency contact procedures and agreed to meet again at the shop in a fortnight's time.

Meanwhile, Kitty was to organise her German course and find an apartment, and two weeks were more than ample to do this. When she first joined the class, Kitty justified starting with the basic course on the grounds that while she spoke a little German she was finding grammar difficult. Her class included several Englishmen, Canadians and Americans as well as a Hindu, an Egyptian and two Turks. One of the Englishmen was red-haired and aged around thirty, who introduced himself as John Smith. 'Oh, yeah,' she said to herself as he sat down next to her. He said that he was a supporter of the British Fascist Oswald Mosley and told her how delighted he was at the Nazis' rapid progress towards power. She had no option but to listen patiently to his rantings.

When she next met Karl, he approved of all she had done in settling in and told her that it was time to get to work. She was to come there at the same time the day after next, pick up the mail and go to Prague. The address was, funnily enough, another tobacconist's. She was to give them the password and hand over the mail. If they had some to give to her, she was to bring it back with her.

Kitty duly collected what Karl had called the mail – a small package which fitted snugly and unobtrusively in the bottom of her handbag – and set off on her first 'active service' assignment. She was excited but nothing like as wound up as the time she had smuggled the ill-fated parcel of cash into Canada for Lamberti. Maybe that could simply be put down to age and experience, but maybe too she was bolstered by the sense, shared by most intelligence professionals, of confidence that what you were doing was in a good cause and that, if it came to it, you could count on a powerful country to back you up.

She took the overnight sleeper and arrived in Prague as the sun was rising. She was travelling on her American passport, which, as usual, meant that she was treated with wary respect at the border. Like every other first-time visitor, she was immediately smitten by the City of a Hundred Towers, with Hradcany Castle silhouetted against the morning sun, the bridges over the Vltava and the medieval streets lined with chestnut trees.

Following her briefing to the letter, she went straight from the station to the mail-drop, without checking into her hotel. She easily found the tobacconist's on a quiet leafy side street. There were no other customers. When the assistant asked politely what she wanted, Kitty told her. 'I'm looking for some American cigarettes called Duncans.'

Duncans were not widely smoked in America, let alone in Europe, so using them as a codeword was pretty safe. 'We're out of them right now. We'll be getting some in next week. Tuesday, I would reckon,' the girl replied, nodding her head to direct Kitty through the door behind the counter. Kitty cooled her heels for two tense hours until a tall, fair-haired man with blue eyes slid quietly in, introduced himself as Janos and apologised for keeping her waiting. He had sensed that he was being followed and had taken even greater care than usual to shake off any surveillance.

'You're new,' he said in evident surprise. 'I'd expected to see Margaret. Is she okay?'

'She's fine,' Kitty shrugged. 'I'm here because that's what our boss decided.'

'You mean Gursky?' he asked.

'I'm sorry,' Kitty said in embarrassment. 'I don't know his name.' It was Janos's turn to be embarrassed.

'Well, it doesn't matter. You'd have found out soon enough anyway,' he reassured her. They exchanged mail and chatted about nothing much until Kitty began to gush about the wonders of Prague. Janos, realising that he had a captive audience, began to reel off anecdote after anecdote about the city and its people, rounding them off with the fable of how in the days before good mortar had been developed, the stones of the Charles Bridge had been bonded together with egg whites.

Kitty and Margaret took it in turns to do the Prague run, and Kitty became quite friendly with Janos, who was gloomily convinced that the Czechs would be the Nazis' first target after they seized power. Sometimes they met behind the shop, sometimes they swapped packages via a brush contact on the street. Kitty always went to great lengths to check for surveillance on her way to and from any meeting. Usually there was nothing, but one day after she had taken a package from Janos she sensed someone was following her. She stopped by a shop window and saw the reflections of two men on the opposite pavement. They might be watchers, but she needed to make sure. She walked quickly down the street. One of the men disappeared, but the other kept following her. When she came to a tram stop, she let one go by and then jumped on the next one just as it was pulling away. The man who had been behind her appeared out of the blue and took a running jump on to the steps of the tram. She was now certain. The worst thing was that she was carrying mail. She had to shake off the tail at all costs. But how? She got off the tram at the next stop and walked into the nearest shop. 'Do you speak German?' she asked the man behind the counter. He shook his head. 'English?' He shook his head again. She went into another shop with the same result. Third time lucky. '*Ja, Ja, natürlich*,' the red-faced butcher smiled.

'I need your help,' Kitty told him breathlessly. 'There's a man following me. I don't know what to do. I'm a decent God-fearing woman. My husband and children are waiting for me at home and all of a sudden this man starts getting fresh. I wonder if there is another way out of here so he doesn't see me.'

'You're in luck, *gnädige Frau*,' he said. 'My back door opens into the courtyard and you can get from there into the next street. This way please. And if that lowlife does try to come in here, I'll teach him how to behave with decent women!' Kitty slipped out of the door across the yard into a little alleyway. She was relieved to see that it opened into a busy street, where she lost herself in the crowd. She changed cabs twice on her way to the station and only relaxed when the train pulled out of Prague.

When he heard what had happened, Karl was very worried, particularly about Janos. That evening Margaret arrived in Prague and left a message at the tobacconist's ordering Janos to drop everything and lie low. They later heard that he had gone to France while things cooled off.

'You can't go back to Prague,' Karl told Kitty. 'We'll find another route for you, but there's enough for you to do here anyway.'

They began to use Kitty's apartment as a safe-house for meetings and photographing documents for the courier package. Gursky used it several times to meet his agents. One of these was Braun, who worked for a well-known arms dealer. Braun handed over several prototypes of a new firearm together with its handbook and details of the countries that were interested in buying it.

In 1932, Vasily Roshchin arrived in Berlin. Four years previously, he had organised the infiltration of Van and other Comintern congress delegates across the Chinese border. His mission now was to set up a 'factory' to produce passports, identification and other paperwork for illegals. For her next assignment, a trip to Paris, Kitty was given a new passport with a false name but her own photograph. It was handed to her by her friend from Harbin, Yunona Sosnovskaya, whose husband Erich Tacke was the INO illegal in Berlin. They were very pleased to see each other again and got together a couple of times more before Tacke was transferred. Kitty had been reborn as Eleanor Davis, an American citizen born in Chicago, a move dictated by the need not to have her real name noticed too often as she crossed and re-crossed the frontier. She also kept her original passport.

Kitty's first trip to Paris, in December 1932, was more than usually tense since this was her first crossing with a forged passport. She had been briefed and she knew from her own experience that frontiers were best crossed at night when the customs and immigration officials were less inclined to be inquisitive. That proved to be the case when the train pulled into Strasbourg at 2 a.m. Even though the officials seemed to be just going through the motions, Kitty's heart skipped a beat as she handed over her passport, but it was stamped and given back to her without questions. She dozed off and woke up in Paris on a grey December morning with rain streaking the carriage window.

Her first impression of the City of Lights was how dark and gloomy it was with the pavements covered in grimy slush. She had expected to see svelte Parisian ladies, but instead she saw a mass of dowdy women splashing along the streets clutching shopping bags, heads bowed in the teeth of the snow and rain, most of their umbrellas blown inside out. Ever afterwards those umbrellas were her abiding memory of Paris. The mail-drop was in a café and, after handing over her packet, she was told that she needed to come back in a couple of days to pick up mail for Berlin. Chilled to the bone, Kitty went back to her hotel, swallowed a handful of aspirin and spent the next two days in bed with flu, another memento of Paris.

Back in Berlin life went on. Kitty made a point of giving her landlady presents from time to time remembering the old German proverb that 'small gifts nourish a big friendship'; in return the grateful landlady would often invite her in for coffee. One day she mentioned casually that the police had been around asking her what the five or six students she had as tenants were living on. Though they had not asked specifically about Kitty, Gursky was very worried when she told him since other illegals had reported similar inquiries by the police. Gursky, whose code name was MONGOL, reported all this at his first meeting with the legal *rezident* ARTYOM, who frowned. 'I've already told Moscow we've got to provide plausible cover for the income of all our illegals. Unfortunately they've only managed to do this for a few of them so far, including you.'

ARTYOM was Boris Berman, who had been appointed the legal *rezident* in 1931 at the age of thirty. His father had been the owner of a modern mill, which seems to be the reason why at one point Berman was expelled from the Party as being 'of bourgeois origin'. However, he was soon re-established and became an officer of the OGPU in 1925, and was posted to Germany in 1931. He was tasked with penetrating and producing intelligence on all the political parties, the financial and industrial sectors, military organisations and cultural bodies as well as the German intelligence services. Later he was to become the deputy chief of the INO.

Reminded of his business cover, Gursky laughed, 'Here's my latest advert.' Berman took the newspaper folded to page three, where there was a large box proclaiming: '*The Lotus Company: Handkerchiefs; Top Quality Irish Linen; Appenzel Embroidery.*'

'What or who the hell's Appenzel?' Berman grumbled.

'Some place in Switzerland that's famous for needlework, at least that's what they tell me. Trouble is, the firm is losing money. Not to put too fine a point on it, it's nearly broke. I've asked my brother in Harbin if he'd be interested to buy some shares and make me his commercial agent. He agreed, but so far I haven't had any money from him. I'm also negotiating with the Moscow Trade Syndicate to rent a warehouse. That would make a big difference.'

'Getting back to our illegals,' Berman said. 'I've suggested to the Centre that we set it up so that their money comes from various wealthy relatives abroad. But they still haven't got back to me, so we'd better organise it ourselves.'

ARTYOM reported to the Centre that he proposed sending GIN to New York to bring money back to Berlin for herself and GYPSY, and to send GYPSY herself a little while later. He also advised Moscow about the police inquiries. At the beginning of the autumn Margaret made a trip to New York, and Kitty followed her as soon as she got back from Paris. She was still feeling poorly and the sea air failed to work its usual magic. She spent most of the voyage in her bunk. Kitty had four days in New York before the next liner sailed for Germany, seeing her family, visiting her father's grave and arranging for money to be wired to Germany.

When she got back, her classmate John Smith expressed perfunctory interest in where she had been, but before she could answer he launched into a frenzied diatribe about his discovery of Nietzsche and his message for Germany and the world. Kitty thought to herself that if an Englishman, albeit a Fascist, could get so besotted with ideology, what price the Germans. Each day brought more evidence that the Nazis, worried that their popularity might be waning, were pushing ever more aggressively to seize the reins of power, if not through the ballot box then by a *putsch*. Nazi units began to arm themselves. Intelligence on their moves reached MONGOL, and GYPSY couriered it out of Germany on its way to Moscow.

There were two illegal *rezidenturas* in Germany and one legal. The latter controlled the general thrust of their operations, but the illegals maintained their own communications with the Centre, using a system of couriers operating via third countries. A 1932 assessment of the work of the Berlin *rezidenturas* noted that:

Agents' reports and documents have shed extremely valuable light on the foreign policy of the German government. As well as political intelligence we regularly receive information on German intelligence operations conducted via the Foreign Ministry and have identified some of the individuals involved.

One example in Kitty's files is intelligence from a source in the immediate entourage of Chancellor Franz von Papen about the latter's talks in Paris in June 1932 on the creation of a military alliance between France, Germany and Poland, directed against the Soviet Union. The first stage in this alliance was to be an attack on the Ukraine. The participants in the talks also hoped that Britain would become involved and seize the Caucasian oilfields on the pretext of liberating Georgia.

Some of this intelligence was obtained by the legal *rezidenturas* and some by the illegals. And Kitty, as GYPSY, played a part in passing it on its way to Moscow. Just after Christmas 1932 Kitty went to Paris again, carrying reports, one of which was her own, on a bizarre party she had gone to, with Karl's approval, with the rabid John Smith. Even allowing for Smith's Fascist sympathies, she had been staggered to find the two of them the guests of honour, and the only ones not in brown uniforms with swastika armbands. Her report to Karl highlighted the self-confident aggression of the guests and especially the claim by one older Nazi that, since Hitler now had the backing of German industry, he would be in power within the month, a forecast that in the event was only five days out. Because of the rush of holiday traffic the sleepers were booked solid and Kitty had to take a day train. Crossing into France at Strasbourg her heart sank when the young gendarme took his time leafing through every page of her passport. He looked at her hard and demanded, 'What state is Chicago in?'

'Illinois.'

'Full marks. That's what I learned at school too. But your passport says "Indiana".'

Kitty thought furiously. It was on the tip of her tongue to say that Chicago, the Windy City, was indeed in Illinois, but that the eponymous little town where she had been born happened to be in Indiana. But she remembered at the last second that she had written 'USA, Chicago, Illinois' on her customs declaration.

'Madame,' the gendarme said calmly. 'You've got a false passport. I don't know how or why you've got it but I'm not letting you into France with it.'

'There must be some mistake,' Kitty exclaimed. 'I'll speak to your superiors.'

'As you wish, but you'd do better to just take your passport, Madame,' the gendarme said in a level tone, 'and give it back to whomever sold it to you. Ask them for your money back.' What was she to do? For appearance's sake, she grumbled a bit more, then grudgingly retrieved her passport and got off the train, reckoning to herself that she had got away lightly. The gendarme did not make any notes and would forget her name before too long. To have been detained and questioned, and forced to admit that the passport was a fake, would have been bad enough. But if the rolls of secret film had been found too, she would have been in a real mess. As it was, she was lucky.

Stubborn to the point of being pig-headed, Kitty decided, contrary to common sense and basic tradecraft, to cross the frontier by bus, using the same passport. Luckily for her the gendarme who looked at it was no expert in American geography and she passed through without a hitch. Her trip back was also trouble free, though she took care to travel via Saarbrücken rather than Strasbourg. When he heard what had happened, Gursky blew his top, gave Roschhin's passport 'factory' hell for its carelessness, and didn't spare Kitty either, berating her for not checking the passport herself. She promptly burst into tears, sobbing that if he felt she wasn't up to the courier job, she would do something else or even go back to America. He did his best to calm her down, but the tears took a long time to stop.

Three developments at the beginning of 1933 had a profound effect on history. On 3 January the ailing Hindenburg ceded total control to the Nazis and made Hitler Chancellor. On 4 March Franklin D. Roosevelt became President of the United States and, as one of his first measures, officially recognised the Soviet Union. A few days previously, as Kitty watched the baleful glow over the Berlin rooftops from her bedroom window, the Reichstag had burned to the ground. When the Nazis rounded on the Communists as the guilty parties, Willy Münzenberg's Communist propaganda apparatus swung into action, producing volumes of evidence, much of it superficially plausible, but much also soon later demonstrated to be spurious, to try to prove that the blaze was not the work of a lone mental defective but arson instigated by the Nazis as an excuse to settle scores with their opponents and cement their grip on power. But whatever the truth of the matter, the Nazis lost no time in taking advantage of the opportunity and the wave of reprisals began in earnest in March, with left-wingers, Jews and many foreigners caught in its wake. One consequence was that the *rezidenturas* lost a number of agents, and several illegal and legal officers were obliged to leave Germany.

ARTYOM wrote to the Centre that such legends as they had been able to construct for the illegals, including GIN and GYPSY, would not stand up to close scrutiny, given the intensified interest being taken in foreigners generally, and that they would probably have to leave Germany to avoid getting caught up in answering questions and possibly being exposed. In the event, they did not leave and operations continued.

(Meanwhile back in New York, Earl Browder was introducing his friends to his new wife, Raisa Luganovskaya, and their son Feliks. Two more sons were to be born in later years. When challenged about the fact that Raisa had entered the United States illegally because they were not married, Browder produced some dubious Russian documents falsely purporting to show that he had divorced his first wife, Gladys, in 1926. Kitty, of course, did not rate a mention.)

It was reported in May that Janos had been arrested in France, so there was a risk that a counter-intelligence investigation might lead back not only to GIN and GYPSY, about both of whom Janos knew a great deal from their Prague meetings, but as far as MONGOL himself, since Janos had met him and knew his real name. There was a further risk that since GIN was living with Abraham Einhorn (alias Harry Terras), she could be caught if the latter's apartment was raided. (Their relationship was deeper than anyone seems to have suspected at the time. When Margaret was hauled before a US Grand Jury in 1952 to be questioned about her alleged work for the Soviets, she said she had actually been married during her time in Germany to a man she named 'James Meadows', about whom she claimed to know curiously little other than that he was an American helping refugees escape the Nazis. She told the Jury they had lived together for three years 'until one day he just vanished'. It seems almost certain that 'Meadows' was in fact the elusive Einhorn. The Jury proceedings went nowhere in large part because the FBI stayed their hand, hoping that under pressure Margaret would finally 'spill the beans'. She was made of sterner stuff.)

There is no record of what happened to Janos, but the Centre decided that MONGOL, GIN and GYPSY should spend a few months out of Germany. A few days later Kitty found herself back of the deck of the *Komsomol*, on which she and Earl had sailed from Hamburg to Leningrad all those years before, but this time in a rather more relaxed frame of mind, with the risks of the Third Reich behind her for the moment and Moscow to look forward to. She made friends with the crew, who teased her about the odd way she pronounced the name of Ilyusha, the first mate, a total professional on duty but something of a lad in his spare time. One of the things he taught Kitty was dominoes, which she spent happy hours playing with the crew.

No one met her when she reached Moscow so she made her own way to the address she had been given, where she was kept waiting a long time in the lobby before a man eventually emerged from an office and said to her in Russian, 'Hello, please come in and take a seat.'

While she gazed idly around his rather nondescript room, the man flicked through a file on his desk and then said, 'So, they call you GYPSY. So will we. How was your trip?'

After listening politely, he continued, 'Here's the form you need for the hotel and these are meal coupons. Settle yourself in, have a bit of a rest, and we'll be back in touch in a week or so and decide what we're going to do with you.'

The hotel was distinctly further down market than the Savoy, where she had stayed with Earl, and could be more accurately described as a hostel. She had to share a room with two other women, Ulrike, a German, and Ilona, a Hungarian, though whether these were their real names and what they actually did, she had no idea.

Kitty spent a week catching up with Moscow, and found that May was a far nicer time to be there than January or February, though the city centre was one big building site. The Metro was being excavated, the old buildings in the Okhotny Ryad were being torn down and Gorky Street was being rebuilt. She soon got bored, but had absolutely no idea whom to turn to. After about a fortnight, she was summoned back to the same office, where the same anonymous man suggested that she might like an official, all-expenses-paid spell at a sanatorium in Sochi, on the Black Sea. However, she would first be required to undergo a physical examination. Even though both concepts were quite alien to her, she played gamely along with the drill of giving specimens, being X-rayed, allowing doctors to prod her and listen to her chest, and reading – with difficulty – the optician's test card. She was so taken with the whole process that the Russian word for it, *dispanserizatsiya*, entered her vocabulary, even though she found it a bit of a tongue-twister.

Armed with a voucher for the sanatorium and a first-class rail ticket, she spent two whole days chugging southwards marvelling at the changing views of Mother Russia, drinking tea from the samovar, which, as in all Russian trains, bubbled day and night at the end of the carriage, and enjoying the whole experience. Once the passengers in her compartment – an army officer and his wife and a portly engineer, all also headed for a break in Sochi – realised that she was not the foreign tourist they first took her for, but actually worked for the Comintern, they took her to their hearts and taught her to play the Russian equivalent of the children's card game 'Go Fish'. It was the most relaxed and enjoyable time she had ever had, and Sochi itself was just as big a treat, with warm, humid breezes, imposing white buildings, friendly guests and staff, and wonderful meals. True, Sochi's pebbly beach was a tad uncomfortable compared to the sandy sweeps of Long Island and Far Rockaway, but she soon got used to it.

Kitty stayed at Sochi for just over three weeks; it was something out of a story book, and she even had a little holiday romance with one of her fellow guests. She got back to Moscow in the heat of July, picked up a fresh supply of meal coupons and waited nearly a month for the office to get in touch. She had been told simply that she was being held 'in reserve', but eventually the call came; presumably someone at a high level in the Centre had decided that a three-month sidelining was enough. She was given a new passport and crossed back smoothly through Poland into Germany, ready for work.

CHAPTER 7

Nazi Dances

At about the same time that Kitty returned to Germany, Vassily Mikhailovich Zarubin arrived in Berlin from Paris to take up his post as the new illegal *rezident* with the codename BETTY, evidently a tribute to his wife Elizaveta Yulevna, herself an outstanding intelligence officer, codenamed ERNA, who accompanied him.

Zarubin, a Muscovite born and bred, was the son of a railwayman and had served in the First World War and then the Civil War in Russia. He had joined the Cheka in 1920, targeting gangsters, arms smugglers and drugs traffickers. He began his overseas intelligence service in 1925 in China and later served in Finland and Denmark. The Zarubins had been posted to Paris in 1929, where he had operated as illegal *rezident*, with a cover job as a partner in an advertising agency. His assignment covered intelligence on Germany as well as France, and he regularly passed the Centre secret intelligence obtained from a source inside the German embassy.

Zarubin joked in his memoirs that he was transferred to Germany because of his Aryan appearance, and with his blue eyes and neatly combed blond hair, he looked more the archetypal Aryan on a Nazi poster than many of the Third Reich's leaders. He was a fine balalaika player, had a good voice, and when asked where he had learned to sing he had told his daughter, 'I don't tell anybody and I don't put it in my personal file, but I learned to sing in the church choir!' His sister Anna also worked for the intelligence service, as did his wife ERNA. ERNA had been born Elizaveta Rozenzweig, but perhaps because it was felt it would help her career not to have a Jewish name had been 'rechristened' Gorskaya when she joined the NKVD in 1925. Born in Romania, she had studied history and philology at the University in Czernowice, the Sorbonne and the University of Vienna. Pavel Sudoplatov, then head of the NKVD's Department of Special Tasks, recalled that:

> Her manner was so easy and sociable that she naturally made friends. Slim with dark eyes she had a Semitic beauty that attracted men and she was one of the most successful agent recruiters. She spoke excellent English, German, French, Romanian and Yiddish. Usually she looked like a sophisticated upper-class European but she had the ability to change her appearance like a chameleon. When she worked in the United States she blended right in.

Perhaps the most chillingly memorable in a long list of remarkable and successful assignments was Liza's part in the entrapment of her former husband, Yakov Blyumkin, once a leading hothead in the Social Revolution Party, who had been sentenced to death for his part in the 1918 assassination of the German Envoy to Russia, Count Mirbach. Pardoned as a result of Trotsky's intervention, he had become an officer in the Cheka even though the assassination had been expressly forbidden by 'Iron' Feliks Dzerzhinsky, the Cheka's founder. By the late 1920's Blyumkin was *rezident* in Constantinople. Around the same time Trotsky himself went into his exile on the Island of Prinkipo in the Sea of Marmara. For reasons which were obscure – maybe on a straightfoward surveillance mission from the Centre, maybe because Trotsky was his friend and mentor, maybe as part of a delicate attempt to set him up – Blyumkin went to Prinkipo to see Stalin's exiled arch-rival and came away with several letters from Trotsky to former colleagues in Moscow. His visit in itself was probably enough to seal his fate in Stalin's eyes, and carrying clandestine mail for the pariah compounded a cardinal sin. Word went out that Blyumkin was to be brought back to Moscow *coute que coute*. It has been said that, urged by her bosses to 'forget bourgeois morality', Liza was persuaded to play a key role in the operation that followed and, according to one account, was actually in the Lubyanka when Blyumkin was dragged away to the basement to be shot. He is said to have stammered in bemusement, 'Liza, you have betrayed me.'

With Blyumkin buried in a pit in one of the OGPU's killing fields outside Moscow, Liza married Zarubin and proved herself to be a bold and resourceful partner on his assignments in France and Denmark.

(Liza was Zarubin's second wife, his first having abandoned him for a more senior officer, Naum Eitingon, who had trained many of the illegals and had himself served in Shanghai, Spain – where he made the contacts he later used in organising Trotsky's assassination in Mexico City – behind enemy lines in the Second World War, and in Turkey, where he led an abortive mission to assassinate the German Ambassador Franz von Papen. Zarubin's daughter Zoya went to live with her stepfather and she also became an intelligence officer. Ever the survivor, and arguably a better model for John le Carré's Karla than the East German spymaster Marcus Wolff, Eitingon was imprisoned from 1951 to 1953 for his alleged role in the so-called Zionist spy plot, and again from 1957 to 1964 accused of being an accomplice in many of the long and bloody laundry list of crimes laid at the door of the vicious, disgraced NKVD Chief Lavrenty Beria.)

The Berlin in which the Zarubins arrived was a city whose bustling crowds seemed dominated by brown and black uniforms, its air heavy with tension and fear. Neighbour denounced neighbour, the nights were punctuated by arrests, Jews were beaten and reviled, and the foreign community felt itself under suspicion and siege. A cynic might have observed that several of these characteristics were also to be observed in Moscow, but the Zarubins had been away from home for many years. As the tension rose, many foreigners left the country, but the two illegal *rezidenturas* in Berlin continued to operate. An assessment of its operations in 1933 by the INO's Third Department noted that, 'Thanks to timely precautions and organisational restructuring we avoided any major complications in our work.'

Some of the agents were put 'on ice' and some transferred to other countries. The most valuable and reliable assets, many of whom had been recruited by Walter Krivitsky in the 1920s, building on the German Communist Party's own clandestine intelligence unit and its so-called *Zersetzungsdienst*, or 'subversion service', were transferred to the illegal *rezidenturas* headed by BETTY, who masqueraded as a talent scout for a Hollywood studio, and YEVGENI (Fyodor Parparov).

Both *rezidents* inherited reliable agents from their predecessors, among them BREITENBACH or A/201, who worked in the Gestapo and was well-informed about official investigations into the left wing, foreigners generally and, in particular and very valuably, Soviet of targets. He was a serious and conscientious agent, who provided a great deal of unique intelligence, including advance notice of the date of Operation Barbarossa, the German attack on the Soviet Union. Other agents provided secret documents from the Foreign Ministry and the Nazi Party leadership, information on the Party's intelligence service and its assets in the Soviet Union (in German embassies, consulates and businesses), on the political situation in Germany, on its foreign policy, on counter-intelligence measures against Soviet espionage and military intelligence services, and the German Communist Party, on the German army, and on the intelligence and counter-intelligence services generally. There was also a huge amount of scientific and technical intelligence, covering shipbuilding, submarine diesels and batteries, gas mask filters, aircraft and engine production, and the synthetic production of diamonds, petrol and rubber. One agent, codenamed RADIANT (or STRAHLMANN, an engineer at AEG named Klaus Behrens), provided intelligence, seemingly out of science fiction, on German experiments using high-voltage current at long range to stop vehicle engines.

All this intelligence was processed, photographed and then taken out of Germany by couriers, including GYPSY, but the sheer volume of agents and material meant that the couriers as well as the *rezidentura* staff had to get involved in meeting agents and collecting their information. Accordingly, GYPSY was assigned to work with an agent codenamed NASLEDTSVO (LEGACY), a forty-two-year-old engineer named Fritz Talbe, who worked for Bamag. He was well-educated and well-informed, and not only provided material to which he had access through his job but had somehow managed to penetrate Bamag's inner sanctum and was able to get information on all the organisation's latest technology. His principal motive in working for Soviet intelligence was money, prompted by his wife Gertrude's ambition to build a house in the country. As often happens in the espionage game, even working for money somehow changes the agent's psychology, and in this case both husband and wife gradually became opposed to Hitler and German militarism. One of the reasons for this may have been their terror at the thought of sacrificing their teenage son to the war they knew was looming.

For whatever reason, LEGACY was diligent in providing interesting intelligence but had just one foible. When he had agreed to spy, he had said that he would only come to a rendezvous if his wife could accompany him. This was a breach of tradecraft but the *rezident* had reluctantly agreed.

Kitty was by now using a new passport, and she had to sign up for more language courses and to rent a new apartment. The passport she had been given in Moscow was useless because it had Soviet-Polish and Polish-German border crossing stamps, and her own passport was also temporarily dangerous as there was still a risk that Janos might have compromised her. Thus, for the time being, both these passports were kept in a safe place.

Once back in Berlin Kitty went to the tobacconist's safe-house, where she met Liza Zarubina (ERNA), a meeting she remembered vividly for the rest of her life. Liza became her friend and her oldest comrade, even though she was a year younger, and remained close to her until the day she died.

Despite her hard professional edge Liza was well regarded by her colleagues for her readiness to take up the cudgels on their behalf with Moscow if she felt one of her subordinates had been badly treated. Kitty's file for instance shows that when MONGOL's salary was slashed on the grounds that his business cover should provide him with an income, she fired off an angry letter to the Centre, explaining that it was not a matter of money (although MONGOL could not earn much through his cover job since he was totally focused on his intelligence work) but of personal dignity and of disrespect to a career officer.

Liza spent a long time talking to Kitty, who told her her full life history, especially the recent years in China and Germany. Liza then explained to Kitty a new assignment she had for her.

'Oh, do you think I could manage it?' Kitty hesitated. 'I'd have to talk to him about scientific stuff but I . . .'

'You won't have to do anything like that,' Liza reassured her. 'All you have to do is to take whatever he gives you, bring it back here and then give him money, if he has earned it. The first meeting is tomorrow at Bülow Allee in the Tiergarten, at 6 p.m., the third bench on the right. The two of them will be sitting there. If there's anyone else on the bench, don't go near it until they've left. You sit down next to them and light a cigarette with this lighter. He gave it to us as a recognition signal. Then you say, "It was the same sort of weather this time last year." He'll say, "Yes, but it was three degrees warmer," and after that you can talk about whatever you want. When he gives you his material, come straight back here with it. Check for surveillance on the way there and back. Got it? His money's in this envelope.'

Kitty walked through the Tiergarten trying not to look around her too obviously, and telling herself that every man she saw in uniform was not a policeman and that the business-suited man coming towards her was not a plain-clothes detective. She saw the bench and the couple from a long way away, and walked up, muttered an apology for disturbing them and sat down. She pulled out a packet of cigarettes (although she did not smoke) and the lighter. The minute she flicked it the woman exclaimed, 'Where did you get that lighter?' Forgetting the recognition phrases Kitty blurted reflexively, 'Take a guess!'

'Of course, of course. Fritz, you know this young lady . . .'

'Shush, Trudle, shush,' her husband reassured her. 'How do you do? Judging from your pronunciation you're not a Berliner.'

'You're right,' Kitty replied. 'I'm Dutch. But I like your city very much, especially the parks.'

'You mean this place?' the woman laughed cynically. 'Are you a Catholic?'

Kitty, in fact a devout atheist, hesitated for a moment, not knowing what answer Gertrude wanted.

'Anyway it doesn't matter. This isn't a city, it's Sodom and Gomorrah, and I shouldn't be at all surprised if twelve years from now it's in ruins, just like in the Bible. That's why we're in a hurry to build our new house and move out there. Did you bring the cash?'

'Of course,' Kitty replied, 'and did you bring what I need?'

'Sure,' the man replied. 'Here you are.' They exchanged envelopes unobtrusively, agreed the details of their next meeting and went their separate ways.

For a while they continued to meet regularly, and then LEGACY suddenly vanished off the radar screen. The Berlin *rezidentura* sent alarm signals warning the Centre that he had failed to attend a fixed rendezvous, and the agreed fallback, and they reported that

GYPSY was sure that he could not have got the times and places wrong. It was suggested that either he had been taken ill or had been arrested as a result of some carelessness on his part. It was noted that Kitty had introduced herself as Dutch and that he did not know her real name.

It turned out, however, that LEGACY was neither ill nor in custody, but had simply moved to his new house outside Berlin.

After some debate the Centre agreed that Kitty should be tasked to intercept LEGACY on his way to his office because, as Zarubin noted, he would now need even more money to furnish the house. When Liza briefed Kitty about renewing the contact, Kitty thought that it would be better to try to intercept Gertrude, who would presumably have established a reasonably fixed shopping routine in her new area; anyway, she was the one who called the shots. 'If she wants him to co-operate, he will, and if she doesn't, he won't.' Liza agreed.

Kitty spent two or three days sitting with a book on her lap in a little square not far from LEGACY's new house and finally saw Gertrude walking towards the shops with the self-important swagger of a proud new homeowner. As she approached, Kitty put her book in her handbag and went up to her.

'You!' exclaimed Gertrude, her eyes wide with surprise.

'Yes, me,' said Kitty calmly. 'Surprised to see me?'

'Why should I be?' Gertrude smiled politely. 'Very nice to see you.'

'How have you settled in to your new place? I bet you've got nice new furniture and a new gas stove and you're showing it all off to lots of visitors.'

'If only, if only. This is a pretty posh neighbourhood, you know, and we still have hardly a stick of furniture in the place. We can't possibly have anyone around.'

'What's the problem?'

'We're very short of money.'

'So what's the problem?' Kitty repeated. 'We can fix that,' and

LEGACY began to work again. Over the period he co-operated with Soviet intelligence, he was paid 35,000 marks, but the value of what he contributed ran into many millions.

As well as meeting LEGACY, Kitty continued with her primary assignment as a courier and was used by BETTY's *rezidentura* to maintain communications with France, where a special group, headed by AMBROSIUS, who had previously served in Berlin, had been set up to handle the couriers from Germany and process their deliveries. At the beginning of 1934 Kitty had to cross the French frontier again. In the early years of the Nazi regime, frontier controls were actually relaxed and tourism flourished, despite Hitler's suspicions about contact between Germans and foreigners. In fact, the biggest risk lay on the French side because, in the 1930s, France had become a centre of international terrorism and the scene of several headline-grabbing kidnappings and murders of politicians, Russian-exiled leaders and even King Alexander of Yugoslavia. Backed by a nervous public, the police and counter-intelligence services treated incoming foreigners with deep suspicion.

In the event, Kitty only made two or three runs before AMBROSIUS was recalled to Moscow because he was having problems with the work and his wife was found to be under surveillance by the French authorities.

The Centre's routine circulars to *rezidents* frequently included reminders that, in the interest of security, illegals were forbidden to associate with one another, unless there was an operational need, but this rule was just as frequently flouted. The fact was that people operating under constant stress in a foreign and hostile environment felt especially lonely and homesick, and needed to share what they were going through with a kindred spirit. For many at the courier level, including Kitty and Margaret, months could pass with nothing for them to do, when they were either waiting for mail or had to be sidelined because something had gone wrong somewhere. At one point the *rezident* reported on Margaret that, at forty, 'she is feeling old age looming and is frightened of ending up alone. She would like to work in the USA, which would give her the chance to take a break among people she knows, while at the same time building a legend for work in the future.'

It was the same with Kitty, about whom Zarubin reported to the Centre in April 1934, claiming that she had a short attention span and was a little lazy. Despite having been in Berlin for some time, she had not got to grips with photography, and he felt that she had been underutilised, or, more accurately, had not been kept sufficiently busy, as a result of which she was inclined simply to sit out her time in Berlin until her residence permit expired and then return to New York, 'where she believes she will find something more suited to her personality and her abilities'.

In Zarubin's opinion Kitty's frame of mind was mainly the result of sitting twiddling her thumbs for months on end, and he observed that her mood improved the more she was given to do, such as safe-keeping, delivering messages, making mail runs abroad, arranging for her flat to be available for photographing mail, and the other run-of-the-mill tasks of the *rezidentura*. He also noted that she was a very willing colleague, who approached her work conscientiously, but just did not find it satisfying. One day in April 1934, leaving Kitty's flat after they had spent the evening together, Margaret yelped and clutched at her side.

'What's the matter?' Kitty asked, worried.

'I don't know,' Margaret replied. 'It may be appendicitis. I've had a twinge or two before, but nothing as bad as this.'

'I'll call an ambulance.'

'No, don't! You know we're not supposed to be seen together . . . Oh!'

'I'm going to call one anyway,' Kitty insisted.

Margaret, in pain, begged her not to phone for an ambulance, so Kitty suggested that she try to get herself downstairs and sit on the bench in the little garden across the street. Margaret practically crawled downstairs and tumbled on to the bench, and Kitty then called the ambulance. She gave the address, but not her name, and told the operator, 'I can see a woman on the bench across the road who looks as if she's in a pretty bad way. Please come and see what's wrong.' The ambulance arrived in eight minutes. A few days later Zarubin reported to the Centre that Margaret had been successfully operated on for appendicitis and felt fine. In reply, the Centre cabled that Margaret was to go to Moscow for radio training.

The illegal *rezidenturas* had been debating the question of radio communications for a long time and, as early as 1931, the Berlin illegal *rezident* KARIN had written to the Centre:

> Given our limited financial resources we cannot afford to keep couriers on constant standby. I note that Radio Moscow and Radio Leningrad are used for commercial purposes; if you tune in you can hear the State Fur Combine or some other business talking for hours on end to their subsidiaries around the country; sometimes they transmit in cipher. It occurs to me that we could use radio for our work too, mainly for transmitting directives.

By the time Margaret returned from Moscow in 1934, the *rezidentura* had obtained a transceiver and decided to have a trial run at a radio link with the Centre, which suggested two or three test transmissions a month. Their first radio station was a large villa in the suburbs owned by a rich aristocrat, who spent most of his time in his flat in the city, and whose butler Gustav was a *rezidentura* asset. Gustav spent the day in Berlin looking after his master and would go back to the house at night, ostensibly to keep an eye on it. The radio could not be kept there and had to be brought by car from a safe-house late at night. The first time they did it, it was pitch dark when the Mercedes crunched up the villa's gravel drive, and the only light was in a little window in Gustav's attic room. Margaret and two men got out of the car and one of them rang the bell while the second opened the boot of the car and, with a great deal of effort, pulled out the suitcase with the radio in it, which weighed fifty pounds.

'God, it's heavy,' he grumbled.

'Don't make such a fuss, hurry up, hurry up,' Margaret urged him in her heavily accented Russian. They all went upstairs and Gustav disappeared into the mahogany-panelled study, where he sat comfortably at the elegant desk, playing the role of the baron, reading a leather-bound book, the blinds safely drawn and a glass of brandy ready to hand. Meanwhile, in the loft one of the men opened the shutters and lowered the aerial wire down the outside wall. He also bypassed the meter, so that it would not show a spike in power usage after they had finished operating. Margaret put on the earphones and sat down at the set, slightly nervous at operating for real for the first time. She tuned in, checked her watch and, exactly on time, heard a man announcing, 'Attention, attention. We are now transmitting information on the water level of the rivers in the Yenisei Basin. Angara . . .' There followed a list of rivers and a whole lot of numbers, which Margaret wrote down in a frenzy. But reception got steadily worse and the voice eventually disappeared completely.

'Can't hear them any more,' Margaret muttered, looking at her colleagues as if it was her fault.

'Don't worry,' one of them reassured her. 'The hardest part is always the beginning.' He glanced at his watch. 'Anyway it's our turn now. Off you go.'

Margaret took a sheet of paper and began to tap out numbers, but there was no answering 'message received' signal. 'Not to worry, that's enough for today,' she was told.

After two or three sessions Margaret got the hang of the procedure and was able to keep the circuit open, but there was still a major logistical problem because the transceiver had to be lugged to a new safe-house for every session, forcing the owners to stay up most of the night waiting for and looking after the illegals, while the latter were taken away from their regular duties for almost a full day. Moscow soon ordered a halt to communications, announcing that the radio should be hidden in a safe place and suggesting that the link should only be used again if there were special circumstances. When, a few years later, such circumstances arose, it again proved impossible to use the radio effectively.

Zarubin's most reliable safe-house was the apartment of Elena, the attractive thirty-five-year-old widow of a civil servant, who lived there with her sixteen-year-old daughter. One day Elena told him that her brother Erich Tacke, whom she had not seen for fifteen years since he had vanished almost overnight to China, had turned up unexpectedly. He said that he wanted to settle down and had rented a bed-sitting room, the address of which he had given to Elena. He had also asked a lot of questions about their old friends and expressed a particular interest in who was working where. Zarubin was astonished, for he had known Erich when they had worked together in China; he also knew that he had recently been in Berlin as an illegal and had then been posted back to Moscow. The Centre had not told him about Tacke's return, but he realised that the 'need to know' principle was being applied and that whatever assignment Tacke was on was nothing to do with him, though he guessed that he had not obtained the Centre's clearance before making contact with his sister.

Several days later, BREITENBACH reported that the Gestapo had received a report from a man named Meissner, a former Social Democrat, who had told them that he had run into Tacke, whom he knew from the time they had been together a few years previously in Moscow. Though they had come to a gentleman's agreement to keep quiet about one another, 'as a decent German and a repentant Social Democrat he now felt unable to maintain that silence'. Clearly Tacke's freedom, and even his life, was at risk. Accordingly, Elena's daughter carried a message to Tacke to come and meet someone whom he would know when he saw them, so no recognition phrase was necessary. Liza remembered that Kitty had mentioned Tacke, so she was sent to the initial rendezvous, where they recognised each other instantly from Harbin.

When he subsequently met Zarubin, Tacke told him that he had gone to his sister's flat because the Centre planned to transfer it from Zarubin to him for use as a safe-house. He had met Meissner, he explained, because he had liberal leanings and might be of use. Tacke was put in a safe hiding-place, given a Czech passport and sent back to Moscow.

After he had left, Kitty telephoned the woman who had rented him the bed-sitting room and asked about 'her friend'. The landlady told her that he had gone off to Hamburg a long time ago. 'Funny you should ask,' she added. 'Another of his friends came round a while back with two mates and was very upset when I told him he had left.' Clearly Tacke had escaped just one step ahead of the Gestapo.

In fact, it had been Zarubin who had told Liza to involve Kitty, concerned that yet again she had too little to do, while attempts were being made to find new lines of communication following AMBROSIUS's recall from Paris.

Liza soon gave her another job, which was to handle a man called Stadtler, an engineer who worked in a factory in which Soviet intelligence was interested, and who had recently come to the *rezidentura*'s notice. He needed to be thoroughly checked out and Liza suggested that Kitty should use a private detective. This was quite safe, she told her, as long as one was not taking an interest in diplomats, civil servants or Nazi functionaries. Kitty found a newspaper advertisement for the Calcius Private Detective Agency and, when she called, a plain and weedy secretary accompanied her into the proprietor's office, where she met Herr Calcius himself, a thin, nervous man wearing a *pince-nez*. He laid his hands flat on the empty desk top and fixed Kitty with a long, shrewd, but at the same time rather avuncular, look. She felt that she had passed some sort of initial test.

'How can I help you?' he asked.

'Maybe I should begin by telling you who I am,' she replied.

'Fräulein, we haven't the slightest interest in who our clients are. We don't even want to know your name, your address, or your telephone number. Give us any name you like, just so that we can open a file.'

'Okay then, Giselle.'

'Okay, Fräulein Giselle. What exactly is your problem?' The secretary came back in without a word, put two cups of coffee on the desk and went out again equally silently. The office walls were hung with diplomas, pennants and photos, one of which showed a much younger Calcius in a police uniform from the pre-1914 era.

'The fact is that my sister is going out with a man called Stadtler. Here's his address. She's head over heels in love with him but for some reason our parents don't like the sound of him, even though they've never met him. We'd like to know everything we can about him, for a start, is he an Aryan? What does he do? Where did he go to school? What sort of relationships does he have with women? Who his friends are, and . . .', she hesitated in feigned embarrassment, 'his financial situation.'

Calcius listened, his eyes half closed, without making a note. It was a story he had heard before, and he knew exactly what needed to be done. He was well wired in to the police and other useful organisations, and had a good network of concierges and domestic servants who would provide information in exchange for small sums of money. He understood very well that the main concern of a solid bourgeois family like Fräulein Giselle's was whether Herr Stadtler would be able to keep their beloved daughter and the inevitable children in the style to which she was accustomed.

Calcius set about the job diligently and soon gave Kitty all the information she needed, adding that he had also heard that Stadtler was going to be in a particular café to celebrate Fasching, the German holiday. It was the one time in the year when people let their hair down completely and when there were no inhibitions about women approaching men they found attractive. Kitty, who had already seen Stadtler on another occasion, had no difficulty in spotting him across the crowded café, obviously enjoying himself. The café was fitted out with a system of pneumatic tubes, connecting each table, which had its own number, with a central clearing desk, thus allowing flirtatious and anonymous messages to be exchanged. Kitty scribbled, 'If thirteen isn't unlucky for you, you should know that the lady sitting under it would like to dance with you.' Stadtler took the bait and came over. The relationship developed and Kitty was soon able to introduce him to her 'cousin', in fact a Soviet illegal, who in due course successfully recruited him.

In the autumn of 1934 Kitty took some time off and went to Italy, unburdened by any secret papers, and although she was using a false passport, she was relaxed. The train took her across Switzerland to Milan, and, after brief visits to Verona, Padua, Venice and Florence, she arrived in Rome, where she spent the rest of her break. Bored with Italian food, she was delighted to spot Babington's English Tearooms at the foot of the Spanish Steps, which had been founded in 1893 by Miss Anna Babington and her friend Elizabeth Cargill, and offered a menu of overwhelmingly traditional, nostalgia-inducing English dishes that had made it a mecca for British and American tourists and expatriates. Kitty found an empty seat and gave the waitress her order, while the formidable Miss Babington, still going strong at seventy, barked instructions at her staff from behind the counter like a general at the Battle of Waterloo.

'Quite something, isn't she?' observed the man sitting next to Kitty. 'You know, no matter how often I come here, I can't take my eyes off her. She's just a lady who runs a café but she's so dignified. Take a look at that family tree,' he added, pointing at a beautifully drawn chart on the wall. 'One of her ancestors was Sir Anthony Babington, one of the Catholics who was executed in 1586 for plotting against Queen Elizabeth. And Sir Donald Cargill had his head chopped off in 1681.'

'Yes, nasty times,' Kitty declared, somewhat at a loss for comment.

'Chopping off a few aristocrats' heads was kids' stuff compared to what's happening in Germany today,' her new acquaintance said with evident feeling. He introduced himself as Gerhard von Bose, a lawyer at the German embassy. Once he knew that Kitty was, as she claimed to be, a Londoner, he made no attempt to hide his detestation of the 'Nazi scum' who had shot his brother Herbert, Vice Chancellor von Papen's private secretary, in the bloodbath that had followed 'The Night of the Long Knives', when Hitler had decimated the SA.

When she returned to Berlin, Kitty reported the contact to Liza and, with the Centre's approval, work began to profile and check von Bose as a potential asset. That initiative, and many others, came to a halt in the tide of spy mania and xenophobia that engulfed Germany later in 1934, when the Gestapo rolled up a spy network being run by a young Polish officer named Jurek Sosnowski, a consummate charmer, with seemingly inexhaustible financial resources and sexual energy. In the legend created by Polish intelligence, he was alleged to have been cashiered from his regiment for having an affair with his commanding officer's wife, and women certainly made up a large part of his eclectic network. They included Frau Falkenheim, a Swiss *femme du monde*, Rita Passy, a Hungarian nightclub dancer, and Frau Nazmer, who worked in the German General Staff's Inspectorate. In turn, the latter recruited a Frau von Jena and three young girls who 'needed some pocket money'. Sosnowski also had a couple of men, the heavily indebted Colonel Biddenfuhr and a Lieutenant Rotloff, who worked in the War Ministry. In just twelve months Sosnowski managed to get his hands on 150 secret documents, the keys to General Guderian's safe and a draft of the German plan for the invasion of Poland, but his network was betrayed to the Gestapo by Rita Passy, 'out of jealousy'. Frau von Falkenheim and Frau Nazmer were executed in 1935, and Frau von Jena was sentenced to life imprisonment. Sosnowski was swapped for a German woman spy who had been arrested in Poland, but, like Stalin a few years later, the Polish General Staff concluded that most of the intelligence Sosnowski had produced on Germany's plans had been fabricated, and he was locked up. In 1939, for reasons which remain murky (though he may well have been the same 'Sosnowksi' who, renamed 'Dobryzhinski', was turned by the Russians and run against his fellow countrymen), he was recorded as being in the Lubyanka, where he gave Soviet intelligence the names of those of his agents whom the Gestapo had not identified. They were subsequently recruited. What happened to Sosnowski himself is again obscure though, if indeed he was 'Dobryzhynski', he was later shot by his new masters.

Increasingly apprehensive about growing European tensions and the possibility of war, the Centre made every effort to create special 'communications *rezidenturas*' in countries that were likely to remain neutral if war broke out, and Kitty was given the assignment of covering Sweden and Denmark. Her task was to find safe-houses and select courier agents, whose cover jobs would justify them making trips to other countries and carrying mail. The new *rezidenturas* were also required to develop ways to conceal intelligence material and carry it clandestinely in containers that incorporated rapid-destruction devices, and create new formulae for invisible ink. The Centre had very high hopes for Denmark, convinced that the country would remain neutral whatever happened, but these were dashed when the Germans invaded in 1940.

A Latvian codenamed ERVIN, who had played an active part in the Civil War and who had joined the Cheka in 1924, was appointed the *rezident* in Copenhagen in 1934, where his cover job in the mission was as a lowly filing clerk under the alias Lukin. Initially the Centre had considered sending Margaret to Denmark, but it changed its mind and told ERVIN that 'GYPSY from BETTY's group' would soon arrive from Germany to handle his clandestine mail, instructing him to meet her in the Thorwaldsen Museum on a particular day and time.

The day before she was due to leave Germany, Kitty ran into John Smith on the street, in the middle of a group of young men of college age, all of them lugging bundles of books tied up with string.

'Hey Kitty,' John shouted. 'Why don't you come with us?'

'Where are you going?' she replied with curiosity.

'You'll see,' he chuckled. 'There's going to be some fireworks.'

Kitty couldn't resist joining the crowd, which grew steadily in size as it approached the city centre. Most were young men also loaded down with books and many had blazing torches. The crowd, estimated by some observers to be 40,000 strong, soon turned into an organised torch-lit procession and, on the Opernplatz, the square between the Opera House and Berlin University, the books – an eclectic catalogue of works by Proust, Freud, André Gide and Hemingway, among many others – were stacked into a huge pile on to which people began to throw their torches. As the bonfire billowed, it was fuelled with more and more books. When the flames grew so hot that the crowd was forced to back away, Kitty saw a small man limp through the throng and scramble awkwardly on to a makeshift rostrum draped with swastika flags. She recognised him as Dr Goebbels, and as he spoke Kitty was astonished that such a puny frame could produce such a melodious, slightly hypnotic voice, and use it to say such terrible things.

'Once more the spirit of the German people has found its voice!' he declared. 'This fire is the final sunset of the old era and the dawning of a new age.'

His eyes searched the crowd and he seemed to be looking and pointing directly at Kitty as he yelled, 'There's the mother of a German child who one day will tell him about this fire. Let him take pride that she was here on this glorious night amongst you, my dear *Kameraden*.'

The people around her seemed to look at Kitty with curiosity and envy, and John Smith had the good sense not to say anything. Twenty thousand books went up in flames that evening, and for years afterwards Kitty had nightmares about it.

A couple of days after leaving the madhouse, Kitty found herself, by complete contrast, in Denmark, where time seemed to have stood still; everything was quiet and orderly, and the Danes took pride in how small their country was, rather than in its size and power. With its absence of traffic, its flocks of cyclists – many of them old folk on bicycles as old as they were – its quiet streets that turned into drawbridges when a large ship needed to pass through, Denmark seemed to be living proof of the adage that good things come in small packages.

After giving herself a couple of days to settle in, Kitty phoned Lukin at the Soviet mission, but had the impression that he did not know why she was calling. She had to say her name two or more times before the penny finally dropped. The Thorwaldsen Museum, where they were to meet, had been built in honour of Denmark's most famous sculptor and contained much of his work, which is probably why their rendezvous in Room 23 was completely deserted. ERWIN, a smallish man with burning eyes and tousled hair, appeared on the dot as agreed, asked whether she was Frau Trachtenberg and confirmed that he was indeed Lukin. He immediately launched into an explanation of why Kitty's situation as a courier was quite tricky. Summertime was less of a problem, he asserted, for entering Denmark from Germany as a tourist by steamer from Stettin, or by rail, did not seem to attract much attention, and in fact Germans did not even need passports. The border guards paid a little more attention to foreigners, who simply needed some form of identity papers. The problem was the winter, when virtually no one came to Denmark to ski, and it would strike the frontier guards as unusual for any individual to cross the border more than once during the whole winter, which would apply to Kitty. He also pointed out that, according to a new German directive which was being applied rigorously, foreign students who lived in Germany and who did not pay taxes could only take fifty Reichsmarks out of the country with them when they travelled, which would hardly go anywhere when it came to living expenses.

'Do you think I could manage two round trips in the winter?' she asked.

'I doubt it,' he replied, 'and you'd need to find something here that you can say you are studying. It could be anything from Danish as a foreign language to Hamlet's influence on Shakespeare. I'm joking, of course. Anyway, you'd better think of something.'

'What about the money?' she enquired.

'That's going to be a problem. They should have found you a rich sponsor in the States, who you could say was giving you an allowance. The difficulty isn't just that we haven't got anything in our budget to support you, but you need a legitimate reason to explain whatever money you have. I'm amazed they didn't think about all of this.'

They agreed on their next meeting and went their separate ways, fretting. Kitty was anxious because she had no confidence in what ERWIN had said, and what he might do, and he was concerned because the last thing he needed was a new problem to worry about. A fortnight later the Danish press exploded with the banner head-lines: 'Russian Spy seized in Denmark', 'The Hands of the OGPU reach the Öresund', 'Time to Rein in the Russians', 'More Vigilance Needed Towards Foreigners', which all told the story of a Russian spy caught red-handed as his Danish agent passed over secret infor-mation.

It appears from the archive that this was an operation conducted by the Soviet military intelligence service, the GRU, which allowed Zarubin to take the high ground when expressing his concern to the Centre at the implications of the fiasco, and on the prospects for developing the organisation's communications. Because the situation in Denmark had deteriorated, he felt that it had become too risky to send couriers across the frontier more than once every four months. A courier arriving one day might find himself arbitrarily stopped from returning the next.

'It has rained on our parade,' Zarubin complained, 'or, more accu-rately, our "cousins" have brought the rain on. It seems to me that we have made a fair old mess of things in Denmark.' In reply, the Centre declared that the GRU operation had been blown as a result of a completely unacceptable breach of the elementary rules of tradecraft. Apparently, the GRU had been using Denmark as a base for operations against Germany, blind to the fact that Danish counter-intelligence was in close contact with its German opposite numbers. The Centre concluded that, in the circumstances, GYPSY could only be used as a courier once the summer tourist season had started, which meant that yet again Kitty found herself with nothing to do for quite a long time. ERWIN gave her a little money and she signed up for language courses, though she hardly went and did almost no work. She was bored and miserable, and was overjoyed when ERWIN finally dispatched her to Stockholm.

Kitty took the ferry to Malmö and then crossed southern Sweden by train, where she was to meet and exchange mail with ANTON, a member of the German underground, whose real name was Ernst Wohlweber, a former submariner who had run the dockworkers' union in Hamburg before escaping to Scandinavia when Hitler had come to power. He had built a sixty-strong network throughout the Baltic ports to provide intelligence and to conduct sabotage operations if war came. Kitty's lasting memory of the trip was ANTON himself, a calm, self-confident and unflappable man, who always thought two steps ahead; he was the type of man to whom she was attracted. Their relationship, however, was entirely professional and, after several more trips to Stockholm, Kitty was posted to Moscow in October 1935.

CHAPTER 8

Back to School

M oscow had changed a great deal since Kitty was last there, and all the more in the eight years since she had first arrived with Earl. There were more cars on the streets, the people were better dressed and the homeless children who used to huddle around the tar cauldrons for warmth had disappeared. Although she could not have known it, Stalin, ever paranoid and fearful that the hundreds of thousands of waifs, strays and orphans created by the Revolution, forced collectivisation and mass deportations, might represent a potential breeding ground for radical opposition, had shipped count-less thousands of them to state orphanages and imposed severe penalties on juvenile offenders.

With the city's rebuilding complete, there were actually fewer tar cauldrons in evidence. Impressive new buildings lined Gorky Street and Kitty marvelled at the splendour of the newly opened Metro, which put the subways of New York, Berlin and Paris to shame with its light-filled stations, a stark contrast with the grey perpetual twilight which shrouded the Moscow streets at the end of October. They must have seemed like fairy-tale palaces to her.

Kitty was sent to a hostel at Kuntsevo on the western ring road just outside the city. Although ration cards had been eliminated in 1934, she still needed coupons to eat the monotonous, though ample, food in the cafeteria. She shared a room with a French girl named Annie, and Hannah, a German, and there were several other foreigners on the same floor. With the exception of Ludwig, a veteran of the First World War, Kitty was the oldest student.

At her first interview, conducted on the day after her arrival, Kitty learned that, like all the others in the hostel, she was there for intelligence training in the adjacent school. Each student had their own hand-tailored programme, built around their experience, their native language and the country in which they were destined to serve. Kitty's classes included a Russian course, tradecraft, counter-surveillance measures, radio work, photography, the use of invisible ink and, of course, political instruction, the latter being a priority. Despite the fact that all the students were almost by definition sincere believers in the Soviet system, their ever wary tutors never lost sight of the fact that their pupils lived outside Russia in an environment which, if not actively hostile, was certainly foreign, and that they had read foreign newspapers and listened to foreign radios, and that by the nature of their clandestine work they were compelled not merely to listen patiently to what their political opponents had to say, but to give every impression of sharing their views. Consequently, they knew practically nothing about everyday life in the country in whose interests they had volunteered. Their curriculum was therefore carefully crafted to ensure that even those who were evidently convinced had their convictions reinforced, while those seen as having the potential to waver were put painstakingly back on the right track. The need for this political tuition was all the more important because, in those complicated years, there were three contradictory aspects to life in the Soviet Union.

The first was that of endless trials of 'enemies of the people', the constant 'unmasking' of political leaders in whom everybody had believed the day before, firing squads, spy mania, the midnight knock on the door, lawlessness by those supposed to uphold the law, secret denunciations, terror and the total absence of personal freedom.

The second was the genuine enthusiasm of the work force and its as yet unsullied belief in a glorious future. There was national pride in the huge new public works projects, there were cheerful new music and new movies, and the first Soviet flights across the North Pole; in short, as many Western fellow travellers reported, most Russians believed that their country 'would soon become the happiest and most powerful in the world'.

The third, which dominated and shaped the other two, was the burgeoning, overweening cult of personality surrounding Stalin.

The political education instructors at the intelligence school had crafted their course skilfully, by emphasising the first and second aspects, and explaining the third only as and when they had to. The students' timetable was strict, as was the overall regime; they had to have a good reason to leave the campus and were required to report on all their friends and other contacts. Even some of the specialist subjects were politicised, and before learning about clandestine operations, the students underwent a course entitled 'Leninist Principles of Secrecy', run by a small, dry stick of a man who introduced himself as Comrade Gennady, and who told them that he had been in the Party since before the Revolution and had acquired his excellent German in Switzerland while in exile there with Lenin. His opening remarks were a reminder of Lenin's dictum that, 'It was harder to trap a dozen clever men than a hundred idiots': 'There's an Arab proverb that goes: "If you want to keep a secret from your enemies, keep it from your friends." So the main aim of *konspiratsiya* is to conceal on-going secret operations. Everything else in your work is secondary. If you aren't able to pull off a mission, that's a fifty per cent misfortune. If you do succeed but it then gets blown, then that's a hundred per cent misfortune for you, for the operation and for other people.'

How intelligence officers should behave was another of his themes: 'You can't operate by rules which don't admit the possibility of things going wrong. There are no such rules any more than there are people, or intelligence officers, who never make mistakes. The smart oper-ator is one who knows how to correct a mistake easily and quickly. And remember one more thing, the intelligence officer mustn't keep quiet about his mistakes or try to cover them up, even if they seem trivial or if they relate to intimate aspects of his or her life.'

Gennady's course was popular and interesting, not least because he illustrated his advice with real-life examples, and Kitty was very disappointed when one day he simply failed to turn up and never reappeared. When she asked about him, the senior instructors averted their eyes and swiftly changed the subject. Despite this loss, Kitty enjoyed the counter-surveillance course, which began by studying the theory. Like every other teacher before and since, the instructor reckoned that his subject was the most important in the timetable and started by quoting a British manual, which asserted that, 'in many cases, surveillance is the sole means of establishing a suspect's connections and obtaining evidence that will stand up in court'.

'So you see,' he emphasised, 'how important it is for you to detect surveillance and, if need be, get away from it. You need to be constantly alert, don't get over-confident and never underestimate the skill of the people who are on your trail.'

All of the practical examples used in Kitty's lessons related to the British Security Service and Special Branch, and it was not hard for her to deduce that she was being trained to work in Britain. After the theory came the practice, and Kitty virtually committed the street map of Moscow to memory before going out on her own, strolling the streets, taking the tram, the bus and the Metro to develop a route which would give her several good opportunities to check if she was being followed. She knew that on these training exercises she had to behave naturally and not give any indication that she was aware of hostile surveillance. The object was to spot whoever was trailing you and to be able to give a detailed descrip-tion of them when you were debriefed later on. Along the way, you had to fill or clear a dead-letter box and also execute a brush contact.

Of course, this was not the frightening or risky operation it would be in real life, more a battle of wits in which both the environment and the adversary were friendly, but vigilance was still required. On one occasion a complete stranger came up to Kitty and whispered, 'You're being followed!'

'By whom?' Kitty asked in surprise.

'Those guys there,' the woman told her, with an unobtrusive gesture towards two surveillance officers whom Kitty had not yet spotted.

'Thanks,' Kitty said, as the woman disappeared into the crowd. Kitty was uncertain whether to approach the watchers and tell them that the game was over, but decided to pretend nothing was amiss and continue on her route. At her debriefing, the instructor said that she had done absolutely the right thing, since in a hostile situation the woman's approach might have been a put-up job to get Kitty to give herself away by her reactions.

Kitty also worked on a team that ran surveillance on foreigners suspected of espionage, a task she enjoyed, and she even managed to spot her target dropping a letter in a postbox. In line with the training manual, after the target had moved on, she immediately dropped a piece of plain paper in the postbox so that the original, suspect letter could be identified easily and recovered.

Kitty did quite well in her language class, and by the end of her training spoke and read Russian reasonably well. She also learned about invisible ink, from making it by mixing over-the-counter medicines with certain chemicals to the techniques required to develop the writing. She was also much amused by what the trainers called Aesop language, which was used to supplement the secrecy of invisible ink by the addition of a simple code to disguise the meaning of what had been written. An ostensibly innocuous remark such as 'a visit to Auntie' might mean the dispatch of a courier, or 'Uncle's illness' could tell a reader that a recent batch of film was of poor quality. Passports were known as 'shoes', and the argot allowed what would otherwise be highly incriminating messages to be concealed in what appeared to be a quite innocent text.

Whitechapel c. 1900, Kitty's birthplace.

Kitty Harris, a photograph taken for
a false passport.

The two loves of Kitty's life: Earl Browder (left) photographed after his arrest in 1919, and Donald Maclean, the Foreign Office diplomat who spied for the Russians. Kitty was not only his case officer but also his lover.

The leading figures of the American Communist movement in the 1920s: Jay Lovestone, William Foster, Charles Ruthenberg, Anna Damon and Max Bedacht.

Earl Browder (right) with Tom Mann in China, late 1920s.

Liza and Vassily Zarubin,
Kitty's long-time NKVD controllers.

The Bund, Shanghai's famous waterfront,
in 1937.

The KGB headquarters in Moscow.

Moscow Centre, as the actors in this story knew it – a rare view of the OGPU's
headquarters in the early 1930s.

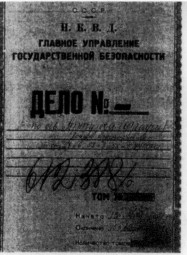
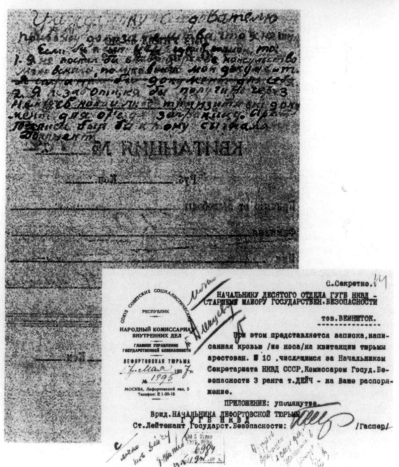

Artur Artuzov, head of the INO, the OGPU's foreign department –
a photograph taken just before his arrest during the purges of the 1930s,
and the note written in his own blood declaring that he wasn't a spy.

Kitty with a hairstyle and glasses
deliberately designed to create
a forgettable appearance.

Theodore Mally, the illegal *rezident* who ran
the Cambridge Five. Kitty was posted to his
rezidentura in Paris in 1936.

Alexander Orlov, who trained and
developed the Cambridge Five.

Arnold Deutsch, illegal *rezident* in
London from 1933 and recruiter of
the Cambridge Five. He was Kitty's
immediate superior in London.

Kitty in a rare moment of relaxation.

Karl Gursky, *rezident* in London 1941-3.

Grigory Grafpen, Kitty's last controller in London.

Itzhak Akhmerov, Soviet illegal and husband of Browder's niece Helen Lowry.

Naum Eitingon, a key Soviet illegal who masterminded the assasination of Trotsky in Mexico City.

A portrait of Vicente Lombardo Toledano, Kitty's contact in Mexico.

Her most important courses were photography and wireless procedures. Both Zarubin and Gursky had tried without success to teach Kitty how to photograph documents, but concepts such as exposure, shutter and focal length remained a total mystery to her. It often happens that someone with a quick mind, with a good ear for languages and who is otherwise very adaptable finds themselves totally at sea when it comes to technical matters, however skilled the teacher, and in Kitty's case her trainer was Vilyam Fisher, who was later to become famous as the spy Rudolf Abel.

Fisher had been born in England to a family of Russian political emigrants. His father, one of the Russified Germans who had settled in Yaroslavl Province, and his mother, who came from Saratov, had been expelled from Russia in 1901 for revolutionary activities. Vilyam was an exceptional student and was admitted to London University at the age of sixteen, but a year later the entire family went back to Russia. Vilyam qualified as a radio operator in the Red Army and, from 1923 onwards, was as an officer in the Soviet foreign intelligence service. He carried out a number of important missions abroad working as a radio operator for various illegal *rezidenturas* and returned to Moscow in 1935 as an instructor for intelligence probationers.

Despite exposing dozens of metres of film and using up hundreds of sheets of photographic paper, Kitty got nowhere because she forgot to take the cover off the lens, or she got the light wrong, or took the photograph from the wrong angle. Her instructors complained to Fisher, who tried patiently to give Kitty guidance. 'What on earth am I going to do?' she sobbed. 'It looks as though there's nothing I'm good at. But I'm trying as hard as I can.'

'Well, you'll just have to try harder,' Fisher replied. 'It was Rousseau who said that real education came less from knowing the rules than from doing the exercises. So go and do more exercises.'

Kitty did as she was told and gradually her performance improved to the point where the photographs of documents she produced were more or less legible. In parallel with photography, she also underwent radio training and proved quite nimble with the Morse key, achieving within the first month the 'magic' level of sending and receiving eight groups a minute. Her trainers then worked on speeding up her transmissions, and she also managed, though not without difficulty, to get the hang of assembling the radio and taking it apart. However, when it came to radio theory, for which the trainee needed an elementary grasp of maths, if only for such mundane tasks as working out the length of an aerial, she was at a complete loss. The trainers and Fisher himself tried everything they knew, but Kitty always produced numbers that were wildly off the chart. Finally, it occurred to Fisher that the problem was that Kitty actually had no idea of basic arithmetic. A few questions established that she had never even learned her multiplication tables, and she was told that she must have extra maths lessons with a personal tutor. She burst into tears, cursing herself, the world, her parents who had not taught her properly, and all those people who were forcing her to deal with such dreadful things, but in the end she went along and learned the essentials. She then moved on to practical work and spent February and March 1936 exchanging training transmissions with a station in Sverdlovsk. While she hardly covered herself with glory in this phase of her training, she was thought to be adequate and a note on her file mentions that

> She easily gets muddled when dealing with technical
> aspects. She has completed a full course in receiving and
> transmitting and has a basic grasp of aerials and calibration.
> She can put together a basic receiver and transmitter. She
> undertook duplex training from 13 February 1936 to 21
> March 1936. She can be regarded as trained. She knows
> how to handle our model of transceiver.

The senior staff of the INO decided to see how GYPSY would cope in an operational situation, and in April 1936 posted her to MANN's illegal *rezidentura* in Paris. MANN's real name was

Theodore Mally, and he was also known as MALY ('small') and HUNGARIAN, the latter demonstrating, since he was in fact Hungarian, the transparency of many of the code names used in those days. The son of a civil servant, Mally had been fascinated by religion from boyhood; he had joined a monastic order and enrolled in the Theology and Philosophy Faculty at the University of Vienna. However, he soon became disillusioned and, although he had been ordained, gave up Holy Orders and enlisted in the army. He passed out of training school as an ensign in 1915 and was soon promoted to second lieutenant, only to be taken prisoner when the Russian army attacked the Carpathians in 1916.

In 1918 Mally enlisted in the Red Army and fought with it until 1921, when he was taken prisoner in the fighting against the Czechoslovaks in 1919, an event which later became one of the factors in his subsequent downfall. After being interrogated in Admiral Kolchak's counter-intelligence headquarters, he was locked up first in the Krasoyskarsk prison and then in a prisoner-of-war camp, from which the Red Army liberated him. In those days to have been a prisoner of war was not regarded as particularly compromising, and in 1921 he joined the Cheka; by the early 1930s, he was working overseas for the INO. In France in 1932 he recruited a retired officer of the French general staff named Cadoux, who was a valuable source but who soon fell under suspicion, forcing Mally to leave for Moscow in a hurry.

Mally also had a number of other good results in that period. One of those working in his *rezidentura* was the illegal Dmitri Bystrolyotov. Codenamed HANS, Bystrolyotov had pulled off some notable coups, including getting his hands on German codes and recruiting a French military intelligence officer, from whom he obtained Austrian, Italian and Turkish code material as well as some secret German documents. He was also responsible for handling Ernest Oldham and John King, both cipher clerks in the Foreign Office in London. Working together, Mally and Bystrolyotov also ran a brilliantly conceived operation in which a brand new Italian machine pistol and a new type of gas mask were acquired by the Berlin *rezidentura*. While Kitty is known to have had a hand in some of their operations, there is no detailed information on her personal file, which mentions only her work as a radio operator.

In 1936 Mally was transferred to London. Kitty was posted there too, but she continued to divide her time between London and Paris, going backwards and forwards as a courier. In those days travel between France and England was probably the easiest frontier crossing in Europe, for when the cross-Channel ferries docked, there were so many passengers swarming on and off that the harassed immigration officers could do little more than glance at passports. Towards the end of 1936, Mally's *rezidentura* was supplied with new radio equipment which was much more sophisticated than the basic sets on which Kitty had trained, and the Centre was asked to send her to Moscow for retraining, which she began in January 1937. The outcome was discouraging, and her instructors recorded at a review meeting that, despite two years of radio work, any more technical training would be a waste of time and that she should only be used as a radio operator in an emergency.

Kitty waited several days before she was called upstairs to be told her future. When she went into the office, she met a man with deep-set, half-closed eyes, thin lips and the large ears Russians think are a sign of musical ability. This was Walter Krivitsky, a highly experienced intelligence officer, the same age as Kitty, who had been born Samuel Ginsberg in the little town of Podvolchisk, which at that time belonged to the Austro-Hungarian Empire. He began working for the Red Army's intelligence service in 1920, and from 1923 he worked in Germany, France, Italy and Holland. In 1931 he became an officer in the INO and operated in Holland until 1937. In March of that year he was recalled to Moscow, where he witnessed the arrest of many intelligence officers, some of them his personal friends. Krivitsky himself survived the purges and was assigned several trained agents to upgrade his overseas staff, something he had requested, but never dreamed, as the Grand Guignol rolled on, that he would be granted. On top of that, he was actually allowed to leave Russia. In his memoirs he recalled meeting Kitty in Moscow:

Among the woman agents who had been recommended to me was an American called Kitty Harris, formerly Katherine Harrison. I was told she was the former wife of the US Communist Party leader Earl Browder and therefore highly reliable. At that time I needed a woman agent in Switzerland and the holder of an American passport was particularly welcome. When Kitty Harris came to see me and gave me her dossier in a sealed envelope, it turned out that she was also staying in the Savoy Hotel. She was about forty, dark-haired and of good appearance. She had been connected with our intelligence service for some years. She spoke positively about Browder and especially his sister, who was working for our service in Central Europe. I approved the assignment of Miss Harris to a foreign posting and she left on 29 April.

Kitty returned to Paris using a Soviet passport in the name of Elizaveta Stein, but sloppy staff work meant that she was detained for twenty-four hours at the frontier, when the border guards found that she was carrying $100 she had been given for travel expenses. Soviet citizens carrying foreign currency were regarded with extreme suspicion.

When she finally reached Paris, she found a personal letter and a little parcel from her old teacher Vilyam Fisher. He wished her every success and sent her as a joke an electric plug from the training school, as well as some books and notes that he had promised her. It was at this point that, although Kitty was still classified as a radio operator, her career with wireless drew peacefully to a close, though not to her great regret.

Ahead of her lay Kitty's finest hour. She would be working under Mally (who had inherited the illegal *rezidentura* from Alexander

Orlov, codenamed SCHWED ['the Swede']), Grigory Grafpen (SAM) and Arnold Deutsch, alias Stefan Lang, all of them outstanding men whom destiny was to take in various extraordinary and diverse directions, but who all made vital contributions to Soviet intelligence, not least their part in recruiting or running the famous 'Cambridge Five'.

CHAPTER 9

The Three Musketeers

As the Roaring Twenties slumped into the Depressed Thirties, Britain's Conservative Government was about to depart from power. Though its time in office had been marked by growing official concerns about Soviet ambitions, espionage and subversion, fuelled by such episodes as the Zinovyev Letter, many young people, including some very bright upper-class idealists, found themselves captivated by Communist dogma. They contrasted the seemingly inevitable decline of the West with the vibrant Soviet Union, rolling out its Herculean Five-Year Plan, a land free – or so its apologists claimed – of unemployment and making maximum use of the country's vast resources. Russia was 'unique . . . a benchmark for world society'.

Among them was Kim Philby, who later wrote:

I always felt that my ideals and convictions, my sympathies and desires were on the side of those who were fighting for a better future for mankind . . . the embodiment of these ideals was the Soviet Union. That led to my struggle taking the form of working in Soviet intelligence. Joining the ranks of Soviet intelligence was not just a random event. On the eve of the

143

Second World War the Soviet illegal Stefan Lang was able to see the possible ways in which my future might go. When he began to talk to me about the possibility that I might work for the British Secret Service, I thought that he was fantasising. Possibly in the beginning he was. But his fantasy was based on his experience of life and later became reality.

Stefan Lang, of course, was Arnold Deutsch, the illegal *rezident* in London and Kitty's immediate superior, whose initiative had brought the Cambridge Five into espionage. Deutsch's real intelligence work began in 1933, when he began to operate illegally in Britain, at a time when British policy towards the Soviets was far from friendly, and when Moscow considered it a priority to learn the real intentions of those at the centre of power.

In one of Deutsch's reports to the Centre he described his efforts to create a spy network and referred specifically to Philby and his co-believers:

All of them came to us when they graduated from Oxford and Cambridge. They shared Communist convictions. This came about under the influence of the revolutionary movement which had caught the imagination of certain strata of the British intelligentsia and especially the two strongholds of British intellectual life, Cambridge and Oxford. Eighty per cent of the top Civil Service jobs in Britain are taken by Cambridge and Oxford graduates, since only rich people can afford the fees. There are some poor students on scholarships but these are the exception. A degree from either place opens the door to the higher levels of public and political life.

Deutsch was born in 1904, the son of a minor businessman, had started out as a village schoolteacher in Slovakia and had joined the revolutionary movement at sixteen, arriving in Moscow in 1932 to work for the Comintern. Several months later he was recommended to Soviet intelligence and, thereafter, operated under the alias of Stefan Lang. His intelligence training did not take too long since he already had considerable experience, including working underground, had acquired tradecraft skills and spoke several languages. In October 1933 he began working operationally in London, a city which struck him as peaceful and well-ordered. He took his time to feel his way around and settle down, and in 1934 he enrolled at London University, majoring in psychology, but he was also trawling for students he could use for intelligence purposes. His main target was upper-class students, but they seemed to be few and far between in London.

Deutsch made a careful study of the system by which British civil servants were selected for the principal Ministries and Departments of State, and his detailed memorandum, forwarded to the Centre, and as long and weighty as a doctoral thesis, was the 'beachhead' from which he launched his clandestine invasion, one which would be narrowly targeted rather than scatter-shot:

> There were of course young people ready and willing to join us. But before they could be recruited they needed to be checked and their abilities and career opportunities carefully assessed. Once recruited they had to be trained in the rules of tradecraft and their approach to their future careers carefully mapped out.

To succeed, Deutsch needed not just to be extremely careful but to be armed with powerful arguments, and he relied principally on the human factor, for he was no cloak-and-dagger spy. Pressure, blackmail, high-speed car chases, shoot-outs and the other staples of spy fiction were never part of his life. Nor did he regard money as a useful tool, quite apart from the fact that he had limited funds at his disposal anyway.

His essential strengths were his fascinating and attractive personality and his uncanny insight into people's hearts and minds, traits he would mix and match, depending on his assessment and feel for his target. In the end however, the decisive factor was always ideological conviction. During his period in London, Deutsch recruited more than twenty sources, the overwhelming majority of whom worked for Soviet intelligence out of conscience rather than from fear.

All his agents we now know about were Cambridge graduates, but he also recruited students from Oxford who were no less talented and committed, but none of them has ever been identified publicly. While every one of his agents made their mark, the so-called Three Musketeers from Cambridge are the best known, and Kitty is linked with all three, and in particular Donald Maclean.

It was an inflexible rule of Soviet intelligence that a target could only be recruited after he or she had been carefully vetted and approved by the Centre, but in Philby's case the letter to the Centre about him, written in invisible ink in July 1934, turned out to be literally illegible. Having received no reply from Moscow, Deutsch and his *rezident*, Ignati Reiff, decided to go ahead with the recruitment at their own risk. As it happened, they were just in time because a day or two later Philby would have joined the Communist Party of Great Britain and therefore would have been off limits as an agent because the Centre was convinced that all members of the Party were under surveillance and that any attempt to recruit them would be counterproductive.

Philby was assigned the code name SYNOK ('little son'), which, for tradecraft reasons, was written in German as SÖHNCHEN, in the hope that in the event of a leak, the other side would think that the Germans were involved. SÖHNCHEN was initially recruited for 'anti-Fascist work' and was drawn into Soviet intelligence only gradually, a process that was completed by the new illegal *rezident* in London, Alexander Orlov, codenamed SCHWED. Orlov, who had been born Leiba Lazarevich Feldbin to a Jewish family in Bobruisk in Byelorussia, had an amazing career and his contradictory personality sets him apart in the Pantheon of senior Soviet intelligence officers. Orlov had always wanted to be a soldier and had enrolled as an officer cadet, passing out in 1917. He became a Bolshevik in 1920 because he 'believed in Lenin's programme and promises', and, despite everything that happened to him afterwards, he is claimed by some to have remained a believer in Communism until the day he died.

After several administrative jobs, Orlov served in the Red Army from 1919, with which, as a senior counter-intelligence officer, he fought on the Polish front, took part in operations and sabotage behind enemy lines, and was also involved in intelligence gathering. His wealth of experience made him one of the Red Army's leading experts in counter-intelligence and sabotage, and he earned high marks from Artur Artuzov himself.

After the Civil War, Orlov went back to college and then worked in the legal system, before joining the OGPU in 1923. By 1926 he was working in the INO and was given his first overseas posting to Paris; he always worked abroad thereafter. It was in Paris, then the second largest *rezidentura* in Europe after Berlin, that Orlov, posing as 'Lev Nikolayev', pulled off his first major disinformation operation by passing to the French General Staff what purported to be a German plan to occupy the demilitarised Rhineland and to invade France eighteen months later. At the beginning of 1928 Orlov was posted to Berlin, using the alias 'Lev Feldel' and working in the Soviet trade mission, which provided cover for the collection of scientific, technical and economic intelligence. In 1932, again using his Nikolayev alias, he posed as a member of an official Soviet trade delegation sponsored by General Motors to visit Detroit. When he got to London, he was able to give Deutsch a great deal of help in training and developing the Cambridge Five.

The Cambridge Five began with Philby, and when he was asked by Deutsch to produce a list of fellow undergraduates who might be potential recruits, Maclean headed his list while Burgess was at the bottom. Like the others, Maclean's life has been well documented. He was born in 1913 on 25 May, his birthday falling one day after Kitty's. He was the son of a Cabinet Minister and a high-minded mother. Maclean's father had died in 1932, hence his code name WAISE ('orphan' in German) or SIROTA (the equivalent in Russian). When Maclean went up to Cambridge at the age of eighteen, he plunged into politics, spoke at the university's Socialist Society and gained a reputation as a writer and speaker. He made no secret of his support for Communism and even told friends that he planned to go to Russia to work as a tractor driver or teacher. Describing Maclean in a letter to the Centre Mally wrote:

> I like the new people very much. They are very different, very individual but I think they are all honest . . . <u>WAISE</u>: the first thing to be said is that he is certainly very good looking. There is something feminine about him not only in his facial expression but also in his body language. But he is half a head taller than me. He is modest, clever, looks at everything from the Comintern point of view, disciplined but still very young, inexperienced and therefore frightened. We do not have a safe-house where we could have a relaxed conversation. We meet somewhere way out in one of the suburbs in a little restaurant but when we get on to ticklish subjects and name names he shivers in fright in case someone might hear us. He is an idealist and we need to be very careful how we deal with him so as not to destroy his idealism. He regards us as Gods. We have by the way established that he has indeed told all his friends that he has put his 'youthful indiscretions' behind him and thrown himself completely into his work.

Like Philby and Burgess after him, Maclean had to renounce his left-wing views and connections when he was recruited in August 1934. In February 1935 a woman officer at the Centre, known only as 'K', opened a file on Maclean, based on a suspicion that he was spying for British intelligence. Who the long-vanished K was, or what led her to decide that Maclean was a British spy and how she intended to investigate him, are all questions to which today there are no answers. In any event, no one other than K thought that Maclean was a spy and the *rezidentura* treated him as a reliable agent from the outset.

As the son of prominent parents, Maclean moved in the right circles and was well connected. His mother's friends and acquaintances included several ministers, among them Sir John Simon, the Home Secretary, a connection which led Orlov to suggest to the Centre that he be planted in the Home Office. However, as things developed, it was felt more promising to place him in the Foreign Office, where he was appointed a Third Secretary in early 1936, on the back of excellent results in the Civil Service examinations and references from all the right people.

Maclean's post in the Foreign Office gave him access to many top-secret papers, and he soon became an important source of valuable intelligence in such quantities that, in May 1936, Mally told the Centre that the *rezidentura* was overwhelmed by Maclean's material and a special assistant was needed to handle the work. The Centre agreed that an independent section should be created to handle the Maclean 'take' and promised to send the highly experienced Dmitri Bystrolyotov as soon as he could settle his personal affairs.

Unfortunately, Bystrolyotov's personal affairs were finally settled only eighteen years later, when he was freed from jail and rehabilitated after being imprisoned on a trumped-up espionage charge.

It was at this point that Deutsch recalled that Kitty had been idle since her radio, along with two others in Berlin, had been taken off the air. Kitty's job at that stage was to run a safe-house (in fact a flat) where Mally and Deutsch met their agents. She was pivotal to the operation and, in October 1936, Deutsch reported that in the previous week the *rezidentura* had been unable to complete as much work as it had wanted because GYPSY had gone to Paris and there was no other apartment available. Kitty had come to know Philby,

Maclean and Burgess during their visits to the flat, though not especially well at that stage because all she had done as housekeeper was to meet the visitors, bring them coffee and biscuits, and sometimes cook supper. They might exchange a few words, but she had played no part in the serious business conversations. In that year she changed flats twice so as not to draw attention to her visitors.

One day an obviously flustered Deutsch had turned up unexpectedly and explained that he had 'to take off in a hurry. Tell all our friends not to turn up here until they get the agreed telephone message.' The reason for Deutsch's hurried departure, which was to last for three months, was sheer bad luck. He kept a meticulous list of his expenses, including payments to his agents, in a folder which a woman colleague, codenamed STRELA ('arrow'), held for safekeeping. One day it vanished, and STRELA swore that she could not have lost it. When Deutsch told the Centre, he was ordered to leave England immediately and work with his valuable network ground to a halt. Finally, desperately searching her apartment one last time, STRELA found the ill-fated folder tucked underneath the cushions of her sofa and rushed to tell Mally, who reported the good news to the Centre, which in turn lifted Deutsch's exile.

(Though not identified in Kitty's file, no doubt for security reasons, STRELA was in fact Edith Tudor Hart, the darkly attractive Viennese-born photographer and friend of Philby's Austrian first wife Litzi Friedmann. Married to a Welsh doctor, Alex Tudor Hart – also a Soviet asset who had been recruited by Deutsch after running a field hospital in the Spanish Civil Was – it was the twenty-six-year-old Edith who escorted a nervous but enthralled Philby to his first meeting with Deutsch in London's Regents Park. It is not clear at this distance whether the danger-packed folder was mislaid at Edith's studio in Mayfair's Duke Street or in Brixton where she moved when Alex – described by one of Edith's family as 'a madcap idealist' – opened a surgery. Edith's professional reputation lives on; major London galleries still promote her work and a book of photographs by Edith and her brother Wolf Suschitzky appeared only a few years ago under the title *Eye of Concern*; their joint work was the focus of a recent exhibition in Berlin.)

When Deutsch returned to London and asked Kitty to notify his agents, she passed on the agreed telephone signal by calling Philby on MAIda Vale 7858 and asking 'if Miss Shirley Stevens was there?' For Maclean she enquired about 'Dr Wilson's surgery hours', while with Burgess, then living characteristically beyond his means in a flat at 38 Chester Square, she called SLOane 4847; when he answered, she simply blew twice into the mouthpiece.

Her work as housekeeper picked up again, and at about this time she did another small but important job for Deutsch which he had given to her not just out of operational necessity, but to make her feel wanted. Guy Burgess had been tasked to penetrate MI6, the Secret Intelligence Service, and, with a helping hand from Maclean, he had become friendly with David Footman, an SIS officer who was also an established and respected author. Burgess, then working at the BBC, suggested making a radio programme on his latest book and Footman took the bait, agreeing to meet Burgess in the lobby of the Langham Hotel, across the street from the BBC's imposing headquarters.

Since Kitty knew Burgess, Deutsch instructed her to keep an unobtrusive eye on how he handled himself, and to watch what was going on in the lobby so that he could compare her comments with Burgess's report. The meeting was crucial since it was the first serious attempt to penetrate British intelligence. Burgess was noticeably excited, which he attributed in his debriefing to his worry that Footman might not turn up, but overall his account of the meeting squared with Kitty's. Burgess and Footman became firm friends, and Footman helped Guy become first a freelance asset for SIS and then a member of its staff. In turn, Burgess later helped Kim Philby to enter SIS.

Deutsch reported that Kitty was clamouring for more work and had asked for permission to go to photography school. At the back of his mind in passing this on was the thought that she might be useful in handling Maclean, and, with the Centre's approval, Kitty enrolled. When Deutsch and Mally then suggested that Kitty should be assigned to receiving and photographing Maclean's material, the Centre replied that GYPSY had been trained as a radio operator and should concentrate on that, adding that she could only take on other assignments if they did not adversely affect her primary responsibility. Even though Kitty was by then not working as a radio operator, Mally understood that the Centre's elliptical reply was a polite way of saying 'No'. However, in September 1937 Deutsch reported that Kitty was very depressed. In his opinion, she was losing confidence in herself and thought that the organisation did not want her. Deutsch promised to convince her otherwise, but it was not just that she had too little to do that had depressed her. Alarming rumours had reached her from Moscow.

One gloomy autumn day, with time hanging heavily on her hands but not much cash in her purse, Kitty was window-shopping in the West End when she sensed that someone was watching her. She turned casually and saw a woman who had been standing behind her rush forward to hug and kiss her, sobbing, 'Kitty, Kitty, how are you my dear?'

It took Kitty a moment to recognise Dorothy Pelz, who looked much older than when she had last seen her, her eyes puffy with tears. They had been friends in Chicago, and, although they were not that close, Kitty knew Dorothy and her husband to be a decent, honest couple who had never gone in for big-time politics, always having been quite content to remain cogs in Browder's organisation. Some time back, as Kitty recalled, Arthur Pelz had gone to Moscow to work for the Comintern, but she was astonished to learn that he had been arrested in Moscow on espionage charges.

The two women talked for half an hour. Kitty thankfully was sufficiently disciplined to refrain from saying that she had a line to Moscow through which she could vouch for Arthur and get what was obviously a monstrous mistake put right. She merely told Dorothy how sorry she was, and that she hoped things would get sorted out in Moscow and that justice would be done. When they said goodbye, she told Dorothy that she couldn't give her an address as she was just passing through London.

Kitty reported the encounter to Deutsch, who, being the decent man he was, reacted by making a robust plea in Pelz's defence, telling the Centre that GYPSY had met a woman friend whose husband had been arrested. She had known them for sixteen years and was convinced that they were honourable members of the Party. Perhaps Deutsch was being naïve, and maybe he had wondered what his cable would achieve, because of course he received no reply, but the cable itself was conscientiously added to Kitty's personal file at the Centre.

This was probably Deutsch's last message from London because he was recalled to Moscow in September 1937, in Mally's wake. That month Maclean had been 'put on ice', the *rezidentura* having been instructed by the Centre to 'tell him this is necessary in order to consolidate our work and maintain secrecy and that it has absolutely nothing to do with all the things that are going on here at home'.

What was going on 'at home' in Moscow was a positively Jacobean tragedy, a wholesale bloody purge of the intelligence service, the full scale of which only emerged in 1999. According to figures published in 1999 under the auspices of the new Russian intelligence service, the NKVD had a staff of some 24,500 in 1936. By January 1938, 5,898 of them had gone: 1,373 had been arrested, 3,048 either dismissed entirely or placed on reserve, 1,324 transferred to other departments and 153 executed. No information was given on the subsequent fate of those arrested. Among the victims was Mally, who was shot, and Artur Artuzov. A recent history of Soviet counter-intelligence reproduces the note Artuzov wrote to his interrogator, Veiynshtok, on a prison receipt form, declaring, 'I am not a spy!' A covering memorandum by the head warder to the commandant of the Leforotovo prison pointed out with clinical detachment that the plea had been written in Artuzov's own blood 'from his nose'. The memorandum shows that Artuzov was held at the disposal of 'the Head of the Secretariat of the NKVD of the USSR Commissar of State Security 3rd Class, Comrade Deutsch'. A short while later interrogator Veiynshtok himself was shot.

Deutsch managed to get back to London for ten days to put his leaderless agents 'on ice', and in December 1937 Kitty was also recalled to Moscow because she was known to Walter Krivitsky, whom she had met in Moscow the previous spring.

Horrified by what he had heard and seen in Moscow, and expecting to be arrested himself at any minute, Krivitsky had been summoned by Frinovsky, the NKVD's Deputy Commissar, on 22 May 1937. Expecting the worst, he concealed his emotions when, instead, he was told that there were no allegations against him and that he should return that evening to his post in Holland. His colleagues assumed this to be some significant, if dimly understood, mark of favour by Stalin's toady Yezhov, the head of the NKVD and main architect of the purges, but whatever the real reason, Krivitsky, scarcely able to believe his luck, arrived in The Hague on 27 May, where he met his NKVD colleague Ignac Reiss. The two veteran clandestine operators had a long talk about what was happening at home and what it meant for them personally, and a month later Reiss defected from Paris after circulating to his friends and close colleagues, including Mally and Krivitsky, copies of a letter he had sent to Stalin. The response was a manhunt for Reiss, and a hit squad caught up with him in Switzerland on 4 September.

This episode persuaded Krivitsky that he too would never return home but that, unlike his unfortunate friend, he would find somewhere safer to conceal himself. He therefore hid from his former colleagues in various parts of France until 5 December 1937, when he sent Trotsky's son, Lev Sedov, an open letter declaring that he had broken with Soviet intelligence completely.

Krivitsky sought sanctuary in the United States, where, among the valuable insights he gave the FBI, were a good sketch of Kitty and information on Margaret Browder. He told them that Margaret was using the name Jean Montgomery (the real Montgomery was an American journalist on *PM*, a newspaper where one of Kitty's sisters also worked) and working as a radio operator for the Soviets in Central Europe. When Krivitsky was found dead of a gunshot wound to the head in a Washington DC hotel in 1941, the police declared the death a suicide, but that judgment remains controversial. There is also some debate about the nature of the operations for which Krivitsky was recruiting when he was in Moscow, and in his memoirs he relates how, just prior to the interview with Kitty, he had been asked by Otto Spiegelglass, an experienced OGPU assassin, to assign Margaret to him for 'an important job in France for which he needed especially reliable people', which Krivitsky suspected might have to do with the OGPU's hunt for Reiss. According to Krivitsky, Margaret travelled to Amsterdam in July 1937 and then to Paris, but whether she participated in the subsequent operation remains unknown.

The INO Directorate was naturally anxious about the security of all the intelligence officers working abroad who were known to Krivitsky and wanted to establish precisely the nature of their relationship with him. Dozens of people were investigated, among them Margaret Browder, but luckily for Kitty her own case was put in the hands of Ivan Nikolayevich Kaminsky, a first-class intelligence officer and a thoroughly decent man, who had himself only recently returned from overseas. Although they had not known each other for long, she probably got closer to him than any other officer in the organisation. He was forty years old and had fought in both the First World War and the Civil War, when he had been seriously wounded while leading his regiment. He began to work for the INO as deputy *rezident* and then *rezident* in Poland, Czechoslovakia, Latvia, Italy and Finland. He was later transferred to illegal work, where he had his share of triumphs and disasters, and in the spring of 1934 Kaminsky, then an illegal *rezident*, ran operations against émigré groups in France, Belgium and Holland. Another operation took place in Switzerland against a group of Ukrainian nationalists headed by Colonel Konovalets, who were planning to bomb the Soviet delegation to the League of Nations and assassinate Maxim Litvinov, the Soviet Foreign Minister. Kaminsky managed to infiltrate his own agents into Konovalets's entourage, but the operation was blown when the husband of Kaminsky's assistant took fright and reported the whole thing to the police. Kaminsky and his associates were arrested, but refused to say a word at their trial and went on hunger strike. Although they were subjected to psychological and physical pressure, the prosecution failed to prove their involvement in espionage or even to establish their true identities.

Since Konovalets had been successfully typecast by Soviet propaganda efforts as a terrorist, Swiss public opinion was in favour of anything that could be done to get rid of him, and the press came out in support of Kaminsky. As a result, Kaminsky was released and returned home, while Konovalets was expelled. The plot against Litvinov collapsed and in 1938 Konovalets was murdered in Rotterdam by Pavel Sudoplatov.

Upon his return to Moscow Kaminsky was promoted to the head of the INO department responsible for supervising operations in Western Europe, including Great Britain, and he quickly realised when he looked into Kitty's case that she was not implicated with Krivitsky and that her security was not at risk providing she could be given a new, preferably authentic, passport. He decided to send Kitty to the United States and Canada to obtain two real passports, and then return her to Britain, where she was to put all her energies into working with Maclean, as it was clear that she would never make a good radio operator. Indeed, Vilyam Fisher had noted in her file that, although she had been given very detailed training, 'she is incapable of working as a radio operator'.

Two memoranda on the file record her application for Soviet citizenship. The first declares:

To the Praesidium of the USSR.
    <u>Regarding the granting of Soviet citizenship to</u>:

Harris, Kitty Natanovna born in London 24 May 1899
spinster, British subject, worker, member of the Communist
Party of America, elementary education, seamstress.
<u>Declaration</u>
I wish to bear the high and noble title of Citizen of the
USSR, to play an active part in the building of Socialism,
and to fight against all enemies of the Soviet State.
(Signed) Kitty Harris 21/12/37

The second, an extract from Minute 93 of 26 December 1937 of
the Presidium of the USSR, states simply:

Petition heard.
Decreed: accepted for citizenship of the USSR.
Signed: M. Kalinin

Kitty left for America in late December 1937, travelling on her
original American passport. Despite an awkward moment at the
Finnish border when she was told that she needed a visa and had
to argue her way across, she reached Stockholm, but was discon-
certed to find that the next sailing for New York was a month away.
Undaunted, she took a train to Paris and then to Le Havre, where
she boarded the *Manhattan* bound for New York.

Kitty found disembarking in New York a little nerve-racking for
she was using her own passport, and she was worried that the authorities might have been given her name by Krivitsky, but there were
no problems. As soon as she was safely ashore, she went to see her
sister, with whom she stayed for the rest of her visit, thereby avoiding
the need to produce her passport in an hotel. Her primary mission
was to get two passports, one American and one Canadian, both
genuine but both in false names, and she had introductions to two
people whom she had been told would be able to help her. However,
the first said that he could do nothing since the official with whom
he had a connection had told him that getting a passport was

currently impossible, and the other had simply vanished and Kitty was unable to find any trace of him.

While Kitty may have been clueless with the camera and a rotten radio operator, when it came to other professional problems she was not the sort of person to throw up her hands in despair, so she started canvassing her contacts for help. Of the people she knew well, the 'Red Milkman' had disappeared, Pelz was in a Moscow jail facing an espionage charge, and Lamberti was too dangerous even though, as she found out, he had continued his trades union front and never been exposed. As for her first lover, Peter Skonetsky, he had moved to New York, put the delusions of his youth behind him and become a trades union leader. Although Kitty had not been cleared by her controllers to meet him, and she was not absolutely sure of his loyalty, her intuition told her that he would not betray her. At worst he would refuse to help, but he would never turn her in to the FBI.

When she telephoned, Kitty was taken aback at his evident pleasure at hearing from her. He said that he would cancel all his appointments and come straight over to see her. When they met in a quite expensive restaurant in mid-town, she saw that the bright young man of her memories had become a middle-class *homme de famille* – with a daughter and two sons – who was running slightly to fat.

Kitty recounted her cover story – that she was 'working for the Comintern in Nazi Germany' – and told Peter that she and Earl weren't together any more. When she asked if he had any idea of what was happening in Germany, he seemed to be totally disinterested and, instead, wanted to reminisce, a feeling of nostalgia perhaps fuelled by a couple of stiff cocktails he had downed before they even reached their table.

'Do you remember the lake?' he asked. He fell quiet for a moment and then suddenly blurted out, 'You know, I'm very unhappy. I don't love my wife and I only put up with her for the sake of the children. I've always remembered you, Gypsy, and I've always wanted you. When we first saw each other today, I thought that you'd got older just like me, but now you seem just like you were all those years ago. What a fool I was. We'd have been so happy together.'

Kitty kept in mind her real purpose in meeting Peter, but she could not help getting caught up in reminiscing about the long lost past. They sat, sipping their wine and looking back. They couldn't stop talking, although Kitty was nagged by the thought that she had to get down to business. Should she leave it for the next time they met? That would be less crude but, on the other hand, if she asked him now while he was feeling so good about their meeting, he might find it harder to refuse. Reluctantly, and with some difficulty, she managed to turn their conversation to Germany, the Nazis and the difficulties of her job, but she still could not bring herself to make the final leap. Then, screwing up her courage, she told him that he was the only one who could help her. Though he had had quite a lot to drink and his mind was evidently on other things, he was immediately alert.

'What's happened?'

'I often need to cross a frontier or to live somewhere under cover,' she explained, 'and I can't use my own passport all the time. I need two more, one American and one Canadian, in another name. I'd be terribly grateful if you could help.'

Suddenly completely sober, Peter sat and thought. 'Will you swear that they won't be used for anything against America?' he asked rather coldly.

'Of course,' Kitty exclaimed without hesitation, 'our work is against the Fascists.'

Reassured, he agreed to help her, but only half way: he could get an American passport but not a Canadian one. Kitty breathed a sigh of relief because now they were back to being comrades in a common cause. Several days later they set off on a trip to Toronto, a trip also back to the time when they were young and alone together, and one that turned into a honeymoon.

Kitty wrote to Kaminsky from New York with a brief account of how she had got the passport. She added a few comments at the end about the increasingly tense international situation and about how the American press was running an anti-Soviet campaign. She also confided in him that she would be very pleased to get good news about her brother Abe, who at that time was fighting in Spain, and signed the letter with her new code name, NORMA. The document is in her file, together with a request:

> To NIKOLAI
> Ask NORMA to describe the circumstances in which she got the passport.
> (Signed) DOUGLAS
> (Countersigned) MOROZ (FROST)

(DOUGLAS was the code name known to have been used around this time by the hitman Spiegelglass.)

Against each name other than hers is a neat note in pencil, 'Arrested', so there was nobody left to pursue the question and it was never followed up, a chilling reminder of the conditions under which Soviet intelligence officers operated in 1938 and 1939, and testimony to the guts that it took just to go into the Centre in the morning, knowing that you might not be going home in the evening.

Equipped with her new passports, Kitty travelled from New York to London, where the new *rezident*, Grigory Grafpen, was expecting her. Codenamed SAM, Grafpen was a young but experienced officer who had worked in America in the late 1920s and 1930s before being posted to London in 1938 as *rezident*, using official, Soviet mission cover, with the task of re-establishing contact with the agents who had been put on ice and to explain to them why contact had been broken off.

CHAPTER 10

London by Night

Even before Kitty left New York, the Centre cabled Grafpen to report that a female staffer, NORMA, was being sent over and was to be used for full-time liaison with Maclean, whose code name was now LIRIK (LYRIC POET) replacing the former WAISE/SIROTA.

The Centre gave Grafpen the agreed date and place for the rendezvous (an encounter originally misinterpreted by John Costello as a meeting between Kitty and Maclean himself), and the recognition phrases they were to use. In a follow-up letter they enclosed a snapshot of Kitty, annotated that, 'those concerned should be aware she no longer wears glasses and that she has changed her hairstyle'. At 4 p.m. on the agreed day, Grafpen went into the restaurant above the Empire Cinema in Leicester Square and took an unhurried look around. The matinee audience was mostly pensioners and the restaurant was almost empty, since they watched their pennies and preferred to have a bite to eat at home before they went out.

Sitting at one of the tables was an attractive woman, who looked nothing like the photo but who, as agreed, was reading A. J. Cronin's

The Citadel in a black dust-jacket with the title printed in white. Grafpen ostentatiously switched his copy of *Time* magazine from one hand to the other as part of the drill and approached her table. 'Have you seen my friend Karl?' he asked.

'I saw him on the seventh of January,' she replied. They nodded at each other politely and Grafpen sat down next to her. After enquiring about her trip and whether she had settled in, he then reassured her that she wouldn't have time to get bored as she would soon be given something to do.

However, when Kitty was on the point of leaving for her first meeting with Maclean, she was suddenly instructed to suspend operations. At the very last moment a directive from the Centre had declared that NORMA was only to contact Maclean if the *rezidentura* was sure that he was in the clear as far as 'a certain matter was concerned'. The crisis concerned the Woolwich Arsenal spy ring, which had been run by Mally and Deutsch and which had been penetrated by the British Security Service. One of the ring's prime movers, Percy Glading, knew Mally personally albeit under his alias 'Peters'. Deutsch and Mally had run the Woolwich operation and the Cambridge Five in parallel, and the take from both sources had often been sent to Moscow in the same diplomatic bag. Indeed, the archive files contain a memorandum from Deutsch informing the Centre that 'we are sending you the films from LIRIK as well as the shrapnel samples received from G'.

The British Security Service's agent, Olga Gray, had infiltrated into the CPGB's King Street headquarters, where she had caught Glading's eye, probably as planned since the Service would have had its eye on Glading from his time in India as a Comintern emissary in the 1920s. He had recruited her to run a London flat as a safe-house, where Russian case officers could meet their agents. After watching the ring for several months, the police arrested Glading and his associates on 31 January 1938, by which time Mally and Deutsch had fortunately left London.

Keeping Maclean and others on ice proved in this case to have been prudent. None of the Five came to notice and they could be safely reactivated, although the Centre expressed justifiable concern that LIRIK might 'be lost to us because we've gone far beyond the time period agreed for establishing contact with him'. However, the diligent Maclean had continued to make his visits to the rendezvous on the days and at the times he had originally agreed with Deutsch, and eventually his patience was rewarded. Instead of a tall, well-built man like Mally, or a hard-charging Orlov type, he saw approaching him a nice, rather low-key girl who, to his considerable surprise, he realised he knew. She gave him the recognition phrase and he quickly recovered from his initial shock, which Kitty had been quick to spot, and responded with the matching words as they both started to laugh.

'You hadn't expected to see a lady, had you?' Kitty asked, slightly flirtatiously.

'Frankly no, but it's a pleasant surprise. Our work can sometimes get boring and now I've got the opportunity to show I can behave like a gentleman,' he replied, echoing her somewhat playful tone. He invited her to join him at a restaurant, where they chatted, joked and laughed at nothing at all, and she found it very easy to get on with this tall and attractive man whom she had not seen for so long.

He wanted Kitty to inform their comrades in Moscow that he was glad to be back in touch and that he would do whatever he was asked. He then advised her to rent a flat in a nice part of town, which might be more expensive but would be better from a security point of view.

'Why?' asked Kitty in surprise.

'Because,' he said, 'it would be difficult to explain it away if one of my friends saw me going into a dump in some God-forsaken part of London. That reminds me, you need to think up a story as to how we come to know each other.'

They decided that they had met by chance at a performance of *A Midsummer Night's Dream* at the Old Vic, and, as they were saying goodbye, Maclean asked her to tell Moscow that things were going well for him at the Office and that he thought he was about to be promoted. There was a posting to Paris on the cards.

'Will you come with me?' he asked jokingly. 'After all, we'd have to go on working there too.'

'Absolutely,' Kitty exclaimed, thinking to herself that the chances of the Centre agreeing to such a thing were remote. As she was still living in a hotel and Maclean would be carrying documents, they agreed that their next meeting would be at his place.

Tradecraft dictates that it is always undesirable to meet at an agent's home even if the contact agent is a woman, and Kitty made every effort to find herself a suitable flat. It needed to be in a decent building but preferably without a porter or a liftman, and in the end she was successful. However, in the meantime, she continued to visit Maclean in his two-roomed bachelor's flat in Chelsea's Oakley Street, its walls hung with what she figured was a recent Cambridge graduate's standard paraphernalia – team photographs, pennants and an impressive-looking parchment degree certificate; books were piled high on the table and there was a decent choice of wine.

On her first visit Kitty began by feeling slightly awkward, but she soon felt at home and looked around inquisitively.

Donald joked, 'I don't know what to do. On the one hand you're my new boss but, on the other, you're a woman, and either way I'm the one that has to take the orders. So what's it going to be, dinner first and then work, or the other way round?'

'I think dinner can wait,' Kitty retorted with a hint of asperity, wanting to show that she really was the boss.

'Fine,' said Donald, unfazed. 'Let's get on with it.' While he pulled out the papers he had brought and arranged them on the table, she got the camera ready, sorted out the accessories and started to shoot. This was her first session under operational conditions and she had a hard job stopping her hands from shaking. She tried to remember every line of the manual and everything her instructor had said;

the image of Fisher's severe but intelligent eyes glinting behind his spectacles floated unbidden into her mind. It was not an easy session, and she used three rolls of film before she felt that it had gone all right. They congratulated each other, and Kitty put the canisters at the bottom of her handbag to give to the *rezident* in the morning while Donald gathered up the documents and put them in his brief-case. When they sat down, Donald brought out a bottle of 1913 Bordeaux and switched off the overhead light, and they settled down to a supper which Kitty thought was just the sort of schoolboy food a bachelor would serve up.

Kitty did not tell Donald that this was her first photography session because she wanted him to think that she was an experienced case officer. Within the limits allowed by tradecraft, which was never far from her mind, she told him a couple of things about her life and then the conversation turned to Moscow.

'How are things at home?' Donald asked, and Kitty noted with satisfaction that, like her, he referred to Moscow as 'home'. She was well aware that something was wrong and that sometimes innocent people like Pelz were arrested, but, as she told Donald, she genuinely believed that those who confessed in open court to spying, sabotage, terrorism, or Trotskyite and other hostile acts, were really guilty. Donald nodded and said, without a smile, 'Kitty, would you please tell Moscow that I fully agree with the Soviet courts' verdicts in destroying the enemies of the people. I'm one hundred per cent on your side and I'm getting down to work with great enthusiasm.'

The next day Grafpen's report on the meeting, quoting Maclean verbatim, was sent off to Moscow, together with the canisters of film, and Kitty found a suitable flat in Bayswater which nearly met all the requirements of tradecraft, apart from one serious drawback: it was located on the ground floor. In his report Grafpen noted:

(a) You can easily see in from the street or if you stand in the space between the windows you can hear what people are saying inside; the same is true for the glass door which leads out into the hall from the dining room (it doubles as the kitchen) where LIRIK and NORMA eat. In two or three months we are going to have to change flats.

(b) All the equipment is kept in the flat and could be discovered if it were searched while she was out. But she can't stay home all the time – for instance she has to go shopping – and the caretaker probably has a spare key to all the flats. This worries us a lot.

The Centre was even more worried and sounded the alarm in its reply to Grafpen: 'Your message on the set-up of NORMA's flat raised the most serious concerns . . .'; it also noted that the flat was an extremely poor choice since it could be targeted so easily for surveillance and eavesdropping. What was Grafpen going to do to make sure that this could not happen? How long had she rented it for? How was the equipment kept? What were the neighbours like? How did Kitty explain to people why she was at home most of the day?

'We repeat that LIRIK is to be cherished as the apple of your eye,' the Centre admonished Grafpen in a rather un-Soviet quote from *Deuteronomy*. 'He deserves to be your highest priority.'

Whatever the Centre thought of the flat, Kitty felt very much at home there and tried to turn the rooms into a comfortable little nest, somewhere where Donald really wanted to come rather than felt he had to, especially the kitchen-dining room, where they spent the nicest part of those first few meetings. Maclean's job as a Third Secretary in the Foreign Office gave him access to a large number of secret documents, among them all correspondence directly relating to the Western European Department, where he worked, and to Spain, the country with which he dealt specifically; he also saw many ministerial papers. Security consciousness in the Foreign Office was not of the highest, and when officials left their rooms to go to a meeting, they rarely bothered to put away secret documents, presumably on the mistaken understanding that gentlemen did not read each other's mail. Furthermore, they were allowed to take papers home to work on them, a fertile opportunity for a spy, and one that Maclean took advantage of with enthusiasm.

Over the period they worked together in the safe-house, Maclean handed Kitty a vast quantity of documents, which, as the files show, the senior levels of Soviet intelligence and the country's leaders (for the most part, in this period, Stalin, Molotov and Beria) evaluated as 'important' and often 'very important'. Even if he had accomplished nothing else, Maclean made an invaluable contribution by passing over the plain texts of enciphered cables. Regardless of their content, side by side comparison of the plain text with the transmitted version allowed the British diplomatic cipher to be cracked. In addition, of course, Maclean supplied a vast range of internal papers, such as letters, reports, memoranda and plans – the core of diplomatic paperwork – which were not transmitted in code, and these too he dutifully lugged along to the flat for Kitty to photograph.

Even with security as lax as it was, there were some papers whose sensitivity made them absolutely impossible to remove from the Foreign Office, and these Maclean memorised. He had a retentive memory and he relayed to Kitty his conversations with colleagues, statements at official meetings and verbal directives given by senior officials. He also had a lot of friends in the Foreign Office, about many of whom he knew things they might prefer to remain unknown, thus enabling him to give his controllers reliable guidance about other potential targets for recruitment. Maclean also provided some SIS material to which he had access, which called occasionally for urgent counter-measures. One example was the intercepted Comintern cable traffic which SIS distributed to the Foreign Office, and which in turn travelled back to Moscow via Maclean. Despite his disclosure of the source, the traffic continued to be intercepted, and when he sent the Centre the next batch of cables, Mally advised that Maclean was depressed because he had interpreted the fact that the traffic was continuing, despite his warning, as meaning that his efforts were wasted. Mally said that he himself failed to understand why Moscow had not got a grip of the Comintern and flushed out the '*provocateur*' who was knowingly allowing the use of a compromised channel of communication.

The Centre replied that it was no less concerned and asked the *rezidentura* to assure LIRIK that strict measures had been taken. They re-emphasised that all LIRIK's messages were considered extremely interesting and of high value. Indeed, LIRIK's next batch comprised of seven rolls of film and twenty-eight typed pages, including a report from an SIS agent in the USSR, an SIS report on a meeting of the German General Staff, SIS intercepts from Spain, a War Office memorandum and a Foreign Office report on British arms shipments to Portugal, the Baltic States and Iraq. In one of its replies the Centre drew attention to the interesting point that, for the first time, SIS intercepts had included American traffic, meaning that the British had now begun to spy on their 'special relationship'.

A document which stands out in the Maclean record is a report on Soviet foreign policy obtained by SIS from an agent in the Soviet Foreign Ministry, meaning in effect that the British were running a counterpart to Maclean in Moscow. When Mally sent this to Moscow, the Centre replied immediately that measures were being taken to identify the British agent. The archives do not show whether the source was tracked down, but, as this took place in 1937, it is at least certain that innocent people would have suffered in the ensuing molehunt. Certainly during this period hundreds of Foreign Ministry officials were arrested and shot, or sent to the Gulag, charged with being spies for various countries, maybe the hapless SIS agent among them. In any event, SIS's source promptly dried up, an example of disastrous handling of a sensitive product which Maclean himself almost experienced, in the relatively trivial case of the Soviet ship *Komsomol*, sunk by one of Franco's warships while en route to Spain. The fate of the crew was unknown, and Kitty had burst into tears when she read the press report since she had fond memories of the ship that had carried her to Leningrad not so long ago, of its cheerful first mate Ilyusha and of playing dominoes with the crew. Had they drowned or were they rotting in a Fascist jail?

Kitty's concerns were shared in Moscow because Mally was instructed by the Centre to find out what had happened, a task he assigned to Maclean, whose subsequent report, quoting confidential sources, was passed to Moscow. For unknown reasons, and in defiance of the principles of *konspiratsiya*, it was decided to release to the Soviet press the news that the crew were alive but in prison, and shortly afterwards the Centre advised that the *Komsomol* cable had been very well received and asked the *rezidentura* to express their thanks to Maclean, and to reassure him that publication of the information in the Soviet press would not have the slightest impact on his work. The resulting publicity enabled the Soviet authorities to exert pressure for the crew to be freed after a year behind bars.

There was a similar incident when the Centre decided to send NELLY, one of Deutsch's secret UK contacts, to Nationalist-occupied territory in Spain. She was an experienced illegal, a Party member who used to travel to India as a courier and who had an entrée via her husband to Mosley's British Union of Fascists. Deutsch only used NELLY in emergencies and, as he was not in regular touch with her, he asked Kitty to approach her to set up a meeting with him. Kitty calmly went to the address she had been given, only to find the door opened, to her utter amazement, by John Smith, her Fascist 'friend' from Berlin.

'Kitty,' he exclaimed in astonishment. 'How did you find me?'

'That's my little secret,' said Kitty thinking furiously as she asked herself, 'Who is he? What's he doing here? Is he one of us? Why shall I say I'm here?'

'Well, do come in,' Smith purred in a very friendly tone. 'I can see you don't want to tell me, but I reckon our people in Berlin gave you my address. Eh? Aren't I right? You can't have found me from the telephone book. My name isn't John Smith, it's actually Harold Stowman.'

When sending Kitty to meet NELLY, Deutsch, who could not have anticipated this bizarre and unwelcome development, had given her only the most flimsy cover story, that the two women had met at some unspecified evening class.

'I'm just passing through,' Kitty said. 'I'm going to Paris tomorrow. You're right, actually. It was our friends that gave me your address. I dropped in literally for a couple of minutes just to tell you they said "Hello" and they look forward to hearing from you.'

'And is there anybody here in London you can put me in touch with?' he asked.

'No,' she replied. 'I don't know anybody here myself.'

He then invited her in to have a cup of coffee and to meet his wife. A nice looking young woman stepped into the hallway and was introduced as 'Jane'.

When John disappeared into the kitchen to make the coffee, Kitty took the opportunity to explain to NELLY who she was and to make the arrangements for her meeting with Deutsch. Before John returned, NELLY had time to tell her that John was a member of the BUF and that she used him as an unwitting source of intelligence on the organisation. Soon afterwards, as planned, NELLY left for Spain.

Maclean soon fell into a routine of visiting Kitty's flat twice a week, his briefcase bulging with papers, and in one of his reports he wrote:

> . . . the situation is that I am authorised to take home
> papers that I am working on, but sometimes I also bring out
> papers that pass across my desk and that are classified
> Secret (and over the last year Top Secret too) but which
> are not related to my work. I also bring cables. If I was
> made to open my briefcase when I was coming into or out
> of the Office, it would be easy to explain that the papers

which were classified 'Not to be Removed from the Office' had got in there by mistake and nothing would happen.

The Centre valued Maclean very highly and did their utmost to minimise his risk, ordering the *rezident* not to make any attempt to task Maclean to procure specific items of intelligence if doing so might adversely affect his feeling of security; nor was he to permit the *rezidentura*'s appetite for intelligence to override security considerations. 'Maclean is your most valuable source, you should draw the appropriate conclusions,' the *rezident* was warned.

When he visited Kitty, Maclean would first head off to Oakley Street and then leave his flat a little while later and take a taxi to some randomly selected street corner, where he would pay it off, walk on a little way and then hail another. Sometimes, if he thought there was the slightest risk, he would repeat the manoeuvre, get out on a street near Kitty's and complete his journey on foot. He had a very good sense of time and always approached her front door at exactly half-past nine, when she would be happily waiting for him in eager anticipation, dressed accordingly.

'Good evening, Miss,' he would greet her jokingly, sometimes handing her a bunch of flowers or box of chocolates, and she would give him a mock curtsey. Their relationship was developing at two levels, one strictly business, the other playfully friendly.

'What's the bee brought today?' she might ask, and Donald would wave his briefcase and answer in the same vein, 'A lot of nice, sweet honey.'

Usually they got straight down to work, and Donald never interfered in Kitty's ministrations with the camera. Instead, he leafed through the Foreign Office papers he had brought, putting to one side those he reckoned were of little interest. This practice once caused a problem with the Centre when the *rezident* received a complaint that 'many pages seem to have been left out during the photography'.

The *rezident*, worried and frightened, shot back the explanation that Maclean was discarding papers he felt had no value, but added his assurance that henceforward 'everything will be photographed consecutively'. The Centre grumbled that the *rezident*'s explanation was not wholly satisfactory and that there was no need to photograph every single document, since it was not worth overloading the diplomatic bag with uninteresting material, or unnecessarily prolonging the photography session.

Sometimes Kitty made her own mistakes. One evening she decided that the lens was dusty and ran it under the tap, but the lens slipped through her fingers on to the cast-iron sink and cracked. It was far too late to run out to the camera shop and buy another one, so Maclean had to take back the papers he had brought that evening and return with them again three days later. On another occasion the Centre, clearly very alarmed, cabled that three entire rolls of film with material from Maclean had turned out totally blank. The Centre's concern was not that the intelligence had not reached them, but whether the film canisters had been switched in Kitty's flat after she had taken the photographs. The *rezident* was required to undertake another investigation and provide a full history of the films, including how long Kitty had kept the film in her flat after taking the photographs. Had she left them there when she went out, and had she subsequently noticed any traces of unauthorised entry? If it turned out that the whole episode was another example of Kitty's inexperience, the Centre suggested that she should be helped to improve her skills and not make such mistakes in the future.

Questioned by Grafpen, Kitty claimed, through a flood of tears, that she had not left home after the session and had kept the films on her, so they could not have been swapped.

'It's because I don't have enough experience,' she said in justification. 'I haven't worked much with a Leica and I forgot to put the exposure dial to "T", so that on every shot there was only a brief exposure instead of the usual twenty seconds. When I brought the films in to you, I warned that I wasn't sure whether anything would come out.'

Grafpen remembered that she had in fact asked permission for the films to be developed in London, but the Centre had categorically forbidden it, and he promptly submitted his whitewash of her to the Centre.

Kitty's collaboration with Maclean continued, and she was given the important additional job of taking delivery of oral reports from him which were to be cabled urgently to Moscow. This required both a good memory and a reasonable understanding of the things he was reporting, but she coped pretty well, her only weak point being when it came to anything technical.

One day Maclean brought her tickets for *A Midsummer Night's Dream* at the Sadler's Wells Ballet, which was intended to be a night out, with the added advantage of validating the cover story of how they had met. But when Kitty looked at the tickets, she said firmly, 'This won't work. We can both go to the theatre but we can't sit next to each other and we shouldn't be seen together.' Asking him to change one of the tickets for another row, she explained that such close contact would be a breach of tradecraft. They did indeed go to the theatre, but kept well away from each other.

Maclean generally lacked an instinct for tradecraft and once confided to Kitty that, during some argument in his office, he had come out strongly in favour of the Soviet Union, an admission that horrified Kitty. She apologised but said that she would have to report it to the Centre.

'But what I'm telling you was back before we started to work together,' Maclean remonstrated. 'I promise you I won't do it again. Anyway you can see for yourself that it had no unpleasant consequences.'

Kitty usually photographed Maclean's papers in the maid's room, which was dark and cramped, and she used to change into a lightweight smock before she started the by now well-practised drill. Maclean would stand to one side watching, and would wipe the pages after she had finished with them, but one day she felt him press closer and put his arm around her shoulder. 'You're getting in my way,' she muttered, not especially severely. He carefully moved away but, when she had finished, he hugged her again and began to kiss her neck and her hair. She stood motionless, head bowed and hands by her sides.

Kitty was sorely tempted to give in to his advances but, on this occasion, she held back; instead, she offered him the consolation prize of dinner in a couple of weeks' time to celebrate her birthday. They were both astonished when he revealed that his birthday was on 25 May, and they agreed to combine the celebrations. She was only paid £50 a month by Grafpen and, although she was not on the bread-line, she had to live quite modestly, so buying Donald a birthday present needed thought and careful calculation. After a lot of window shopping, she decided on a pair of cuff links and a tiepin.

Grafpen shared Kitty's financial anxieties and had asked the Centre more than once to find her a notional lover, or relative in America or somewhere else, who could send her money and validate her legend. 'This is very important for us,' he wrote, because the British authorities took a great deal of interest in other people's money, and when Kitty had rented her flat, the managing agents had asked whom she knew in Britain, who her visitors were going to be and why she had no bank account. Because Kitty spent a large part of her day at home, anybody enquiring into her life would find it hard to understand the source of her income or might leap to uncharitable conclusions.

When pleading with the Centre for a solution, successive *rezidents* argued that she had no occupation or profession, and even if they decided to send her off to study, they would need to find some legitimate source for the tuition fees. This was the trickiest part of the process of getting her 'legalised' and was never fully resolved. Possibly someone in Moscow decided that Maclean's regular visits were sufficient, by giving the neighbours the impression that her money came from her mysterious, well-to-do boyfriend. Kitty's actual legend, based on her Canadian passport, allowed her to pass herself

off as having been born in Quebec, where her only surviving relative, an uncle, supposedly still lived. Her father and mother, long
since dead, had been farmers and she had no brothers or sisters.
Her uncle had taken responsibility for bringing her up while she
was young, but then had turned her out of the house in her teens
and she was no longer in touch with him.

The 1st of May was a warm contrast to the cold of April, and
Kitty took a walk in Hyde Park, where there was an anti-Fascist
rally. Not wanting to draw attention to herself, she gave it a wide
berth but noticed that one of the speakers declared he had just
arrived from fighting in the Spanish war. This was a distressing
reminder of her brother Abe, of whom she had received no news
since he had gone off to fight in the American battalion of the
International Brigade. In fact Abe, a sports coach, had joined a
group run by the Soviet illegal Gregorii Syroezhkin, under the name
of Gregory Grande, which was training saboteurs to fight behind
the Franco lines. Abe had taken part in some of their operations,
which had included laying mines, and it was subsequently claimed
that it was one of their own mines, and not, as history has it, a
shell, that blew up the car in which Kim Philby, then a journalist,
was travelling, wounding him and killing his three fellow passengers.

As May flew past, Kitty chose a pattern in an expensive store
and used her early professional skills to make herself a smart low-
cut dress, but at the last minute the eagerly awaited birthday dinner
was postponed because Maclean had to go urgently to Prague on
23 May. The next day Kitty invited her landlady, with whom she
was now friendly, to have a cup of tea as a very low-key birthday
celebration. She told her that in a few days' time she would have
a proper birthday dinner when her friend, who was now away on
business, returned. The landlady, a middle-aged, open-minded
woman, was delighted to hear that she now had a steady boyfriend
but gave Kitty a friendly woman's warning that she needed to 'take
precautions', telling her that her sister who had got landed with an
illegitimate baby was 'the unhappiest woman in London'.

The reason for Maclean's hurried trip to Prague was the worsening situation in Central Europe, with Hitler moving inexorably towards the annexation of the Sudetenland. The British and French Governments had made a half-hearted offer to help Czechoslovakia and a Foreign Office team was hastily dispatched to Prague, where Maclean and his colleagues were housed in the embassy, tucked behind mock battlements under the walls of Hradcany Castle. Maclean's responsibility was the handling of the DEDIP traffic, messages that were regarded as too sensitive to be handled by the cipher clerks and had to be deciphered by an official, and he was thus well-placed to obtain and pass on copies of cables on everything that the Foreign Office was doing in Berlin, Prague, Paris and other European capitals over this critical period. He also passed on information on the organisation of the British intelligence effort in Prague, and one particularly important message was a report on what a cryptographer named Stevens had told him about British successes in breaking all the Soviet codes.

On the evening he returned to London, he turned up on Kitty's doorstep looking, if possible, even more dapper than usual, carrying a huge bouquet of roses, a bottle of vintage wine and a little box in which nestled a locket on a thin gold chain. Kitty had been waiting for him the past few evenings and was dressed to kill. Donald gasped open-mouthed at her bare arms and shoulders, and gave her a long kiss before he even said 'Hello'. Then he got down on one knee and offered her birthday greetings. Kitty could not wait a moment longer and opened the little box with the locket. 'How wonderful!' she exclaimed. 'It really suits me.'

Delighted that she liked it, Donald fastened the chain around her neck, and Kitty wore the locket for the rest of her life. She had hardly handed him his present when there was another ring at the door and, to her astonishment, a frock-coated waiter appeared bowed under the weight of a large insulated hamper containing a splendid dinner which Donald had ordered from a local restaurant. Kitty laid the table, lit the candles, switched out the lights and then went into her room, returning proudly a moment later with a birthday cake on which twenty-five little candles were burning and singing 'Happy Birthday'. Donald joined in, put the cake in the middle of the table and counted the candles.

'Spot on,' he said, 'we should have eaten this on the twenty-fifth, and I'm twenty-five.' He was too well brought up to ask how many candles there should have been if the birthday cake had been for Kitty. They blew out the candles together and tucked into a splendid meal. The restaurant had done them proud, producing dishes Kitty had not eaten before, and some she had never even heard of. To a background of Glen Miller melodies on the wireless, she even found room for dessert, pancakes with maple syrup, a favourite from her childhood in Canada.

This was the evening when the pair became lovers, and it was only at 2 a.m. that a tired but happy Donald slipped quietly away while Kitty remained awake, not only reliving the last few hours but more realistically wondering what she was doing. She was an uneducated nobody, whereas he was a handsome somebody who could have any woman in London; he was also fourteen years younger. They had nothing in common other than the wild passion that had overtaken them that evening and the cause they shared. Her thoughts then moved in another direction, remembering her tradecraft teacher Gennady's dictum that an intelligence officer had to tell his or her superiors everything, even if it had to do with the most intimate aspects of their life.

Could she really bring herself to do that, she wondered. After all, why should anybody ever find out? If she did report it, they might be separated, but in their job maybe being in love might actually be a plus. The next morning she took the difficult decision and told Grafpen what had happened. Clutching at his forehead in exasperation, he fired off a report to Moscow by the next bag. To his surprise the Centre took the news relatively calmly and did not raise the question of preventing Kitty from working with Maclean.

According to Volume IV of *Studies in the History of Russian Foreign Intelligence*, its then head Pavel Fitin remarked, 'What's the problem? Good luck to them! Do you really think it would do our business any harm?' While this might be seen as an indication of unusual sophistication, it is more likely that the judgment was entirely pragmatic as banning the relationship might have upset Maclean and inhibited the flow of some extraordinarily valuable intelligence. In fact, the affair did have an impact on Maclean's performance, as the Centre later complained:

> . . . the LIRIK material in the last two pouches turned out
> to contain only half of each image. What was the problem?
> How does NORMA explain these gaps? Moreover in the
> last batch, many of the pages were almost out of focus
> because the camera was moved. If this is due to carelessness
> tell NORMA that material photographed like this cannot
> be tolerated and is worthless. If it is the result of her nerv-
> ousness, calm her down and boost her self-confidence.

The real reason was Maclean's insatiable appetite, for every one of his sessions with Kitty began and ended with sex, and he sometimes demanded that she interrupt her work for more. Lying in bed with him one day in a post-coital haze, Kitty made a more serious mistake when Donald asked, 'That tradecraft stuff you're so fond of going on about. I bet it means that when your people write about us they use code names. I wonder what they are? For instance,' he paused for thought, 'I could be HUNTER and you could be HOUSE-WIFE, or maybe I'm PIERROT and you're COLUMBINE. Am I close?'

'You'll never guess,' she replied unthinkingly. 'Actually you're LIRIK and I'm NORMA.' She then bit her tongue, since it was quite out of order for her to have told him, but Donald was satisfied.

'Well, LIRIK sounds very nice,' he said, and the next time he wrote to Deutsch he signed his letter LIRIK:

As you will have heard I have no reason to think my position is not quite sound. The trial of Glading will no doubt increase watchfulness on the part of the authorities . . . I shall be very careful and keep a sharp eye out. If I spot anything suspicious as far as I am concerned, we'll stop work immediately. Greetings. LIRIK

The reference to Percy Glading was in connection with the then current Woolwich Arsenal espionage trial, in which Mally's name had come up, coinciding with the arrest of a German intelligence network, which had prompted the usual strident campaign to raise security awareness in all government departments and to clamp down on documents being removed from offices and the destruction of carbons. Like all such initiatives, it soon ran out of steam, but Maclean's indiscretion, by his use of his work name, caused a storm at the Centre, which demanded to know how he had discovered it. The *rezident* categorically denied that he was to blame, and Kitty then confessed. She was reprimanded, but forgiven, and from that point, in June 1938, LIRIK became STUART, and Kitty became ADA. The reply from Deutsch, writing as OTTO, exuded warmth and concern:

The question of security and caution is not an idée fixe. Don't believe anyone who professes to sympathise with you, whether it's about work or your private life. If you manage to keep your secret to yourself (a secret known to two people is no longer a secret) that will be the best guarantee that we will emerge victorious on the ground where you and we have been sent to fight. NORMA will raise with you a few questions on the 'literature' that you handed over at the last couple of meetings. We will be very grateful if you will help NORMA with this. We wish you continuing successes. Write to us. Comradely greetings Otto.

While these letters were being exchanged, there was another unpleasantness at the Foreign Office when an official was fired because of rumours that he had been a Communist as a young man. The same charge could have been levelled at Maclean, but, although he explained in his letter that the man had been fired simply because he was no good, the Centre decided to put Maclean 'on ice' again temporarily. This news came as a blow to him and Kitty, and it took several conversations for the *rezident* to persuade her that the connection had been broken not because of her poor work (as she had thought), but in the interests of Maclean's security. He finally managed to convince her and sent her off on leave to the south coast.

It was standard practice for the British Diplomatic Service to send its young Third Secretaries on temporary attachments to embassies overseas, and when Maclean's turn came, the Centre was initially uncomfortable at the potential loss of such a valuable source in London.

'Everything possible must be done to see that he remains in London,' the Centre demanded, but the *rezidentura* quite reasonably replied that it already had John Cairncross and other sources in the Foreign Office. It must also have occurred to the Centre that Maclean's foreign assignment would stand a budding diplomat in good stead, and when Maclean disclosed that he was destined for Paris rather than somewhere like Montevideo or Bogotá, it was clear that the Centre would offer no more resistance. Nevertheless, a considerable debate ensued about whether he should be handled by FINN's *rezidentura* in Paris, or be retained as a London asset with a new person being brought in to work with him. The problem was that any new person might turn out to be 'an enemy of the people', for in those difficult times nobody could be trusted.

It was decided eventually that Kitty should continue her role, partly because Maclean had requested this himself. The question was then how she should undertake the task, for travelling to and from Paris every week was inconvenient, expensive and, above all, dangerous, and it was Kitty herself who suggested that she should be transferred to Paris. Grafpen concluded for the file that, 'It is intended to use ADA to handle STUART', and the pair were scheduled to leave for Paris in October 1938.

CHAPTER 11

Night Flight

In September Maclean joined Colonial Secretary Ormsby-Gore and two or three friends on a fishing holiday in Scotland, and began storing up for Moscow's benefit the inside information on the European political scene that Ormsby-Gore shared in their relaxed fire-side chats, whisky in hand, when an urgent telegram arrived summoning the Minister to a Cabinet. Less than half an hour later another telegram arrived instructing Maclean to proceed immediately to Paris.

On 28 September Maclean and Kitty left separately for Paris, in the midst of the Munich crisis, with Chamberlain's hollow promise of 'peace in our time' and Hitler's brutal private dismissal of their agreement as 'a meaningless scrap of paper'. Before her departure Kitty had a long talk with Grafpen, in which she argued that her intimacy with Maclean had actually enhanced their work together rather than hindered it. 'In any case,' she reassured him, 'whatever happens, for me work comes first. I want you and our comrades in Moscow to know that.'

Kitty met Maclean for the first time in Paris in a supposedly casual late afternoon encounter in the outdoor café in the

Luxembourg Gardens near the Boulevard Saint Michel entrance. Though they were delighted to be together again, she was obliged to break the mood and get down to business, telling him that they couldn't meet in the Latin Quarter because he might run into some of his friends from university. Also, he had to stick to the rules of tradecraft.

'Do they think I don't?' he enquired.

'Well, there's one more rule for you,' she replied. 'If while you're in Paris you see any member of our service that you knew in England, you have to try to avoid meeting them or talking to them. Whatever you do, you mustn't say that you've been posted here, and you have to tell them that you have nothing to do with us anymore. Obviously if there is such a meeting you have to report it straightaway.'

'Why are they being so strict?' he asked.

'I don't know myself, but that's what you have to do.' Kitty genuinely did not know that these instructions followed the defection of Alexander Orlov, whom the Centre feared might turn up in Paris and identify Maclean.

'One more instruction for you,' she added. 'While we want you to evaluate your colleagues for us, under no circumstances are you to recruit anyone or even make any hints in that direction.'

'So far I haven't met anyone here suitable for our work,' he replied, 'but I'll keep it in mind.'

Kitty had not rented an apartment and, as it was considered too dangerous to take camera equipment into rented bed-sitting rooms, for the time being they exchanged information at meetings in various parts of the city, either strolling along the street or sitting in some small café. Maclean would give Kitty a detailed report about embassy documents, while at his request Kitty would give him political news from Moscow and brief him on the Soviet position on various issues. This was felt to be particularly important because, after Munich, the Western press, at least as read by Moscow eyes, was full of the supposed triumphs of the appeasers and lost no opportunity to attack Russia. At each meeting with Kitty, the *rezident* would go through Soviet press reports and non-secret Foreign Ministry briefings with her, which she assimilated very quickly and drew the 'politically correct' conclusions, sometimes surprising the *rezident* by how well she understood politics. Kitty's file has an evaluation of her written at about this time by Pavel Sudoplatov, who commented that she 'can be described as a staffer with a flexible mind, capable, disciplined, and interested in the work but she lacks concentration and has no feeling for technical matters'.

It was also at around this period that the 'rich relation' problem was solved by a man in the United States known only as 'Sh', who agreed to play the part and provide Kitty with funds, thus permitting her to sign up for courses at the Alliance Française and begin a serious effort to find a flat. In the meantime, she and Maclean continued to meet at various spots round the city, taking every opportunity to combine sight-seeing with business, all the more since they did not look Parisian and had to pass as tourists.

At one of the meetings Maclean said that he was now in the mainstream of the embassy's work and, in his new position as Second Secretary, he was able to see all the papers, including other British mission cables to the Foreign Office, for which Paris was on the circulation list. However, he could not extract actual copies and therefore simply passed on orally what he had read or heard. Accordingly, Kitty made verbatim records, among them an embassy minute on the American attitude to the Czech crisis.

It claimed that in a talk with Hermann Goering, the American Ambassador said that if war came, America would come in on the side of the Democratic countries, to which Goering had stated that there were 100,000 Germans in America who would not allow this. The Ambassador had replied that America had enough lamp-posts to take care of all of them.

Despite the Centre's ban on cameras and discussing secret business in a rented room, Parisian *mores* meant that it was perfectly acceptable to have visitors, so the two of them went back to Kitty's room after each briefing session to pursue other topics. Maclean would leave late in the evening as Kitty watched from the window, thanking fate that they were still together. One day he arrived highly agitated. 'You won't believe who I met today,' he burst out. 'Philby. Kim Philby. He's just got back from Spain.'

'Which side?' she asked.

'He was with the Fascists as a *Times* correspondent,' he explained. 'You know, we're old friends and he was the "First Musketeer". He asked me straightaway if I was in touch with your people, and I had to lie to his face like some petty thief. I had to tell him that I had no contact at all and do my best to get rid of him. But he did find time to say that at a time like this one shouldn't be ashamed of being in touch with your people. I just stood there red in the face and said nothing. I was really ashamed. I told my best friend a lie and, even worse, what I said might make him think badly of me.'

'Don't rack over it. You did exactly what you're supposed to,' Kitty sympathised.

'But as well as what I'm *supposed* to do, I have a conscience and a heart that tell me what I *ought* to do,' Maclean declared. 'I trust him as much as I do myself and yet I had to tell a lie. That's very hard for me to do, Kitty.' She eventually managed to calm him down like a mother comforting a fretful little boy and the episode had its usual ending.

Finally, Kitty succeeded in renting a flat and installed her equipment, and they resumed the old work pattern. Sometimes Maclean bought papers that did not have to be returned but which still had to be destroyed, a process that was messy but effective. They would tear the paper into small pieces, put them in a big enamel bowl, sprinkle them liberally with washing powder and soak them in hot water. Maclean would stir the mixture carefully with a spoon and, as the water cooled, Kitty would knead the mess into something that looked like porridge which she would then pour down the toilet. One flush would usually do it and they managed never to clog the drain.

Kitty and Maclean worked together for eighteen months, but in

Paris Maclean was just one of several Second Secretaries in the embassy, which was just not the same in terms of access as even a lowly Third Secretary in a key area of the Foreign Office in London, and both the quantity and quality of the material he supplied fell off noticeably. At meeting after meeting with the *rezident* Kitty found herself reporting that she had nothing to deliver since Maclean had not come across anything valuable or out of the ordinary, even though he was working very hard, sometimes all night.

'This combination of circumstances is not good for STUART,' observed the Centre as it reopened the question of his intimate relationship with ADA. 'Is this relationship justified? Does ADA report to us about Stuart? Is she detached enough to observe him and notice changes in him that might indicate his loyalty to us?'

Kitty answered the Centre on 31 December 1938:

> In many respects the Paris job is a complete change for him. When he was in London he could live the way he wanted. He had his friends and had a lot of time for reading. Paris is another matter. He has to lead a completely different social life. He has to go to dinners and receptions. His whole life is centred around diplomatic routine. He hates this atmosphere but at the same time is obliged to work here. I know that he is a very good comrade and is not letting this new situation get to him but I think he would appreciate a letter 'from home'. He feels he can trust me and often shares his thoughts with me. So I know a letter would mean a great deal to him.

Her request was met by another warm letter to Maclean from Deutsch, but the morale boost was to be short-lived because he knew that he was not making the same contribution as he had achieved in London. A further message from the Centre in July 1939 noted that Maclean had supplied 'valuable information, especially on the Finnish question but this was something he had memorised and passed on, whereas we need documents'. The reference to 'the Finnish question' concerned negotiations conducted by the *rezident* in Helsinki, Boris Rybkin (who was working under the alias Yartsev), and the Finnish Government, which turned out to be unsuccessful.

Meanwhile, political tension was increasing elsewhere in Europe, exacerbated by Hitler's annexation of Czechoslovakia in March 1939. Moscow had growing concerns about a possible Anglo-German alliance and Maclean, Burgess and other sources provided information on secret talks between London and Berlin, conducted by the British Ambassador Nevile Henderson, the German State Secretary Ernest von Weizsäcker, Hermann Goering's emissary Dr Wohltat, Sir Horace Wilson and others. Simultaneously, as the Soviets noted, the French and British were also holding military talks with Moscow about mutual assistance, in the midst of which, on 3 August 1939, Burgess reported that the British Chiefs of Staff 'are firmly convinced that they can win a war with Germany without difficulty and that there is therefore no need to conclude a defence treaty with the Soviet Union'.

On 21 August 1939 Nevile Henderson reported to London that 'all steps have been taken for Goering to arrive secretly on Wednesday, 23 August . . . everything is moving towards an historic event and we merely await confirmation from the German side', but these contacts were doomed to failure.

Kitty, of course, played almost no part in these developments, for in June 1939 she had given up her apartment and gone to Antibes for a holiday, staying at the Hôtel du Nile and planning to rent a better place when she got back. She returned in August, but inexplicably missed two meetings with the *rezidentura*, which threw the Centre into confusion. Her first failure to attend a rendezvous, and then a fallback meeting, coincided with the signing of the Nazi-Soviet Non-Aggression Pact on 23 August, and although in retrospect there seems little to link the two events, at the time Moscow evidently suspected that there was a connection, all the more since the Soviet Union found itself the target of a torrent of abuse and criticism. Angry crowds surrounded the Soviet embassy in Paris, many previously well-disposed Frenchmen changed their attitude, and a number of people who had been cultivated for possible recruitment took fright or simply shunned any further contact with their NKVD case officers. Some established agents simply ceased to appear at their scheduled rendezvous, and it was against this background that the inexplicable loss of contact with ADA and STUART sounded an alarm. Baffled, the Centre tried to determine whether it was happenstance or a deliberate refusal to co-operate as a gesture of protest. The fruitless speculation continued until September, when Germany invaded Poland and, a few days later, Britain and France declared war on Germany. Then out of the blue Kitty appeared at the Soviet embassy and NAZON, one of the *rezidentura* officers, literally ran downstairs to greet her, in a paroxysm of relief and delight.

Kitty pinned the blame for the lack of contact on NAZON, claiming that he had failed to turn up for the scheduled and fall-back meetings. She said that Maclean had twice gone to the Soviet consulate to try to make contact, but had not seen anyone he knew and had felt it would be insecure to talk to strangers. Both Kitty and Maclean had been extremely upset and surprised to think that their controllers did not want to keep in touch. Since they were in the embassy, and thus on sensitive ground, NAZON could do little more than arrange another meeting at one of their agreed rendezvous, which the *rezident* himself, codenamed KARP, subsequently attended to apologise, admitting that 'it was our fault. Our officer mixed up the meeting days and that's when the problem started.'

Kitty accepted the explanation and told KARP not to worry. 'All's well that ends well,' she said. 'Back to business. I'm fine and in good shape and ready to go to work. Donald also desperately wants to start working again, and we are fully behind what Moscow has done. Donald says that Russia shouldn't pull the imperialists' chestnuts out of the fire. They should sort Hitler out themselves.'

She relayed the latest intelligence Maclean had collected in the weeks of silence. 'Everything is fine with me. I've rented a flat which will suit us well and I've got a three-year *Permis de Séjour*. I've joined a ladies' charity, where we knit warm things for soldiers and put together parcels for the front.'

Kitty's optimism was premature, for soon afterwards the Washington *rezidentura* reported to the Centre that Ben Gitlow, the expelled former member of the CPUSA's Central Committee, had appeared in front of the Dies Congressional Committee investigating un-American activity and had testified that,

> Kitty Harris, Browder's wife, was given $10,000 for the Pan Pacific Trade Union Secretariat and took the money to China. In my opinion Kitty Harris is currently an OGPU agent in other countries and Margaret, Browder's sister, works for the GRU. As I understand it Browder twice stated under questioning that he did not know anybody named Kitty Harris. Kitty Harris was his wife. According to information at my disposal Kitty Harris was obliged to work for the OGPU outside the United States and that at the present time she is working as an OGPU agent in Europe or Asia or other places they might send her.

Gitlow was Kitty's sworn enemy, following an incident recorded in Kitty's file that had occurred years earlier when, in 1927, as a Party Secretary, she had handed him her transcript of one of his speeches, which she had taken down in shorthand. Gitlow had been infuriated by her version and had demanded, 'What on earth were you thinking about when you did this? Your weekend? It's nothing remotely like what I was trying to say. If you can't do the job, don't bother to try.'

'It would help if you learned to speak English a bit better,' Kitty had flared back. 'Then I could get it down more accurately.' This was a low blow. Gitlow had been born in a tiny Ukrainian village in the Pale of Settlement and had a hard time making himself understood in English, something about which he was acutely sensitive. He had never forgiven Kitty for the wounding insult and must have savoured his denunciation all those years later.

The Centre was less concerned about Margaret Browder, as she had been discharged from the agent network a year before the story broke, had returned to America and vanished from Kitty's life, insofar as the archives are a guide. The only further surviving reference occurs in 1946, when she was reported to be receiving a small allowance from NKVD resources and to have been given a loan of $2,000 in cash to start up an antiques business. However, Gitlow's denunciation was a more serious problem for Kitty, who was now widely known to be working with Soviet intelligence. Could she go on doing so without serious risk to herself, Maclean and the Service? After much discussion, the Centre decided that realistically there was no one to replace her and that, since she was using a passport in another name, she could go on working. The ripples from Gitlow's disclosures had barely died away when Walter Krivitsky's memoirs were published in New York, which included a description of Kitty and an account of his meeting with her in April 1937. Accordingly, attention was refocused on the security of Kitty and Maclean and their future, but the Centre opted to allow them to continue. In the final analysis, the risk paid off as neither the Gitlow nor the Krivitsky revelations had any serious consequences for either Kitty or Maclean.

During the Phoney War, the only sign of war in Paris was a blackout and windows criss-crossed with paper tape as a protection against bomb-blast. In those early days there were constant air-raid warnings, so frequent that Parisians rapidly grew to ignore them and made no attempt to go to the shelters. Indeed, not one bomber disturbed the calm Paris sky, only the occasional incursion by an enemy aircraft scattering leaflets. The atmosphere of unreality was enhanced by fashionable women sporting chic new gas-mask cases.

When Kitty complained to Maclean that she had not been issued with a gas-mask because she was a foreigner, he laughed and told her that she would never need one. Kitty and the other charity ladies would go from door to door collecting playing cards, dominoes, board games, footballs, detective stories and even wind-up gramophones to cheer up the troops at the front. Paris newspapers continued to report first nights at the theatre, new exhibitions and charity bazaars.

Maclean was worn out by the endless round of diplomatic functions and was dog-tired when he turned up for his meetings with Kitty, saying that he was working too hard, but still bringing little in the way of material. He had recently been more than usually attentive and loving, but at the same time she sensed an indefinable distancing and became convinced that he was seeing someone else. One evening, armed with a very plausible excuse, she turned up unannounced at Maclean's flat in the Rue Bellechaise, near Les Invalides. Business over, he invited her to stay the night and went off to take a shower. She had not been in his flat for a long time and her beady eye, sharpened by jealousy, noticed that there had been changes, which confirmed her suspicions. Everything was tidier, things had been put away in their proper place, there were two toothbrushes side by side in the bathroom and two towels, and she thought that she could even catch a hint of perfume in the air. While Maclean was in the shower, she opened the wardrobe door and saw a gossamer-thin nightdress hanging next to his suits. Absolutely sure now what was going on, she got into bed. When a smiling Maclean emerged from the shower smelling of Yardley's talcum powder, she kept herself in check and they exchanged a few meaningless words, until she let herself go and ask the fateful question, 'Okay, Donald. Who's the girl?'

'What do you mean?' Donald feigned surprise and gazed at her innocently. 'Whatever gave you that idea?'

'That's my job,' Kitty said with a sad laugh. 'I'm supposed to know it all and notice everything. So who is she?'

Maclean sat on the side of the bed and stretched his hand towards Kitty, but she moved away. There was a long silence. Then, with a deep sigh, he admitted that there was another woman, whom he hadn't known for long, and that he was in love with her. She was a twenty-three-year-old American student at the Sorbonne, called Melinda Marling, and they had met at the Café des Flores. When Kitty asked how he had ended up there, a hang-out for American Trotskyites and all sorts of other riffraff, he replied, 'A friend took me along,' omitting to mention that they had been introduced by an American named Bob McAlmon. Melinda had been staying next door at the Hotel Montana. 'She was sitting there with a load of other students,' he continued, 'and we sat next to them. You know what it's like, a whole lot of talking, yelling and political arguments. I was very taken with her views; she's a liberal, she's in favour of the Popular Front and doesn't mind mixing with Communists even though her parents are quite well off. There was a White Russian girl, one of her friends, who attacked the Soviet Union and Melinda went for her. We found we spoke the same language.'

'In bed!' Kitty retorted.

'We won't talk about that now,' Donald said, 'there's something much more exciting to tell you . . .'

'What on earth can be more exciting for you than bed?' Kitty asked.

'Just listen to me. I've seen quite a bit of her and, of course, she reckoned that I was just a diplomat. But she wasn't too pleased when I was late leaving work, or when I had to say I couldn't meet her because you and I had . . .', he hesitated, '. . . because you and I had a date to work. She wasn't that thrilled at the thought that I was just a Second Secretary. She broke it off. I wanted to make myself look better and more important than she thought, so I came out with it . . .'

'Came out with what?' Kitty asked sharply, sitting up in the bed with a jolt.

'Well, first that I'm a member of the Communist Party.'

'You're out of your mind.'

'It made her very interested in me. But I didn't stop there. I wanted her to think I was somebody special, not like the other men she knew, and so I told her that I wasn't just a diplomat. That I had a secret side to my life and that, in fact, I'm a spy.'

'God Almighty,' Kitty whispered under her breath.

'Okay, so go ahead and condemn me if you like.'

'Did you tell her anything about me?'

'No, but just in case she saw us somewhere together, I told her that my contact was a woman.'

Now that it was all out in the open Kitty felt a surprising sense of relief, perhaps because she had seen something like this coming for a long time and it had finally arrived. As a professional, responsible for a subordinate, rather than as a spurned lover, she was tormented by a different thought. 'Do you know what you've done? I don't mean me or our relationship. You've exposed yourself and you've exposed what we are doing. It's . . .' – she hesitated before pronouncing the terrible word 'treachery' – 'It's not me you've betrayed, it's the people who trusted you.'

When Donald responded that he would continue serving the cause and that Melinda loved him too much to betray him, Kitty snapped. 'Loves you!' she exclaimed. 'You think she loves you? You stupid brainless boy. I'm ashamed of you and ashamed of myself for trusting you for so long.'

'Kitty, I swear I'll stay true to what we believe in,' he reassured her. 'I'll work even harder and I'll do everything I can to make sure that Melinda doesn't betray us. She's actually promised to help me to the extent she can and she's well connected in the American community.'

They went on talking for an hour and were almost friends by the time Kitty left. It was only when she got back to her flat that she let herself go, hurling herself on to her bed, in a flood of tears and hammering and chewing the pillow.

At about this time Melinda wrote to her mother about her new English friend, describing him as a six-foot tall blond, with beautiful blue eyes, altogether a beautiful man. He has all the qualities for a husband (at least, I think). He is the soul of honor, responsible, a sense of humour, intelligent, imaginative, cultured, broadminded (and sweet) etc. Of course he has faults but somehow they don't clash with mine except that he is stubborn and strong-willed. I needed that as I am drifting and getting nowhere.

Maclean's own view of himself, admittedly delivered a few years previously, was more complex and probably nearer the truth. In a light-hearted interview with the Cambridge University undergraduate magazine *Granta*, he had responded as three distinct personalities housed in the same slim body: the camp aesthete Cecil, the hearty hetero sportsman Jack, and Maclean himself, a serious Marxist swot.

The next morning Kitty passed the signal for an emergency meeting with an officer of the *rezidentura*; when he appeared, she told him what had happened, which was later reported to the Centre:

We drew ADA's attention to the danger of all this and suggested she drew the appropriate conclusions about herself and STUART. ADA told us that, as she saw it, what STUART had done could be put down to a schoolboy's inability to take things seriously and that he will go on working with us just as sincerely and enthusiastically as before. It is difficult for us at the moment to come to any conclusion as to who this new girlfriend of STUART's really is . . . the one thing that is clear is that this development will make our work with the source more complicated and threatens ADA's position. We attach great significance to establishing STUART's sincerity and finding out who Melinda Marling is. In the meantime we are maintaining contact with him.

Kitty had the willpower and the sense of duty to go on working with Maclean despite what had happened, and since his 'little secret' no longer hovered unspoken between them, she found it was actually easier to deal with him, and, as she reported, the better side of his personality – 'a sincere and conscientious colleague' – soon re-emerged. She threw herself into her work, but in the first week of May, as the Wehrmacht occupied Denmark, Norway, Belgium, Holland and France, she caused further alarm at the Centre when an urgent cable arrived reporting that she had met Kim Philby, who had apparently expressed surprise that the Russians had broken off contact with him. He had said that he had valuable information and had also mentioned that Burgess was in a difficult situation as a result of the loss of contact. The Centre ordered ADA to be given a serious reprimand and told her that she must inform Philby that she had no relationship with the Russians. At the root of the Centre's concern was the suspicion, happily for him not long-lived, that Philby had been afflicted by doubts following the Nazi-Soviet Pact and might therefore have become unreliable. Moreover, in the tradecraft lexicon, an agent who sought to re-establish contact unilaterally after being put on ice was to be avoided at all costs since he might be a plant.

The hapless Paris *rezident* was forced into another volley of excuses and claimed that there seemed to have been a mix-up arising from the fact that one of his officers was a very poor linguist. He had established that Kitty had not met anybody at all, but that Philby had telephoned Maclean and mentioned that he had been out of contact with the Russians for a long time. Maclean had replied that he himself had not been in touch with them for quite a while and had relayed the news to Kitty, who had passed it on to the *rezidentura* officer, who had got the whole thing the wrong way round. Yet again, Kitty was rehabilitated and was allowed to meet Maclean for the last time as German troops were less than fifty miles from the city, although neither realised that they would never see each other again.

Maclean explained that he was going with the embassy to

Clermont-Ferrand, but that women weren't being allowed to go. For the time being, therefore, they wouldn't be able to meet. He asked her to tell the *rezident* to get one of his people to make contact with him and said that they would probably be moving on from Clermont-Ferrand to Bordeaux, where they could start meeting again if Kitty could get down there. Kitty replied that she didn't know what she was going to do but that, for the time being, she would have to stay on in Paris even after the Germans got there. Maclean expressed the hope that she would try to reach Bordeaux and reckoned that the embassy staff would be going from there to London as quickly as possible, given how fast the Germans were moving; there was no other choice. He also asked her to inform the Centre that, until he was told otherwise, he would continue working at the Foreign Office.

In her report on this meeting Kitty wrote that she knew MacLean was serious in what he said.

LIRIK is a good comrade and the work he does means everything to him. His only concern is that his work should be appreciated. He felt that his work in Paris was not as important as what he did in London. LIRIK is politically weak and doesn't understand the developing situation but there's something fundamentally good and strong in him that I value. He understands and hates the rotten capitalist system and has enormous confidence in the Soviet Union and the working class. Bearing in mind his origins and his past and the fact that he's been totally detached from Party work where he might have grown and learned, LIRIK is a good and brave comrade. I think I could establish contact with LIRIK if that proved necessary. These are my impressions of LIRIK after working with him for the past four years.

Several days before they left Paris Donald and Melinda married, an event no doubt accelerated by the terrifying events on the horizon but more directly prompted by Melinda's pregnancy. Just forty-eight hours before the Germans entered the city Maclean and his young wife and the rest of the embassy staff were evacuated to Bordeaux, whence a British minesweeper took them to England, where he began a new phase of his life and intelligence career.

The material supplied by Maclean to Soviet intelligence from the day he joined the Foreign Office to the moment he left France in June 1940 fills forty-five boxes in the archives, each containing more than three hundred pages. A significant proportion of this vast volume of paper was channelled through Kitty Harris, not to mention the considerable quantity of intelligence which she received from him orally.

Maclean's future career is well-charted, but it should be noted that at some point upon his return from France he would have been informed that Walter Krivitsky had left another unexploded bomb in his path, the defector having travelled to London to be debriefed by MI5, which took him rather more seriously than the FBI. He told his inquisitor, Jane Sissmore, about a Soviet mole 'in the Foreign Office', but misleadingly described him as a Scotsman of good family, educated at Eton and Oxford, and an idealist who worked for Russia without payment. Krivitsky claimed that the spy had access to the papers of the Committee of Imperial Defence and 'occasionally wore a cape and dabbled in artistic circles'. Thrown off the scent by the references to Eton and Oxford, the Security Service gave not a moment's thought to Maclean as a possible candidate, and the bomb failed to detonate for more than a decade.

As a Canadian citizen, Kitty anticipated that she would be interned when the Germans occupied Paris so she was anxious find a way out. She might have been able to join one of the groups trying to get to Britain, and had in fact already talked about this to some of the women in her charity group, but at the last moment they were unable to get hold of a car and everybody decided to go their separate ways, with the *rezident* suggesting that she try to reach Canada. However, this would have meant a visit to the American embassy for a visa and, as she later recalled, 'I felt this would be undesirable because certain traitors working for the American police knew me well. I had the impression that the US embassy in Paris was very active in trying to uncover our comrades.'

An alternative route was from Bordeaux across as yet unoccupied France into a neutral country where there was a Soviet embassy or consulate, and the *rezidentura*, which was doing its utmost to help Kitty during the crisis, even cabled its counterpart in Istanbul. After one unsuccessful bid to get her to Tours or Bordeaux on 6 June, the *rezident* told the Centre on 11 June that Kitty was planning to leave Paris that day, but there could again be no guarantee that she would get away safely because events were unfolding so fast that it was impossible to see what might happen next. The French Government evacuated Paris on 10 June, three days before the Germans marched in, and mass panic seized the city's population. Feeling that she was now about the only person left in the entire 16th arrondissment, Kitty stayed calm, untouched by the hysteria, while KARP finally took it on himself to get her away. He spent the whole afternoon of 12 June in an unsuccessful search for a car and concluded that the solution was to give Kitty one from the *rezidentura*'s own pool. The next day he commandeered a Ford and put enough spare cans of petrol in the boot to give it an extra 200 miles range, apparently not having realised that Kitty had never learned to drive. The inevitably disjointed story in her file shows that a desperate KARP, with none of his own subordinates available to act as chauffeur since they were all up to their ears burning files or making stay-behind arrangements, literally drove around Paris looking for someone, almost anyone, who looked reliable and had a driver's licence.

He found one eventually, cycling aimlessly on the Boulevard de Sebastopol, who agreed to help him by driving 'a lady' out of town for a suitable reward, and they drove to Kitty's building where KARP's wife helped her to pack. By this time the Germans were on the outskirts of the empty city, and KARP drove the car and his new driver, with Kitty sitting alongside, to the eastern edge of Paris, where he handed over the keys and walked home. When he finally arrived, late at night, German motor-cyclists and armoured cars were already on the streets.

On 28 June a Soviet trade official returned to Paris from Bordeaux with a coded message from NAZON informing KARP that Kitty was in a very difficult situation, hopelessly and seemingly permanently stuck in Brives. KARP decided to go there himself and caught up with her a day later, suggesting that he accompany her back to Paris and then send her to the Soviet Union, in the hope that the opportunity would arise at some point to send her abroad again to re-establish contact with LIRIK. Accordingly, Kitty was given her own room in the embassy with a reliable woman to look after her, and a few days later a passport arrived for her from Moscow in the name of the wife of a Soviet diplomat. She left for Berlin on 19 July and arrived in Moscow a week later, taking up residence in the House of the East Hotel.

CHAPTER 12

In the Shadow of the Aztec Eagle

In Moscow Kitty dutifully wrote up her account of what had happened, was debriefed by senior NKVD officers and was told that she was temporarily on the foreign intelligence reserve, which meant yet again endlessly kicking her heels waiting for an assignment. She asked if there was anything at all they could give her to do, but attempts to find her a job as a teacher in Leningrad and Riga were unsuccessful because she lacked qualifications: her Russian was still poor and her Latvian non-existent. Instead Kitty took some leave in the Crimea, where, far from the war, she maintained regular meetings with her NKVD contact in a little seaside villa. She told him that she was 'ready to do anything. I can go to the front, after all I'm a radio operator, or I can go behind enemy lines or I can go abroad. I'd even go to work in a clothing factory, at least I'm qualified for that, anything rather than sit at home day after day.'

Kitty demanded, begged and cried, and her handlers did their best to pacify her, assuring her that her time would come soon and that they would be in touch when they needed her. However, no one contacted her and she spent August and September tutoring a group of young men and women in conversational German. Who they were and where they were being sent, she did not ask, and she was not told. She was then asked to help out in testing young girls in training as radio operators. She envied them and felt rather sorry for them, since she knew their likely fate, and deliberately gave extra attention to the youngest girl, who reminded her of her younger sister, in the hope that this might help her survive a little longer behind enemy lines.

At the end of September Kitty was called in and asked by a senior officer if she was ready to go off again, first to the United States and then possibly to Latin America. 'How much time do I have to get ready?' Kitty asked.

'How much time do you need?' was the reply.

'Six hours,' Kitty said.

She was told that she would have more than six hours; it would take at least a week for her to be briefed and talked through the assignment. On 1 October Kitty took the express from Moscow to Vladivostok, which turned out to be express in name only since it made lengthy stops at every station to let troop, hospital and goods trains overtake them. From the window Kitty saw a Russia gloomy under the leaden autumn sky. In the muddy villages alongside the track, kerchiefed old crones waited stoically, bucket in hand, to get their daily ration of hot water from a wheezing steam engine and pitiful little stalls sold scraps of food on dirty station platforms. The country seemed mired in poverty and misfortune, unlike France, whose defeat had not diminished its beauty and charm in the slightest, nor Germany, where everything was neat and orderly, its people bursting with pride and smugness. But she was still Kitty, more emotion than judgment, and those endless grey spaces, and convoy after convoy of young cheerful soldiers heading west, convinced her that the Soviet Union, her own country, remained invincible and would win in the end.

Kitty arrived in Vladivostok after a journey that lasted fifteen days. After being sent for a medical check-up, she was accommodated in a modest but surprisingly nice hotel. She sailed for America on 22 October on the tanker *Donbass* and, after a call at Petropavlovsk, sailed across a stormy Pacific and anchored in San Francisco on 6 December 1941, the day before the Japanese attack on Pearl Harbor. The local *rezident* Grigory Kheifits, codenamed KHARON, cabled the Centre to report her safe arrival. Kheifits, a sophisticated and highly experienced foreign intelligence officer operating under diplomatic cover as a vice consul, had once worked as secretary to Lenin's widow Nadezhda Krupskaya, and had been deputy *rezident* in Italy before the war. He held a diploma from the prestigious Jena Polytechnical Institute.

Six weeks in a stuffy cabin, the rough crossing and the tension of her impending illegal arrival in America took their toll on Kitty, and she spent a fortnight in a San Francisco hotel, registered as Elizabeth Dreyfus from Chicago, pulling herself together. She then moved to Los Angeles, where she was based until 15 November 1942, initially in hotels and then in her own apartment, making frequent trips to New York, Washington and other cities. Throughout this period she was run jointly by KHARON and the *rezident* in Washington DC, her old friend Vassily Zarubin, who was based under Second Secretary cover at the embassy, using the name Zubilin and codenamed MAKSIM.

Kitty could not have failed to notice what had happened to Earl Browder, with the *Los Angeles Times* reporting on 17 May 1942 that President Roosevelt had commuted the four-year prison sentence handed down the previous year for his old nemesis, passport offences, dating back to 1934. The President's gesture recognised that the Soviet Union had become a valuable ally, rather than a pariah, following the German invasion of Russia, and that the CPUSA's support was considered important.

But Browder was no longer part of her life. Nor was Maclean, who was back at the Foreign Office in London, run by the new *rezident* Anatoli Gorsky, a stickler for detail and precise timekeeping, who immediately imposed a tighter discipline into the relationship and left Maclean in no doubt who was in charge. Briefing Gorsky in 1940, Leonid Kvasnikov, head of the NKVD's Scientific and Technical Section, had stressed the need to check on rumours reaching Moscow from Western Europe about research into some kind of 'super weapon', and Gorsky had tasked his principal agents, Maclean and Cairncross, accordingly. The latter had been moved from the Foreign Office to the Cabinet Office, where he had been appointed private secretary to the Minister without Portfolio, Lord Hankey, and was able to alert the Soviets to the first steps in the TUBE ALLOYS project researching a British atomic bomb.

In the United States similar experimental work was being undertaken to make nuclear fission a reality, much of it concentrated at the Radiation Laboratory in Berkeley, across the windswept Bay from San Francisco, where Robert Oppenheimer, Enrico Fermi and Leo Szillard attracted the NKVD's attention. They were not Soviet agents but Soviet intelligence officers maintained contact with them directly or via intermediaries. In addition, Soviet agents such as Klaus Fuchs, and scientists whose names have not so far been made public, were working in America's secret laboratories. Anatoly Yatskov, Aleksandr Feklisov, Gaik Ovakimyan, Zarubin and his wife Liza, Grigory Kheifits, Semyon Semyonov and other Soviet personnel kept in touch with them personally, or through contact agents.

One of these was Kitty, who spent much of 1941 in Los Angeles and then in New York. Her role as a contact agent and courier focused on the Manhattan Project could be the subject of a story in its own right, but unfortunately the Soviet records for this period remain classified. However, one aspect of the operation concerned two agents, both pre-war Jewish emigrants from Poland. As shown in Kitty's file, KHARON was directed by Moscow to activate them. One was a dentist whose training in France had been financed by Yakov Serebryanskii, a senior NKVD officer who had instructed him to settle in San Francisco in the early 1930s and to wait, maybe a year, maybe even decades, until someone appeared with the agreed recognition phrase. The other had been given similar orders and settled in Los Angeles, where he ran a small grocery store.

At the end of 1941 the Centre learned that these agents were close to members of Robert Oppenheimer's family who had Communist sympathies. KHARON tasked Kitty with their reactivation. The grocery store owner gave her the right answer to the recognition phrase and confirmed that he was ready to co-operate, but the dentist, codenamed CHESSPLAYER, was a different matter. His address was not known and the San Francisco telephone directory listed no less than three dentists with identical surnames and initials. When Kitty made an appointment with the first one and asked him to put gold crowns on the second and third teeth on the right-hand side, the recognition signal, the dentist told her to open and close her mouth and then looked at her as though she was mad.

'Miss,' he said. 'I'm afraid someone has given you bad advice. You don't need crowns.'

The second dentist turned out to be a lady's man, whose immediate reaction after examining Kitty's pearly teeth was to invite her out to dinner that evening, an invitation she ducked politely, but the third proved to be her man. He reacted with consternation and, Kitty reported, even fright to the recognition phrase, but pulled himself together and responded with the correct prearranged reply, 'I think you're wrong, you need the crowns on the left-hand side, not the right.'

Despite his initial apprehension, he soon grasped what was going on and agreed to meet a case officer. Both of these agents played a part in organising the effort to uncover American atomic secrets, together with the ubiquitous Naum Eitingon, who had also played a part in infiltrating the dentist into the country. CHESSPLAYER's wife was a close friend of the Oppenheimer family and from Pavel Sudoplatov's account of the operation, the case officer who ran the dentist after Kitty's initial contact was in all likelihood Liza Zarubina herself.

(A recent fresh look at the wartime San Francisco telephone directory indicates, first, how well the Bay area was served with dentists even some sixty years ago. But leaving aside characters straight out of the pages of Raymond Chandler such as Painless Parker and Sanford Moose, picking the right trio of names without risk of libel is almost impossible since several practitioners had multiple offices and thus more than one listing. There are two sets of three names, however, one with a French flavour, which catch the suspicious eye.)

Kitty's other link to atomic espionage was, probably indirectly, through Earl Browder's niece Helen Lowry, who was last encountered at the farewell party on the *Nordwyck*. She had married the Soviet illegal Itzhak Akhmerov and, by 1941, was back in the United States with him, working under the commercial cover of a small furrier business in Baltimore, conveniently close to Washington DC. A Tartar who had served in China, Akhmerov had studied at Columbia University under a false name to improve his English and had acted as the illegal *rezident* in New York for a while before being recalled to Moscow in 1939. Despite an interrogation conducted personally by Lavrenty Beria, he narrowly escaped becoming a victim of the purge. Akhmerov returned to America with Helen, now codenamed ELZA, in September 1941 using a variety of names, including William Greinke, Michael Adamec and Michael Green, and divided his time between genuine business and espionage and New York and Washington. Akhmerov's cover was so convincing that for a while he was at risk of being drafted into the US army, but he finally managed to get a friendly doctor to certify him unfit. According to his profile in *Studies in the History of Russian Foreign Intelligence*, he ran a source providing intelligence on the Manhattan Project, and as Kitty operated in that circle, a meeting between them is not inconceivable before the Akhmerovs returned to Moscow in 1946.

Kitty was now entering her busiest period as an intelligence officer, and Zarubin decided that she ought to acquire American citizenship legally. As he explained to the Centre, 'In order to put GYPSY on a solid legal footing I am planning to get her married to an American of some substance. She will live on the (West) Coast.' To avoid any misunderstanding, he added, 'It will be a marriage in name only.' The Centre gave its approval and at their next meeting Liza told Kitty about the plan, which she greeted with laughter; however, Liza had to change the subject for a while when she noticed that Kitty's laughter was becoming a little hysterical. When she returned to it, Kitty complained, 'Why on earth didn't you ask me about this before? Or maybe you were remembering that old Russian joke, something about "They married me off without me,"' she sniffed, pronouncing the last phrase in Russian.

'Please don't get excited,' Liza reassured her. 'It's a meaningless formality, a complete sham. If you like, you don't even need to meet the "groom".'

'Absolutely not,' Kitty objected. 'I insist on meeting him.'

The groom turned out to be a former Soviet intelligence asset codenamed BELY (WHITE), an American Jew who no longer enjoyed access to useful information and was living quietly in retirement. When he was introduced to Kitty, he behaved very formally at first, almost as if he was really meeting his fiancée, while Kitty seemed to be overcome by the impish need to tease him. Given his age, she asked archly, how did he propose to fulfil his marital obligations? Wouldn't he be jealous of other men, and wasn't he frightened that she might be unfaithful?

BELY seemed to enjoy this and joined in the banter. 'You know what they call this in Russia?' he said. '"*Smotrina*", or "showing the bride". It reminds me of the Jewish story about this boy who'd been courting a girl for ages but finally told her parents that he wasn't going to marry her unless they arranged a "showing", and what's more he insisted on seeing her with no clothes on. Her parents objected, but finally gave in. But after the boy had given her a good, long once-over, he told them, "I don't like the colour of her eyes."

In your case I like everything I've seen. Why should it be just a paper marriage? Let's do it for real.'

Fortunately, or unfortunately, the marriage never actually happened.

In November 1942 Zarubin realised that it would be dangerous for Kitty to remain in America. Although she was using the cover name Elizabeth Dreyfus, she had kept in touch with her family, had spent some time with her sisters and had also been meeting old friends. His concern was that this behaviour was bound to come to official notice, all the more since she had been denounced by both Gitlow and Krivitsky. Zarubin therefore suggested that she should be sent to Mexico and used for contact with a prominent labour leader, a task which he felt she could handle adequately. Though the Russian files that Igor Damaskin saw refer to him only as SHTURMAN (NAVIGATOR), he was quickly identified by the American intelligence analysts of the VENONA traffic as Vicente Lombardo Toledano. The Centre accepted the proposal; she had been earmarked for Mexico some time previously, and it was only the special circumstances in and around Los Alamos in 1942 that had kept her in America for so long. In cabling permission to Zarubin, the Centre actually suggested advancing her departure date, provided that she could be given solid and reliable cover, but he was cautioned that she should not be allowed to operate independently. Underlying this last comment was Moscow's assessment that while Kitty was a quick-witted and conscientious courier and contact agent, with an outstanding memory, the ability to relay a complex report very accurately and a field operator who knew how to extricate herself from a difficult situation, she was unable to run agents who were her social and cultural superiors, especially those who required a great deal of thorough work and who looked to their handler as an authority. She simply did not have the tough, assertive personality to allow her to take control. Unfortunately this comment was disregarded, as a result of which her assignment proved extremely difficult.

Shortly before she left on her mission Zarubin ordered her 'back to school'.

'Again?' Kitty said in surprise. 'I reckon I'll learn all I need on the job.'

'You're too modest,' he replied. 'We've got another job for you and I reckon you'll do pretty well.'

He then explained that this was a different kind of mission: 'The man I'm going to introduce you to is very well known not just in Mexico but right across Latin America. He's not completely our agent, he's an independent and proud sort of guy. We're sending you to Mexico to work with him in the hope that he'll be more relaxed and accessible in dealing with a woman and that you'll soon get on the same wavelength. How do you feel about it? Are you scared?'

'I once told a friend of mine that the only thing that scares me is mice,' Kitty replied. 'We'll give it a go.'

Zarubin then began talking about the training. She would be reporting directly to him and there would be some technical material she would need to be able to handle, which one of his men would take her through. They then fixed a day and time, and Leonid from the *rezidentura* staff – a tall, taciturn man with tousled hair – picked Kitty up in New York and drove her to Rye Beach on a very roundabout route, constantly checking for surveillance and taking the final few streets to his house only when he was sure that he was not being followed. The house was in a quiet leafy district behind a neat white fence with only a tennis court between the house and the beach. Leonid spoke English rather badly but was an expert in his trade. Once again, Kitty had to do her best to master the intricacies of photography, this time with a modern miniature camera. She had to learn several new techniques, including how to strip the emulsion from a film and to hide photographs and documents in various household items such as pens, pencils, matchboxes, toilet bags, slippers and suitcases. She loved the work and turned out to be very adept at it.

A little while later Zarubin introduced Kitty to SHTURMAN over dinner at an expensive restaurant in midtown Manhattan. Toledano had a black moustache, dark eyes, a dazzling smile and a powerful strong-willed face, combined with the genial air of a countryman and the powerful hands of a workman. All he needed to complete the Mexican stereotype was a sombrero. They got on well together and both said that they looked forward to working with each other. He promised to help Kitty in whatever way he could and to do everything possible for her.

Born in 1894, Toledano was a successful lawyer, who had become Governor of the State of Puebla and had founded the Confederation of Mexican Workers in 1936. Though a committed Marxist, having attended the Comintern Congress in Moscow in 1935 and remaining closely in touch with the Comintern, he and his Movement were sharply at odds with the tiny official Communist Party in Mexico; nevertheless, he had been strongly opposed to allowing Trotsky to settle in the country. In the period he worked with Kitty, his Movement faced repression and a waning of its authority under the conservative regime of President Manuel Avila Camacho. Zarubin must surely also have been aware (but if he was, it did not reach Kitty's file) that Toledano had known Earl Browder, probably in and around the corridors at the Comintern Congress, and certainly when at Moscow's behest Browder had travelled to Mexico City in 1937 to try to mediate in the endless Party squabbling. Toledano had also met Raisa Browder's mentor, Solomon Lozovsky, but whether Toledano knew of Kitty's former relationship with Earl is equally unclear.

For once Kitty's mission had the benefit of careful groundwork, including a notional relative who would be sending her a regular allowance to Mexico. This turned out to be the 'fiancé' BELY she had never actually married. She was also given a contact in a firm in Mexico through which she could receive money in case of need, but ostensibly the reason for her visit to Mexico as a long-term tourist was her enthusiasm to learn about the country's history and customs. She was told that she should not be in any hurry to find a job since this might cause complications with the Mexican immigration authorities, but in the event she crossed the border, without a hitch, on the Aztec Eagle Express.

Upon arrival Kitty was faced with the usual chores of finding an apartment and developing cover. Yet again, she became a student, this time endeavouring to learn Spanish in order to qualify for university entrance. At the same time she started her real work, which involved not only contact with SHTURMAN but other assignments as well, under the direction of the *rezident*, Yuri (LEV) Vasilevsky, who, as KARP, had extricated her from Bordeaux to Paris two years previously. Vasilevsky, who was listed at the embassy under the name Tarasov, with the diplomatic rank of Second Secretary, and was now codenamed YURI, greeted Kitty as a long lost friend.

Hitherto the *rezidentura*'s principal claim to bloodstained fame had been its involvement in 1941 in the assassination, directed by Naum Eitingon, of Leon Trotsky. After Kitty's arrival in Mexico, the *rezidentura* devoted enormous time and effort in a bid to extract the assassin, Ramon Mercader, from prison, although there is no evidence that she participated in this eventually abortive operation, which saw the *rezidentura* involved with every shade of Mexican shyster and bandit. The VENONA intercepts suggest that, in Kitty's time there, Mexico City acquired great importance in the Soviet intelligence system as a jumping-off point for the infiltration of illegals into America, and the acquisition of Mexican transit papers and American visas. Creating and legalising bogus identities involved a time-consuming effort relying on sophisticated support from a well-built network of sympathetic or corrupt officials, in which Kitty's relationship with SHTURMAN was of great benefit.

In one conversation with Kitty, Vasilevsky mentioned that he had fought in Spain, and she explained that her brother had been there too. 'When I saw him in New York, he told me that he had started in the Lincoln Brigade but had transferred to Grigory Grande's special unit,' she said.

'Grande's?' said Vasilevsky in surprise. 'What's your brother's name? His first name not his surname as everyone served under an assumed name.'

'Abe.'

'Abe? Tall, good-looking sportsman?'

'That's him!' Kitty exclaimed.

'Small world,' Vasilevsky concluded. 'I actually served under Grande as well. A first-class guy. It's a pity . . .' He fell silent.

'Did he die at the front?'

'No, not at the front. But let's not talk about that. One day I'll write a book about him. He deserves it. Your Abe was a terrific guy too. Brave, always cheerful, a good trainer and a great comrade.'

A Harris family photograph survives of Abe in Spain, in his three-quarter-length military coat, an officer's cap and neatly trimmed moustache, looking every inch a Hemingway character.

It was rare for Kitty to have this type of personal chat with the *rezident* because their conversations were usually strictly business, in which her work with SHTURMAN was always a tricky topic.

When she had first met Toledano at his office in Mexico, and he had offered her a cup of coffee, she had asked for it 'black but with some milk', which, for some reason, he had found vastly amusing, and, roaring with laughter, he had told her that 'black with some milk' should be their recognition signal.

Switching abruptly to a business-like tone, Toledano then asked how he could help, at which point Kitty slightly lost her head. None of the men she had worked with, including Maclean, had ever asked that. They had all known exactly what was expected of them, and it was Kitty's job to act as their sponge, soaking up every word of their information. Though she had a general idea of the sort of questions in which her superiors would be interested, before she could put them to Toledano she felt that she needed to be far better briefed on the situation in Mexico, and in Latin America as a whole. Putting trivial questions to a man of his status would simply be a waste of time and, noticing her hesitation, he asked, 'When does the new ambassador get here? I heard that it was going to be Umansky. He's a very smart, nice man. I knew him well when he was your ambassador in Washington and we used to meet quite often to talk about regional issues. He had a watching brief for the area. I would be glad to see Umansky here. Tell your comrades that. Also, what news from Moscow? We're cut off from things here. The bourgeois press can't avoid reporting what's happening in Stalingrad and the Red Army's other victories but does it very grudgingly. We've had no news about any recent Central Committee resolutions, about what's happening on the various battlefronts, about your relations with the Allies or about the Soviet economy. Please bring me up to date on everything.'

Kitty was still scrambling to find something to say. 'Who's supposed to be debriefing whom?' she asked herself, acknowledging that he was right about access to news. She remembered her training in Moscow, when her eyes had been opened to the fact that living in the West, under the influence of Western propaganda, there was a lot one did not know. Despite everything that she had learnt, seen and experienced, she remained a true believer. The relationship survived its rocky start and from time to time Toledano would tell her something new and pass on information of real interest.

He helped her to settle in and also lent a hand in legalising an illegal couple, Nicholas and Maria Fisher, codenamed CHETA or THE PAIR, who had arrived in Mexico. According to a VENONA intercept dated 29 April 1944, Vasilevsky was tartly reminded by the Centre that he seemed to have taken no action on a request made the previous December to put SHTURMAN 'on to the task via ADA' of getting them entry visas to Mexico and transit visas for the United States. That they were important is indicated by, among other things, the fact that the New York *rezidentura* was contemplating paying a bribe to an asset close to the White House to procure an American visa for them. That Toledano was rather central is indicated by a further report from Mexico City to New York that he had personally intervened in an arrangement for some $8,500, to be used to ease the Fishers' local paperwork, to be wired to the account of another Soviet asset, Adolf Ariba Alba. Toledano had pointed out that, as a public servant, Alba was known to live off his salary, and the unexplained arrival of such a large sum would be bound to raise suspicions. According to Pavel Sudoplatov, Maria Fisher, *née* Boyko, was a veteran NKVD officer, who had been sent to America with her husband to reactivate an agent network and facilitate operations in America from Mexico.

Another cable from the Centre directed that SHTURMAN was to be approached through ADA to help get papers for an agent codenamed PATRIOT, but for the most part Toledano would ask her for the latest news from Moscow, or entertain her with stories about Mexico, its war of liberation and its heroes. His particular idol was Benito Juárez, the Indian peasant who had become Mexico's president, and about whom SHTURMAN would talk for hours on end.

Kitty's position in Mexico City became even more difficult after Konstantin Umansky presented his credentials on 22 June 1943 in the hall of the Hidalgo Palace, an occasion overflowing with dignitaries wanting to catch a glimpse of the new Russian emissary. Among them was Kitty, who joined the crowd outside craning her neck to catch sight of the ceremonial coach. Umansky, a former commentator on international affairs who had worked for the TASS news agency in Vienna, Rome and Paris before joining the Foreign Service in 1936, was a strong personality with a broad range of knowledge and interests. He had served in the United States from 1941, first as counsellor and then as Plenipotentiary. The writer Ilya Ehrenburg remembered him as a man who loved poetry, music and art and who spoke English, German and French brilliantly.

Kitty, of course, could not hope to compete with someone like this, and it did not take long for Toledano to focus all his attention on Umansky, whose code name in the *rezidentura*'s telegraphic exchanges with Moscow was REDAKTOR ('editor' in English), which was not particularly imaginative considering his journalistic background, and that the code name for TASS was REDAKTSIYA ('Editorial office'). Either Umansky's charm had its effect on Kitty, or maybe Toledano simply managed to persuade her, but she found herself agreeing that he should pass his information to Umansky first. This unwelcome development must have made her realise that she had been sidelined, which would have a negative impact on her standing, but she appeared to be unaffected and took two initiatives, without asking permission, which were bound to get her into even more hot water. The first was to accept Toledano's suggestion that she take a job on his staff, believing that this would get her closer to the people who worked for him and would generally help the two of them to collaborate. Secondly, feeling terribly alone, she resumed writing letters to her sister, also without seeking the *rezident*'s official consent. Inevitably, the *rezident* reported these breaches of discipline to the Centre, adding the comment that, when he had discussed them with Kitty, he noticed that she spoke about Toledano with such warmth and pleasure he could not help wondering whether she might have fallen in love with him.

Vasilevsky also drew the Centre's attention to the fact that Kitty was asking for information about the Russian front, arguing that she really had to tell SHTURMAN more than he could read for himself in the Western press. On the one hand this was justifiable, he commented, but on the other it raised the thought that she might want to play a more significant role because, since she was in love with SHTURMAN, not just as a political figure but as a man, this might make her look more interesting. 'At her age and in her situation men loom large,' Vasilevsky observed.

His report drew a brisk response from the Centre, which told him that Kitty needed to be frequently reminded that her job was not to keep SHTURMAN informed, but to extract information from him. Taking a job in his office without permission had to be viewed as a breach of discipline. Kitty was also ordered to stop corresponding with her family immediately. A contemporaneous VENONA intercept, requesting Zarubin's intervention, shows that the unauthorised correspondence was a two-way traffic, for Vasilevsky advised Moscow that 'ADA is continuing to receive letters from her sister. It is necessary to take measures through MAKSIM.'

In another VENONA decrypt, which probably relates to this period, the Centre directed the Mexico *rezident* that,

> ADA cannot and should not work with SHTURMAN.
> Send your proposal as to how she should be used in the
> future and also state how you are thinking of completing or
> putting through her 'legalisation'. Particulars of her 'parents'
> have been sent to you – this being all that is available to
> us. You may have to think about her legalisation on a
> completely different basis and cover story . . .

For the first, and last, time the Centre went on to express a lack of trust in Kitty and suggested that a dummy 'combined task' should be orchestrated as a way of double-checking her marked interest in Soviet matters which had nothing to do with her work. Up until this point Kitty had never been the target of this kind of vetting and her collaboration with the Service had been based on total trust. Thousands of secret and top-secret documents had passed through her hands without the slightest leak, and none of the people she had met, or who had been named in the material she had handled, had ever come to harm. Nevertheless, she had fallen under suspicion and, unbeknownst to Kitty, the taciturn LEONID, who had trained her in New York, arrived in Mexico. Vasilevsky held a secret meeting with him at which running a check on Kitty loomed large. When he next saw her, Vasilevsky told Kitty that a comrade whom she knew well had arrived from New York. Vasilevsky couldn't meet him because, if he were tailed, a major case would be blown. The comrade was to hand over an important document, and Kitty was asked to meet him that evening. 'Tomorrow,' Vasilevsky continued, 'you and I will have an emergency meeting. You can give me the document and later on you'll take him my reply.'

Everything went as planned without the slightest hitch, and neither document showed traces of any attempt to open them. LEONID returned to New York without any interference, and a Soviet source inside the Mexican counter-intelligence service reported that over the relevant period no signals had been received which might have given grounds for casting suspicion on Kitty. Vasilevsky reported the results of the check to the Centre and was then obliged to talk to Kitty about her behaviour. His instructions on what to say may be contained in a VENONA intercept that ordered him to 'Tell her we require our orders to be carried out without any discussion. Explain to her that she receives orders and tasks only from you and carries them out at your request', while a tantalisingly incomplete fragment in a message soon afterwards reveals the Centre barking, 'We absolutely forbid ADA to . . .'

Kitty cried, tried to justify herself, explained what she had done as best she could, and made a not very convincing job of denying that she had any special feelings for Toledano as a man. She swore that she understood everything she had been told and that her behaviour would change. She would stop writing to her sister, but she asked to be kept informed about how her family was getting on. Vasilevsky's report on their talk recorded with some literary flourishes that Kitty's main disadvantage was her age. On the wrong side of forty, she was in the 'Balzac period' of a woman's life, when she was painfully aware of being alone and sought a relationship with a man, any man. As far as her relationship with Toledano was concerned, Vasilevsky noted that the Centre's reprimand had achieved a positive effect, and she had now gone from one extreme, of unthinking devotion, to another, of blind distrust.

Kitty's change of heart may have been connected with a complex message sent to Moscow around this time, and eventually decrypted in VENONA, in which a frustrated *rezidentura*, reporting on its clandestine dealings with various unsavoury types in its eventually unsuccessful attempt to organise a jail-break for Trotsky's assassin, complained to Moscow that, 'through carelessness on the part of SHTURMAN and MAKSIM, TEKSAS [Alejandro Carillo Marcor, editor of the newspaper run by Toledano's CTM movement] has been put in the picture about the work of our illegal ADA . . .'

As she had promised, Kitty cut her direct contacts with her family, so she now became reliant on the Centre to relay news, as was demonstrated in a VENONA text dated 27 May 1945, in which the Chief of the NKVD's Foreign Directorate, General Pavel Fitin, ordered the *rezident* to

> tell ADA that we have got in touch with her relations and that they are all alive and well. One of her sisters [Nancy Bell] works as before in Amtorg [the Soviet trade organisation] earning $180 a month and another works in the Soviet Purchasing Commission in Washington DC. A third sister [Jessie] used to work for the newspaper PM but recently transferred to work in the TASS agency in which she is employed as a specialist. The mother lives with a female relative and yet another sister [Jessie and Tilly] and is feeling well. Instructions have been given to our *rezidentura* in New York about the regular forwarding to ADA through you of letters from her relations. ADA may write letters through you to her sister who works in Amtorg. Address letters received from ADA to SERGEI [Vladimir Pravdin, the senior TASS representative in New York] for KNOPKA [PUSHBUTTON, a code name ascribed to Nancy Bell] and send them by the first regular mail.

A further intercept, dated 25 January 1945, signed by DAR, Vasilevsky's successor as *rezident*, reported that, since SHTURMAN was now in direct contact with REDAKTOR, he was not giving

Kitty any information and, in fact, had ignored her completely. He added that while SHTURMAN was a major political figure, he was at best a consummate opportunist and, at worst, he was 'as Comrade PAVEL described him', a presumably unflattering comment made by Lavrenti Beria, who based on other examples could well have denounced Toledano as 'an agent of American imperialism and a spy for various foreign secret services'.

By tragic coincidence later that same day, the aircraft carrying Umansky, his wife and a number of Soviet diplomats to Costa Rica, where he was also accredited, crashed, killing everyone on board. (In the spirit of the wartime alliance, the US Government provided an aircraft to carry his remains back to Moscow.)

Since Kitty was now the only Russian with whom Toledano had personal contact, his attitude towards her improved for a while. The nature of the assignments given to her also changed, with the Centre suggesting that her contact with him should be stepped up, and she was tasked to obtain intelligence on the presidential election campaign, the PRI political party, the Ministry of the Economy and other targets. She was also to become more involved in legalising the NKVD's assets and was instructed to avoid giving SHTURMAN the feeling that REDAKTOR's death would mean a break in contact with the Soviets.

For a time it seemed that everything was going rather better, and Kitty worked energetically, providing interesting information, but eventually it became apparent that the opportunities presented by Toledano had been overestimated. Although he was giving her some interesting information, she had the feeling that he was not taking her very seriously, and this was more than she could bear. In a report in mid-1945 the *rezident* informed Moscow that Kitty had become very fretful and demanding, constantly asking him to point out to the Centre that it made no sense for her to remain in Mexico, and that the issue should be settled quickly. In another report the *rezident* noted that life at an altitude of 2,400 metres had a very adverse effect on the nervous system of anyone who was not used to it.

Indeed, at one point in 1943 he was seen in the VENONA traffic asking the Centre for extra funds because Mexico City's 'strange' climate caused his staff's medical bills to be far in excess of the prescribed allowance. Kitty was certainly badly affected and, already debilitated by her overwhelming sense that she was now alone in the world, she underwent a serious operation and had to convalesce in a nursing home. A VENONA decrypt addressed to the Centre explained that 'ADA became seriously ill and was taken into hospital for a double operation, for appendicitis and for the removal of a large tumour'.

The *rezident* was anxious to repatriate Kitty to Moscow, but at that time leaving Mexico was far from straightforward and messages about Kitty's departure were exchanged between the Centre and the *rezidentura* for months. The main problem was that Soviet ships rarely called at Mexican ports, and when they did they always stopped subsequently at either New York or another American port, where the authorities had the right to check and even fingerprint the crews and passengers. In February 1946 the Centre opined that because of her long history of working for the NKVD, work that had been extremely important and had taken her to numerous countries, it would be dangerous to put Kitty on a ship that might call at an American port. She knew a number of very valuable Soviet agents, and in the light of the disclosures made by Krivitsky and Gitlow she had obviously come to the notice of the American, British and probably Mexican counter-intelligence services. She could therefore only leave on a Soviet vessel departing directly from Mexico to the Soviet Union, and it took long and difficult negotiations with the Foreign Trade Mission and Merchant Marine Department before the ship was finally selected.

Meanwhile, Kitty's health had deteriorated sharply to the point of a nervous breakdown and she spent almost all of January in hospital. As the *rezident* reported, she was overjoyed when she learned that her departure was imminent.

In April 1946 Kitty was back in hospital complaining of heart pains and her cardiologist concluded that she was badly in need of a rest. It was not until 16 May 1946 that, accompanied by a returning officer of the *rezidentura* and his family, she finally boarded the Soviet steamer *Gogol* in Acapulco, having overcome a last-minute hitch when the immigration authorities had refused to let her embark because she had no Mexican papers. In her mind's eye, Kitty was already halfway up the ship's gangplank, and she went into hysterics. The immigration officers only relented after the colleague who was accompanying her provided them with a written assurance that her papers were in the Soviet embassy and would be sent to the Immigration Department. The final word on her mission to Mexico, found in her personal file, is addressed to Colonel Andrei Makarovich Otroshchenko, then head of the Foreign Intelligence Directorate, and later *rezident* in Tehran between 1953 and 1955:

I report that today 12 July 1946 ADA arrived in Moscow. She was met on arrival and accommodated in the Grand Hotel, Room 43. She was given 1,000 (one thousand) rubles for the initial period, and one book of restaurant coupons, and her room at the hotel has been paid for up to 20 July inst. I request your instructions as to her further maintenance.

CHAPTER 13

Through Hell and Back

Kitty's health and her age meant that another foreign assignment was out of the question, but she could hardly be simply thanked cordially for all she had done and packed off home to America. She knew too much and too many people. Gitlow and Krivitsky had both exposed her and Earl Browder was also under suspicion. The defection in Ottawa of the GRU cipher clerk Igor Gouzenko also served to make matters worse. America was in the grip of McCarthyism, with the FBI looking hard under every bed for Reds, and there could be no guarantee that Kitty would withstand lengthy interrogation, in which she might give up the names of people known to her who were still on active service.

Kitty never actually said a word about going home. All she wanted to do was rest and get well, but post-war life in Moscow was miserable, even if the euphoria of victory allowed people to overlook their day-to-day burdens. Kitty was overjoyed to meet up again with her old friends, at least those who had survived the terrible purge and the war, but she cried when she heard that the dashing Kaminsky, who had dismissed the allegations against her all those years ago, had died recently and that Arnold Deutsch had been lost

221

at sea. The thought that the fate of so many of her friends remained unknown was especially sad, but it was some consolation to meet up again with Liza and Vassily Zarubin. Liza had just retired from the NKVD and had time to spare, which she and Kitty spent strolling through Moscow or going to the theatre or cinema, as friends rather than as a senior officer and her subordinate.

Given the lengths those whom Kitty regarded as her friends went to over the years to shield her from the whole truth when it came to personal issues, it is highly unlikely that Liza would have told her that Zarubin had been seeing Earl Browder, who had visited Moscow around that time, apparently using a combination of bluff and blackmail to try to get back into Moscow's good graces. Though 'higher political considerations' (actually Stalin's diktat) had forced Browder's removal as the CPUSA's leader, the NKVD knew that it had lost a valuable talent-spotting and agent-handling asset, and a 1945 appreciation noted that 'eighteen people had been drawn into agent work for the NKVD at Browder's recommendation' and identified Browder's brother Bill as one of his lieutenants in maintaining clandestine contact with Zarubin and others. After meetings with Zarubin himself, Gaik Ovakimyan and Raisa Browder's old mentor Lozovsky, the Centre concluded that bringing Earl back into the intelligence fold was fraught with too much risk because he was bound to be under 'meticulous observation', quite apart from the fact that he was a political renegade. Despite the Centre's pessimism, Browder did not return home entirely empty-handed, for on the tacit understanding that he would keep his silence on sensitive issues, he was given contracts to publish Soviet books in America and an allowance of $300 a month for an initial period of a year. Ties were finally severed in 1949, when the Soviets learned that he had apparently offered his services to the arch apostate, Tito.

Meanwhile, Kitty was waiting to be granted a Soviet passport, having been formally congratulated on the award nine years earlier of Soviet citizenship. When she reminded them about this delay, her senior colleagues made enquiries and received an answer they had not expected, in the form of a memorandum dated 2 October 1946 stating that 'the files of the Commission of the Presidium of the Supreme Soviet of the USSR on Matters Relating to the Acceptance, Withdrawal and Deprivation of Citizenship, contain no information on the granting of Soviet citizenship to Kitty Harris'.

Kitty was baffled by the news, although the most obvious explanation was a bureaucratic blunder, perhaps a clerical error in the filing department which, when they looked her up, had failed to realise that Kitty's surname was listed not under 'Kharris' but in the alternative Russian spelling 'Garris' (the Russian alphabet not having the letter 'h') under which she had been given Soviet citizenship in 1937. Frustrated by years of having mistakenly believed herself to be a Soviet citizen, she had no alternative but to start again with a new application, dated 6 December and addressed to the Presidium of the USSR:

> I request that you accept me for Soviet citizenship and hope with all my heart that I will be accepted. I have summarised the reason for my request in the attached questionnaire. I shall be a sincere and loyal citizen. I submit my request with all due gravity, conscious of the responsibility which a citizen of our country must bear. I say 'our country' because I have regarded it as my country for many years. I joined the Communist Party in 1921 and since then have worked to implement the ideals for which every true Communist must work. I will continue this work in the future. My record is clean and I will continue to keep it clean whatever happens.

In her questionnaire Kitty noted that, 'since I am unable to work legally in Canada and the USA, I request permission to make the USSR my permanent home and I promise to make a contribution to the cause in which I have always strived'. While the bureaucratic machinery ground into action, the Soviet Ministry of State Security issued an order declaring it 'undesirable' for foreigners to reside in Moscow, and, as Kitty automatically came within its ambit, it was decided to send her to Riga, even though many foreigners stayed on in Moscow. Armed with a Soviet internal passport issued under an alias, Kitty moved to the Latvian capital on 18 February 1947, to begin what was probably the saddest period of her life. Kitty had no idea what a 'communal apartment' was about, but she soon found out when she was made to share one with a family with hordes of children and a totally alien lifestyle, to which she was quite unable to adjust. While she could cope with the queues and shortages, which she saw as a consequence of the war, the conditions got on her nerves. The noise, the children running up and down, the booming radio on the other side of a wafer-thin wall, and the timetable which dictated whose turn it was to clean up the common parts, took their toll. Once again, her lack of education and her inability to speak Latvian were major handicaps in finding a job. She was finally found a position as an English teacher, but her Russian colleagues, trained over the years to be alert for possible enemies, treated her as a suspicious foreigner while the Latvians, who were predominantly nationalist, hated her as a convinced Soviet patriot.

Kitty soon found herself seriously at political odds with the Latvians because she was too much enamoured with the country she had served and, therefore, over-idealised it. She regarded the people she met as petty bourgeois Philistines, verging on openly anti-Soviet. The hardest thing for her to bear was the feeling that she was completely alone and that it did not matter to anyone whether she lived or died.

The unbearable loneliness kept her awake night after night, her head spinning with distressing, futile and at times stupid thoughts. She began to think that she had been sent into permanent exile as a way of getting rid of her and that she had been condemned to a slow death. She convinced herself that her NKVD colleagues who visited her had been sent to report on her, and as her mind darkened she came to believe that she was being watched day and night.

Becoming increasingly isolated, she never even got close to, let alone made friends with, any of the people who visited her during her solitary life in Riga, and the only breath of fresh air was the opportunity to see Liza Zarubin on the rare and all-too-brief visits she was allowed to make to Moscow. Finally, Kitty wrote to the NKVD leadership on 7 April 1948:

> I am having a very difficult time. I never have a moment's peace at home or at the school where I work and I am sick to death of it. I don't deserve to be treated this way and it is destroying my health . . . I think that someone has made a big mistake about me. That is all I can say. I want to feel that I am a member of the Party.

Kitty's only happiness in that period was to receive an official copy of the minutes of the Presidium of the Supreme Soviet dated 6 May 1947 and signed by the Secretary Alexander Gorkin, recording that she had been granted Soviet citizenship. Even though this was the second time around, she was not given a proper Soviet passport in her own name. But it would not be fair to conclude that the NKVD had simply cut Kitty adrift. Several jobs were found for her, but none proved satisfactory. She was given a thirty-day travel and hotel pass for a holiday in Kemeri, but insisted on coming home after a fortnight. Medical examinations were arranged, but she refused to talk to the doctors. She became more and more consumed by thoughts of the past and, judging by one of her letters to Moscow, her longing for her family: 'Why are there no letters from my family . . . you know what sort of people my family are – you couldn't find anyone better, they're loyal and honourable.'

There were, however, as her file records, 'objective difficulties' that made any unrestricted exchange of correspondence impossible, among them doubtless the FBI's intense pressure and surveillance on the Harris family in America. Tormented by loneliness, Kitty began to ask for permission to return to her family and, in May

1950, feeling that it was unable to cope with her, Latvia's Ministry of Internal Affairs informed the Centre that her continued residence in Riga was undesirable. Moscow registered no objection, but the authorities were unable to decide what to do with her. At this point some paranoid official took it into his head that since Kitty was so keen on returning to her family, there was a risk that she might decide to present herself at the American embassy and request repatriation. In fact, Kitty's loudest threat had gone no further than to declare that if things were not sorted out, she would lodge a formal complaint with the Party's Central Committee. The expedient solution was that she should be 'isolated', and a memorandum to this effect was sent to Evgeny Pitovranov, then the Deputy Minister of the Interior, but he pointed out that she could be arrested only if there were solid grounds on which to do so. While this correspondence was in progress, Pitovranov himself was arrested. His successor did not share his scruples about procedure, as is clear from the summary of her sad story on Kitty's file, written in November 1953, which records that she was 'arrested 29 October 1951 as a socially dangerous element under Article 7-35 of the Criminal Code of the Russian Federation'. It goes on:

> From 29 October to 17 November 1951 seven interrogations were carried out with the aim of revealing whether she held anti-Soviet attitudes and whether she had disclosed the identities of members of our organisation and our agents who were known to her. The investigation found no evidence to indicate that Harris had undertaken hostile acts against the USSR, had contacts with foreigners or disclosed the names of members of our organisation and agents.
>
> During the investigation Harris showed signs of mental disorder and she was sent for forcible treatment at the Gorky Psychiatric Prison Hospital of the USSR Ministry of Internal Affairs on 9 February 1952.

On 22 May 1953 a panel of psychiatric experts concluded that Harris had undergone a temporary mental disorder, which had now abated, that no symptoms of such disorder were now evident and that the forcible treatment could be terminated.

Since by order of the Ministry of Internal Affairs and the Prosecutor General of the USSR no charge is to be brought under Article 7-35 of the Criminal Code of the Russian Federation, the case should be closed for lack of evidence.

It may be significant that the decision to 'isolate' Kitty, which was presumably being actively considered through the summer of 1951, followed closely after the defection in May that year of her former lover Donald Maclean and his co-conspirator Guy Burgess. Given the KGB's extraordinary efforts to conceal the pair after they had been resettled in Moscow, efforts which were intensified when Kim Philby reached Moscow, it is possible that Kitty's isolation was in part motivated by a desire to make sure that there was no possibility of her and Maclean coming into contact.

Even though the 1953 report of her psychiatrists had concluded that there was no legal justification for her continued detention, she remained in custody, and the decision on her future was passed to the top of the Soviet power structure. On 13 January 1954 the Minister of the Interior, Kruglov, sent a memorandum to Georgy Malenkov, then Chairman of the Council of Ministers, and to the Party's First Secretary Nikita Khrushchev:

The Ministry of the Interior proposes: 1. To free Harris and 2. To settle her in one of the regional Centres, to provide her somewhere to live, to arrange a job and to re-establish the previous allowance of 1,500 rubles a month.

The wheels turned and exactly a month later, on 13 February 1954, Kruglov's deputy, General Ivan Serov, wrote with a humane streak all too rare in Soviet correspondence on matters of this kind and even more so for an officer with Serov's reputation for uncompromising brutality, a reputation which was underscored when, as Chairman of the KGB, he masterminded the Soviet invasion of Czechoslovakia in 1968.

To the Head of the Directorate of the Ministry of the Interior for the Gorky Region.

In the case of Kitty Harris, presently held in the Gorky City Prison you are to take the following measures:

1. Prior to the release of K. Harris the most favourable conditions are to be created for her in the prison hospital, whatever she needs by way of underwear and clothing is to be provided and her food is to be improved.

2. In the course of February a room is to be found in an uncrowded apartment with the necessary amenities, and it is to be furnished and prepared appropriately to accommodate K. Harris.

3. A decision is to be taken as to where K. Harris is to work with a view to using her knowledge of English; the job is to be one with which she feels she can cope, and she is to be helped settle in.

4. After K. Harris's release she is to be surrounded by attention and care and given every help in settling into a normal way of life including obtaining whatever she needs by way of clothes, footwear and other essentials.

5. K. Harris is to be registered at one of the city's Clinics and provided with appropriately qualified medical attention. If needed and recommended by her doctors she is to be given the opportunity to go to a sanatorium for one or two months for treatment and rest.

6. On K. Harris's return from the sanatorium she is to be

helped to get on proper terms with the Soviet people among whom she will be living. She is to be introduced into the families of two or three previously vetted colleagues who can guide her way of thinking correctly, and who will be able to keep a covert eye on her; however this is not to go as far as having her investigated by our agents.

You are authorised to spend 20,000 rubles to implement the above measures. Her monthly allowance remains as before. Responsibility for carrying out the above measures is to be entrusted to the Head of the First Section of the Directorate of the Ministry of the Interior.

On 17 February 1954 the Military Collegium of the Supreme Court decreed that the case should be closed and that Kitty should be freed, and on 11 March she was given a Soviet passport in her own name and told that those responsible for her illegal arrest had been punished.

Kitty spent the last years of her life in Gorky, now Nizhny Novgorod, an historic and relatively elegant city on the Volga, with a cosmopolitan background dating back to the great fairs, which were larger than those of Frankfurt and Leipzig, and which from 1640 until as recently as 1928 had brought merchants and traders flocking to its huge market district from China, Europe and Persia. She moved into a nice flat, received a decent pension and gave private tuition in English. She even found friends locally, among them OLIVER, an agent legalised with the name Antonio Gomez Deans, with whom she had worked in Mexico. She also continued to get her greatest pleasure from the letters and little parcels that arrived from her sisters, and from her meetings with Liza Zarubina.

A file note written after a visit Liza had made to Gorky in 1957 recorded that:

Zarubina had last met ADA in June 1951. She reports that ADA has significantly improved both in her mental state and in her attitude. Though it is true that ADA still broods from time to time that her life has no purpose, she nevertheless values life.

ADA is very sensitive, can quickly be thrown off kilter and is prone to pessimistic thoughts, but overall she is a normal human being, who finds it very difficult to be far from her homeland cut off from her family and those dear to her; she is a person who has undergone a major trauma. She has a nasty streak and her own foibles.

In a political sense she is ours. The trip has already produced definite results (in ADA's own words the meeting with Zarubina was a holiday for her) and we may hope that in the future ADA's situation and behaviour will be more peaceful and normal than hitherto.

In her last letter to her family, Kitty wrote:

My dear Nancy, Jessie and family
You haven't heard from me for a very long time. . . I can now tell you that everything is OK and that I am not lonely. I'm dreaming of the day when we will be together.

Kitty's dream did not come true, and she died on 6 October 1966. She was an ordinary woman, cheerful and tearful, timid and brave, amorous and cool. She loved life, her family and men. She loved the country that she served. There was a lot she did not understand, there was a lot she believed in, but, who knows, maybe she understood something we do not and believed in something those who come after us will also believe in. She was given a ceremonial funeral with a KGB guard of honour and wreaths, one of them inscribed: 'To a Glorious Patriot of the Motherland from the Comrades with whom she worked'.

Those younger comrades, born just before or during the war, had no concept of the countries in which Kitty had lived and the changes she had seen in her lifetime; all that was something they only heard about at lectures in their special KGB training schools. They were the children of a new generation, and much of what she regarded as true seemed incomprehensible to them. Kitty left only a small legacy, consisting of a Russian grammar, 305 books in Russian and 89 in other languages, among them works by Turgenyev, Stefan Zweig, Gorky, Anatole France, and a 'Teach Yourself Spanish'. And there was the small locket on a thin gold chain, engraved 'K from D 24.05.37'.

Whether she ever knew before her death that Donald Maclean was in Moscow, and was just as lonely and miserable as she was, is a tantalising but unanswerable question. She would certainly have wanted desperately to know. Her diaries spanning the years 1954 to 1966 contain no clue. Lieutenant Klimov, the KGB officer who went through them, was particularly struck by one extract, which he added to her file:

> . . . the only thing I know is that I am terribly lonely. I haven't got a single friend. My life is in pieces (who will take responsibility for my sufferings? Who will answer for the fact that in thirty years I have only seen my family three times?) Just why have I had to go through this hell?

Klimov concluded in dry officialese that, 'bearing in mind that ADA's diaries do not contain secret information relating to the tasks she carried out for us and are of no historic value, I consider it expedient to destroy them'.

Postscript

Of those she loved, Toledano died in 1968 after a career of considerable distinction. Browder's convoluted life – he had finally obtained a divorce from poor Gladys, his one legitimate wife in 1959 – ended in 1973. Tucked into Kitty's Moscow file is her CPUSA membership card signed by Browder himself.

Donald Maclean died alone in Moscow, a burned-out case, in 1983, and his ashes were later interred next to his parents in an English country graveyard. Agnes Smedley, who had moved to England when she was accused of espionage during the McCarthy era, died in Oxford in 1950 and was buried in China. Margaret Browder died in 1961, silent to the end despite heavy pressure from the FBI and blandishments of immunity.

In December 1944 Kitty's first hero and first love, Peter Skonetsky, flew to Europe with Christmas presents collected by American trades unions for troops fighting in the Ardennes. By one account, he was a passenger on the same aircraft as the band leader Glenn Miller flying from Bedford to Paris when the plane flew into thick fog over the Channel and vanished without a trace.

Yunona Sosnovskaya and Erich Tacke were shot on 21 August

1937, falsely accused of espionage for both the Germans and the Japanese, and posthumously rehabilitated many years later.

Karl Voldemarovich Gursky, codenamed MONGOL, was recalled to Moscow in 1937. Instead of his anticipated posting to Austria as an illegal, he was arrested towards the end of 1938 and charged with working for German intelligence. He was interrogated so severely that he not only confessed, but also deeply implicated Tacke, whom he claimed had recruited him when they had worked together in Harbin in 1927. Gursky alleged that the two of them had made an extra copy of every piece of paper passing through the *rezidentura* and given it to the Germans. He also gave his interrogators another version of the story we have already heard about Tacke's unheralded arrival in Berlin and his meeting with the Social Democrat Meissner.

According to Gursky, Meissner had actually been a member of the SS, and Tacke had also introduced him to an Abwehr officer named Blum. When Tacke returned to Berlin, Meissner had betrayed him and Tacke was obliged to leave town in a hurry. The Gestapo then arrested Meissner for embezzlement. Gursky went on to confess that he had told Blum all about agent BREITENBACH, and had been paid 750 to 100 marks a month for his efforts. Gursky said that he had also disclosed the names of Margaret Browder and Kitty Harris.

Gursky may have said what he did to his interrogators on 9 March 1939 because he already knew that Tacke was beyond harm, having been shot in 1937. Gursky was sentenced to death and his personal file, annotated by Pavel Sudoplatov as 'Reviewed and finding that Gursky, K.V. is a traitor and is dead', was closed and sent to the archives. But Stalin's long arm was for some reason stayed, and on 5 January 1940 the Military Collegium of the Soviet Supreme Court commuted his death sentence to ten years' forced labour in the Gulag and five years' deprivation of his rights. He served out his full time and, after his release, settled in a town in Siberia. He was rehabilitated in 1956 and the local State Security organs even employed him for operations against the Chinese target.

Boris Davydovich Berman, codenamed ARTYOM, seemed destined for great things. His Berlin assignment was a great success; as well as the legal *rezident*, he supervised Zarubin's and Parparov's illegal networks and provided the Centre with a steady flow of important, accurate and timely intelligence. On his return to Moscow, he continued as desk officer for these *rezidenturas*, and Kitty handled assignments for him both overseas and through visits to him in Moscow.

In the dark days of 1937, when some officers fell and vanished overnight while others rose, Berman was suddenly appointed People's Commissar of Internal Affairs for the ByeloRussian SSR, a move perhaps helped by the fact that his brother Matvei held a senior post as Assistant People's Commissar for Internal Affairs of the USSR. While working in Minsk, Boris beame a member of the Central Committee of the ByeloRussian Communist Party and, on 12 January 1937, was elected a deputy of the USSR Supreme Soviet. In 1938 he was appointed to head one of the NKVD's Directorates, but Matvei's star began to wane; he was first of all moved out of the Internal Affairs Ministry, nominally promoted to USSR People's Commissar of Communications and then arrested in 1938. Boris was arrested soon afterwards. They were both shot and posthumously rehabilitated.

The files reveal that Aleksandr Aleksandrovich Ervin, who had run Kitty in Copenhagen, Yakov Zakharovich Shapiro (codenamed AMBROSIUS), for whom she had worked in her first spell in Paris, and Theodore Stepanovich Mally (codenamed MANN), all came to equally tragic ends.

During his Copenhagen tour Ervin was alleged, apparently with some justification, to have developed a serious drink problem. The correspondence on his file on this includes a tough but humane letter from Berman:

I strongly advise you to stop drinking. If for some reason
this is beyond you, then tell me so straight out . . . I would

much have preferred not to write to you in this way but I believe it is better to warn you now than hit you with it later. Greetings, ARTYOM

Ervin swore that he did not have a problem, though he would have had good reason for he was much distressed by his wife's schizophrenia and he had been left on his own with two children. Soon afterwards he was transferred to Berlin, where senior officers could keep a closer eye on him. In 1937 someone, maybe one of his former drinking buddies, testified that he was a spy and a terrorist, and he was arrested in September 1937, sentenced to death on 4 November and shot the same day.

Shapiro, who had qualified as a doctor, was totally unsuited to intelligence work and things did not go at all well in Berlin, Paris, or his last posting in Stockholm. In 1936 he was recalled and dismissed from the Service, and spent the next period working quietly in the Medical Inspectorate of the Ministry of Health. However, in 1937, when former officers of the illegal service were being vetted, it came to light that in April 1933 Shapiro had recommended one Nathan Luriya, later convicted as part of the Trotsky-Zinovyev plot, to the NKVD for recruitment as an overseas illegal. This alone was enough to have Shapiro arrested, and, as inevitably happened in that period, other reasons were soon 'uncovered' to justify charging him with 'hostile activity'. He vanished in the purge, but was rehabilitated in 1955.

Theodore Stepanovich Mally was unquestionably the most outstanding intelligence professional of the three. After leaving London, where he was very successful in infiltrating the Cambridge Five and other agents into positions of interest to the Centre, or opening the door in that direction, as with Philby's job on *The Times*, he knew what was waiting for him in Moscow. As he told a friend, 'If I don't go back, it will be taken as proof that I'm an enemy and everyone will say "What else do you expect of an ex-priest?" I am going back to prove that I'm not guilty of anything and that death does not scare me.' He returned, and was duly arrested and charged with espionage, with much being made of his time as a prisoner of Kolchak. 'We know that's when you were recruited . . .'

On 20 September 1938 Mally was sentenced to be shot; he was posthumously rehabilitated on 14 April 1956.

Arnold Deutsch's London legacy was the recruitment of more than twenty agents, most of them first-class. When he returned to Moscow, he somehow managed to escape the fate of the majority of his colleagues, probably because none of them had denounced him, but he was sidelined for several months and was clearly under suspicion, grimly illustrated by a memo his immediate superior wrote to their section head Dekanozov asking for funds to pay for Deutsch to take Russian lessons. Dekanozov scribbled on the memo: 'Comrade Sten'kin! Don't waste your time. STEFAN [Deutsch] needs to be thoroughly vetted, not sent off to learn languages.'

Deutsch was fired from the NKVD and went to work at the Institute of World Economy and World Politics at the Academy of Sciences. When war broke out, the new NKVD leadership decided to send Deutsch to Latin America as an illegal. After two failed attempts to get him there via the South Atlantic, one of which got him as far as Bombay, and a great deal of trouble, he sailed for America on 4 November 1942 on the tanker *Donbass*, the same ship which had carried Kitty from Vladivostok to San Francisco. Deutsch was listed as a member of the forty-nine-man crew when it set off by the Arctic route from Novaya Zemlya. The ship was attacked by the Luftwaffe on 5 November and again two days later; after reporting a further attack, its radio went off the air and the *Donbass* was presumed to have sunk with the loss of all hands.

It later transpired that some of the crew had been saved and had been held as prisoners of war. When they were released years later, the *Donbass*'s captain reported that he had actually been sunk by the German cruiser *Admiral Scheer* and that Deutsch had gone down when the bow parted from the hull. Though seriously wounded, he had gone on to the end trying to keep the crew's spirits up and help men in danger.

Dekanozov, author of the sharp rejoinder about Russian-language lessons, was himself shot in 1953 as part of the Beria affair.

Vassily and Liza Zarubin died peacefully, he in 1972, leaving behind a large volume of memoirs which is still in use as a training manual, and she in 1987. The purge virtually passed them by although early in 1940 Zarubin was among a group of foreign intelligence officers summoned to 'a conference' in Beria's office at which they were all accused of collaborating with the Gestapo. Eyewitnesses recall that Zarubin responded to Beria with great dignity and as a man totally convinced that he was in the right, and the confrontation ended in a draw.

Though not part of Kitty' s story, it is worth noting that in the spring of 1941 Zarubin travelled secretly to China to re-establish contact with Walter Stennes, a German who was a senior advisor to Chiang Kai-Shek, and a Soviet spy. Codenamed DRUG ('friend'), the former SA member told Zarubin that he had precise information on Hitler's plans to attack the Soviet Union and even gave the date. The information was immediately passed to Stalin, who ignored it. Meanwhile, in April 1941 Liza had travelled to Germany to re-establish contact with AUGUSTA, the wife of a senior Nazi diplomat who had been recruited by the security organs in Moscow. Liza, passing as a German, met her twice and persuaded her to agree to continue co-operation. This produced important intelligence, and Liza also renewed contact with an agent who worked as a coding clerk in the German Foreign Ministry.

When she went to America with her husband in the autumn of 1941, Liza ran a network of some twenty agents, including certain sources of extremely valuable intelligence. Kitty had a role in a number of her operations.

Kitty's last controller in London, Grigory Grafpen, codenamed SAM, was not in the same league as Deutsch. More of an *apparatchik*, he lived in permanent fear that something would go wrong and constantly found himself having to explain away the short-comings and mistakes of his subordinates, including Kitty. Older than most of his service colleagues, he had worked in America from 1909 to 1913 and spoke English with an American accent. He went back to America as an intelligence officer in 1926 and took over the London *rezidentura* in 1937. He was recalled to Moscow in 1938, dismissed from the NKVD in 1939 and arrested soon afterwards. He was one of the lucky ones, getting off with only five years in the Gulag. He was rehabilitated in 1956, awarded the Order of the Red Banner in 1957 and died in 1987 aged ninety-six.

Yuri Vasilevsky, Kitty's *rezident* in Mexico, returned to Moscow in 1944 and continued to work on atomic espionage. In 1945 he travelled to Denmark to organise a meeting with the scientist Niels Bohr and then went to Switzerland for a meeting with Bruno Pontecorvo. He also met Joliot Curie, and was given a bonus of $1,000 and his own apartment in Moscow for what he had accomplished. But he later fell out with senior management and in 1954 he was fired and expelled from the Party for 'treacherous anti-Party activity in Paris and Mexico'. For the rest of his life he continued to bombard the Central Committee with letters attacking the then Chief of Intelligence General Sakharovsky for failed operations and mishandling of agents. His Party membership was restored.

Vasilevsky also found time to write books including, as he had promised Kitty, one on Grigory Grande (Syroezhkin). In Moscow in the 1960s he often used to meet Ramon Mercader, Trotsky's assassin, whom he had been unable to spring from prison in Mexico.

Ivan Nikolayevich Kaminsky, who had supervised Kitty's training, looked into her file after Krivitsky's defection and had been desk officer for the London *rezidentura*, also fell under the wheels of the purge juggernaut and was sentenced to a long term of imprisonment in 1938, only to be recalled to the NKVD when the war highlighted the acute shortage of experienced personnel. There are two versions of what happened to him. According to Pavel

Sudoplatov, he was sent behind enemy lines to Zhitomir, where a local priest who was an agent of the NKVD betrayed him to the Gestapo. According to the official version in *Studies in the History of Russian Foreign Intelligence*, Kaminsky was not released from prison until 1944 and went back to work at the Centre. He was then sent to the western Ukraine, where, because of his experience, it was felt he could be useful in mopping up the nationalists, who killed him in a shoot-out. Either way he died fighting rather than up against a prison wall, shot by a colleague.

As we have seen, Abraham Einhorn, who as Harry Terras recruited Kitty and Margaret, was shot in 1937. It being a small and grisly world, the file note recording his fate was signed by Ivan Kaminsky not long before he too was arrested.

As previously mentioned, it took eighteen years for Dimitri Bystrolyotov, codenamed HANS, to 'sort out his personal affairs'. Before returning to Moscow for the last time he was already tired and depressed, having spent seventeen years abroad on intelligence missions, six of them as an illegal, and had written to the Centre asking to be replaced. ARTYOM had replied: 'Dear Comrade Hans . . . please be patient . . . cheer up and try not to let the two months you have left to do reflect badly on the many years of tremendous work you have done.'

Although he was well aware of what might be waiting for him, Bystrolyotov returned to Moscow. He spent some time working in the Centre, but on 1 January 1938 the NKVD fired him and he was sent to work at the Chamber of Commerce. Almost a year later he was arrested. His interrogators, sadists named Solovyov and Shushkin, broke his ribs, cracked his skull, knocked out his teeth and gave him such a severe kicking that his stomach muscles were seriously damaged, all in all quite enough to persuade him to confess that he had spied for no less than four different countries.

Sentenced to twenty years' imprisonment and five years of exile, he was released in 1954 on the grounds that he was terminally ill, and rehabilitated in 1955. In 1968 he was still able to write that:

I don't feel bitter about being in prison. The best years of
my life were the time I spent in the intelligence service and
I have every right to be proud of what I have done. I'm
glad that I returned to the USSR to accept my fate. I came
back fully aware of what would happen because it was my
patriotic duty. I think I had a good life and I would do it
all over again.

Bystrolyotov, who is said to have had a command of twenty-two
languages, spent his last years writing twelve volumes of memoirs
as well as fiction. He died in 1975.

Fyodor Parparov, codenamed YEVGENI, had run the second
illegal *rezidentura* in Berlin alongside Zarubin. The *rezidents* worked
completely independently but sometimes exchanged information
personally or by couriers, a role in which Kitty was often used.
Parparov had been transferred to Germany in 1938, and he also
worked in France, Spain and Switzerland. During the war he operated abroad illegally, and afterwards he was in charge of compiling
for Stalin a 653-page dossier and biography of Hitler. Ill-health
compelled him to retire in 1951 and he died in 1959.

There is some confusion over the background of Grigory Kheifits,
KHARON, the *rezident* in San Francisco to whom Kitty reported
when she went back to America. One version, for which no evidence
can be found, is that his father had been 'one of the founders of the
CPUSA', who had come to Moscow in the 1930s to work for the
Comintern. His training in Germany left him with a fascination for
physics that later enabled him to hold his own when talking to
atomic scientists, including Robert Oppenheimer. He was the first
to find out about and report on Einstein's secret letter to Roosevelt
urging the creation of a new weapon. In San Francisco he obtained
information on the preparations for developing the atomic bomb,
on which he reported personally to Beria when he returned to
Moscow on 1944. In his retirement Kheifits worked for many years
on the publishing side of a research institute; he died in 1981.

Fritz Talbe, codenamed LEGACY, was still supplying valuable intelligence as late as May 1941. Tracked down again in 1946, he said that he would only be prepared to go on working for the Soviets if they could find his only son, who had disappeared during the war. Over the next three years the NKVD scoured every prisoner-of-war camp and interrogated hundreds of prisoners, but to no avail. At the last dramatic rendezvous when Talbe was told that there was no trace of his son, he cursed Hitler, Stalin and everybody else, telling his Soviet handler that he deeply regretted having helped Russia, and refusing point-blank to have any further contact.

Ernst Wohlweber, codenamed ANTON, was the Stockholm underground leader whom Kitty so much admired. He had what old hands sometimes call 'a good war', his network sinking several German ships through the judicious use of time bombs. When his instincts told him arrest and deportation to Germany were drawing inevitably closer, he gave himself up to the Swedish authorities, 'confessed' to espionage against Sweden and sat out the remainder of the war in a Swedish jail. He later became East German Minister of Internal Affairs, but was dismissed for 'anti-Party behaviour' after crossing swords with Walter Ulbricht. He died in the early 1960s.

Evgeny Pitovranov, arrested just after he had declined to have Kitty locked up in the absence of hard evidence, had been in jail during the purge, ironically on the grounds that, as an NKVD officer, he had been 'soft on enemies of the people'. On that occasion he got himself out with a shrewd calculation that, while appealing to Stalin for mercy would be a waste of time, a professional letter laying out several important intelligence issues for the Leader's consideration might get a different response. He was right and was swiftly rehabilitated.

The reason for his arrest in the midst of dealing with Kitty's case remains obscure, though this may have been part of the turmoil that followed the death of Stalin and subsequently the downfall and murder of Beria. Any setback can only have been short-lived since Pitovranov later became Head of Soviet Intelligence in East

Germany. He was last sighted in 1995 suing for libel a Soviet journalist who alleged that Pitovranov had been responsible for the assassination on Stalin's orders of the famous Russian Jewish actor Solomon Mikhoels.

In 1937 Rudolf Ivanovich Abel and Vilyam Genrikhovich Fisher, codenamed MARK, the INO technical specialists and close friends who had been Kitty's instructors in photography and radio work, were both fired from the Soviet service, in Abel's case because his brother Voldemar had been arrested and shot for 'spying and sabotage on behalf on Germany and Latvia'. When war broke out, they were both recalled by the NKVD and assigned to a unit that ran military intelligence and partisan groups.

Laden with medals and awards, Abel retired early on health grounds and died prematurely, in 1955, not knowing that Fisher, who went on to spend fourteen years as a Soviet illegal in the US, had 'borrowed' his name when eventually betrayed to the FBI and arrested. MARK flatly denied being involved in espionage, refused to give evidence at his trial and resisted the FBI's efforts to turn him. In 1957, aged fifty-four, he was sentenced to twenty years' hard labour, but was released in 1962 in exchange for the downed U-2 pilot Francis Gary Powers and went back to work at the Centre until his death in 1971. He was buried in the Donsky Cemetery in Moscow because, according to his daughter Evaline, the Novodevichy Cemetery would only agree to bury him under the name of Abel, which his family had refused.

Alexander Orlov made his escape to America before the purges caught up with him, 'reinsuring' his and his family's safety by letting Stalin known that if they were left alone, he would not betray the many key secrets he held, including the facts on the Cambridge Five. He died in his bed in 1973. In 1968 the KGB's senior management decided to track him down and re-establish contact with him in order to confirm, once and for all, that he had not given the Americans the benefit of his encyclopaedic knowledge. After a long and complicated search, Mikhail Feoktistov, a talented young officer in the New York *rezidentura*, finally traced his target and met Orlov face to face. Orlov was relaxed, but his wife threatened Mikhail with a pistol, making any serious conversation difficult, though Orlov did find time to say that he had told the Americans nothing beyond what had been published in his books.

The Orlovs promptly moved, and it was not until August 1971 that Feoktistov succeeded in arranging another, and this time more productive, meeting. Orlov assured him that he had not revealed the name of a single agent and went on relate proudly how he had misled the FBI and CIA by concealing any substantive information. He also told him much else of interest.

As Feoktistov recalls, Maria had tears in her eyes when they said goodbye and urged him to 'be true to yourself and never betray your homeland no matter how many millions of dollars you are offered'. Maria gave him a cake for his wife and children, who were waiting for him outside in the car. However, they refused to touch it, frightened that it might be poisoned. Igor Damaskin, then attached to the New York *rezidentura*, allowed his sweet tooth to overcome his professional caution.

The Soviet Union died in 1991, but Kitty's sister Jessie lives on, aged ninety. She and her American sisters never wavered in their beliefs, and until the end maintained, even to other family members, their vow of silence on anything to do with Kitty.

Select Bibliography

Cecil, Robert, *Donald Maclean: A Divided Life* (The Bodley Head, 1988)

Cope Jeffrey, Inez, *The Life and Times of Zoya Zarubina* (Eakin Press, 1999)

Duff, William E., *A Time for Spies* (Vanderbilt University Press, 1999)

Field, L.K., Unpublished Manuscript Collection, Imperial War Museum, London

Klehr, Harvey, Haynes, John Earl, and Firsov, Fridrikh I., *The Secret World of American Communism* (Yale University Press, 1995)

Morgan, Ted, *A Covert Life: Jay Lovestone* (Random House, 1999)

Ottanelli, Fraser M., *The Communist Party of the United States* (Rutgers University Press, 1991)

Sobolyev, V.A. (ed.), *et al*, *LUBYANKA-2* (Izdatel'stvo Obyedinyeniya Mosgorarkhiv, 1999)

Trubnikov, V.A. (ed.), *et al*, *Studies in the History of Russian Foreign Intelligence*, Vol. 4 (Mezhdunarodnye Otnosheniya, Moscow, 1998)

VENONA Releases (National Security Agency, Fort Meade, 1996)

Select Bibliography

Wasserstein, Bernard, *Secret War in Shanghai* (Profile Books, 1998)

Weinstein, Allen, and Vasilyev, Alexander, *The Haunted Wood* (Random House, 1999)

West, Nigel, VENONA: The Greatest Secret of the Cold War (HarperCollins, 1999)

West, Nigel, and Tsarev, Oleg, *Crown Jewels* (HarperCollins, 1998)

Index

KH - Kitty Harris; EB - Earl Browder

A/201 (Soviet agent) 113
Abel, Rudolf Ivanovich 242
  see also Fisher, Vilyam
    Genrikhovich
Abel, Voldemar 242
ADA (KH as) 1, 2, 4, 179, 181, 186,
  188, 194, 195, 212, 213, 215, 216,
  217, 220, 230, 231
Adamec, Michael (alias of Itzhak
  Akhmerov) 205
'Aesop language' 136
  see also recognition signals
AFL *see* American Federation of
  Labor
Akhmerov, Itzhak (Michael Adamec;
  Michael Green; William Greinke)
  illus, 2, 205
Alba, Adolf Ariba 213
AMBROSIUS (Yakov Zakharovich
  Shapiro) 118, 234, 235
American Communist Party *see*
  CPUSA
American Exceptionalism 45
American Federation of Labor (AFL)
  25, 27, 28
  KH at Detroit conference 37
American Negro Workers' Council
  83
American Socialist Party 26–7

Amtorg (Soviet trade organisation)
  83–4, 92, 217
ANNA (Margaret Browder) 87
ANTON (Ernst Wohlweber) 131, 241
Arcos 79
Artuzov, Artur *illus*, 77, 147
  accusations of treachery 153–4
  as head of INO 81
  illegal service and 82
  report on INO 77–80
ARTYOM (Boris Berman) 87, 102,
  103, 106, 234–5, 239
atomic bomb espionage 203, 204,
  205, 238
AUGUSTA 237
Austria: Soviet intelligence in 79

Babington, Miss Anna 125
Bamag 114
Bedacht, Max *illus*
Behrens, Klaus (RADIANT;
  STRAHLMANN) 114
Bell, Nancy (*née* Harris) (KNOPKA
  [PUSHBUTTON] 2, 3, 83–4, 217,
  230
Bell, Thomas (KH's brother-in-law)
  83
BELY (WHITE) (KH's 'fiancé')
  206–7, 209

Beria, Lavrenty 112, 205, 218, 237, 241
Berlin 112–13
  burning of Reichstag 106
  KH 94–7, 100, 103, 105–6, 114, 118–19, 122–3
  rezidenturas 103–4, 113
  see also Germany
Berman, Boris Davydovich (ARTYOM) 87, 102–3, 106, 234–5, 239
Berman, Matvei 234
BETTY (Vassily Zarubin) 110, 113, 118
Beurton, Sonia (Ruth Kuczynski) 61
Biddenfuhr, Colonel 126
Bittelman-Dana-Cannon group (CPUSA faction) 44–5
Blum (Abwehr officer) 233
Blyumkin, Yakov 111–12
Bohr, Niels 238
Bose, Gerhard von 126
Bose, Herbert von 126
Boyko, Maria *see* Fisher, Nicholas and Maria
'Braun' 100
BREITENBACH 113, 122, 232
Bremen: KH in 94
British Union of Fascists 169, 170
Browder, Bill 222
Browder, Earl *illus*, *illus*, 9, 106, 232
  biography: background 36; first meeting with KH 36; marriage to KH 42; involvement in CPUSA factions 44–5, 82, 90; Shanghai posting 46; first Chinese visit 54–5; identified in Shanghai 74; leaves Shanghai 74; major row with KH 75; marriage to Raisa 106; prison sentence commuted 202; in Moscow 222; Soviet link severed 222
  alias as George Morris 73–4
  character 36
  counter-intelligence on 47
  political life 42

relationships: with KH 2, 37–8, 39–40, 61–2, 63, 64, 75–6, 90–1, 106; with Raisa 43, 52, 76, 83, 106, 222
  Shanghai cover 59–60
  and Toledano 209
  value as agent 222
  Zarubin contact 222
Browder, Felix (EB's son) 43, 106
Browder, Gladys (EB's first wife) 36, 106, 232
Browder, Margaret 2, 48, 91
  biography: meetings with KH 41–2, 83, 93–4; recruitment 87; marriage to 'James Meadows' 106–7; appendicitis 119–20; radio communications work 120–2; sent to Moscow 120; Paris assignment 154–5; antiques business 190; return to USA 190; death 232; Prague run with KH 99,100
  alias as Jean Montgomery 154
  code names: ANNA 87; GIN 87, 103, 106, 107
  identification as Soviet agent 154–5, 189, 233
Browder, Raisa (*née* Luganovskaya) 43, 52, 76, 83, 106, 222
Burgess, Guy 148, 150, 151, 187, 195, 227
  penetration of MI6 150–1
Bystrolyotov, Dimitri (HANS) 139–40, 239–40

Cadoux (French agent) 139
Cairncross, John 180, 203
Calcius Private Detective Agency 123–5
California: KH in 201–4
'Cambridge Five' 7, 142, 144, 147–8, 150, 162–3, 235, 242
  KH and 2–3, 150
Cambridge University: suitability for recruitment by Soviet intelligence 144

Canada
  Communist Party 27
  Harris family's emigration to 18
  KH's 'disappearance' 3
  KH's identity as Canadian 156,
    160, 174–5
Cargill, Elizabeth 125
Chen Yen Yuichen 61, 62, 64, 65
CHESSPLAYER (dentist/agent) 204
CHETA (Nicholas and Maria Fisher)
  212
Chiang Kai-Shek 55, 70–1, 237
Chicago 31
  CPUSA in 35, 42–3
  gangland shooting 32
  Harris family moves to 30
Childs, Jack 75
Childs, Morris (Moishe Chilovsky)
  ('Red Milkman') 40, 74–5, 158
China
  border checks 56
  closing of Soviet consulates 61
  Communist Party 57; Stalin and
    55, 58; massacre 58
  EB's visits 54–5
  Soviet intelligence in 79
  see also Shanghai
CIA: ivy league recruitment 7
ciphers
  Maclean's information on British
    167
  Maclean's information on Soviet
    176
  see also VENONA intercepts
codewords see 'Aesop language';
  recognition signals
Comintern
  China and 2, 47, 59–60
  EB and 42–3
  First Congress 27
  International Workers Aid
    Organisation 43
  Noulens in Shanghai 65–6
  OSM 82
  'provocateur' 168
  Sixth Congress 72

  union policy 27
Communist Party
  American see CPUSA
  Chinese see China
  KH's loyalty to 7
Communist Party of Canada 27
Copenhagen see Denmark
Costello, John 4, 161
couriers
  KH as courier: first assignment
    31–4; Far East assignments 62,
    63, 64–5; Harbin assignment 67;
    recruitment by Harry Terras
    84–6; Berlin 114, 118–19;
    London-Paris 140
  KH as selector of 127
  radio communications and 120
  Soviet 3
  Stalin on 81
  use out of Germany 114
cover stories
  Browder in Shanghai 59–60
  in England 174–5
  KH 62, 67, 96, 97, 106, 114–15,
    131, 184, 210
  with Maclean 163–4, 173
  for Skonetsky 158
CPUSA (American Communist
  Party) 2
  in Chicago 35
  factions in 44–5, 82, 90
  Fortune article on 90
  legalisation 35–6
  link with Soviet intelligence 6
  membership 36
  New York and Chicago branches
    dispute 42–3
Curie, Joliot 238
Czech crisis 184, 187
  see also Prague

Damaskin, Igor 1, 7–8
  on KH's birthdate 16–17
  research on Einhorn 88
Damon, Anna illus
'Daniel' (KH's contact) 28, 35

DAR 217
Davis, Eleanor (alias of KH) 101
Deans, Antonio Gomez (OLIVER)
    229
DEDIP traffic: Maclean's responsi-
    bility 176
Deh (KH contact in Hong Kong) 63
Dekanozov, Vladimir 236, 237
Denmark
    GRU operation 130–1
    KH in 128–30, 131
    KH's responsibility for 127
dentist agent: San Francisco 203–4,
    205
Deutsch, Arnold (OTTO; STEFAN;
    Stefan Lang) illus, 149–50, 186
    and Cambridge Five 142, 144, 162
    on KH 151, 179
    lost at sea 221–2, 236–7
    and NELLY 170
    recall to Moscow from UK 152,
        154
    recruitment methods 145–6
    skills 15–16
    temporary exile from UK 150
    and Woolwich Arsenal spy ring
        162
Din (maid in Shanghai) 59, 60
Djarra (KH's Jakarta contact) 62
'Dobryzhinski' (possibly Jurek
    Sosnowski) 127
Donbass (tanker) 202, 236–7
Doriot, Jacques 54
DOUGLAS (Otto Spiegelglass) 154,
    160
Dreyfus, Elizabeth (alias of KH) 1,
    202, 207
DRUG (Walter Stennes) 237
Dzerzhinsky, Felix 81, 111

Ehrenburg, Ilya 213
Einhorn, Abraham Osipovich (Harry
    Terras; James Meadows) 67–8, 72,
    84, 87–8, 93, 107, 239
    identity 87
    recruitment of KH 84–6

Einstein, Albert 240
Eitingon, Naum illus, 112, 204, 210
Elena (keeper of Berlin safe-house)
    122
ELZA (Helen Lowry) 205
émigré groups
    INO action against 155
    White Russians in Harbin 67
ERNA (Elizaveta Zarubina) 110, 115
Ervin, Aleksandr Aleksandrovich
    (ERVIN; Lukin) 127, 129–30,
    234–5
Esther/Esfir (KH's mother) see Harris
Evans, Walter (essayist and photogra-
    pher) 90
evidence: destruction of paper
    evidence 185
exposure of KH 2, 6, 141, 154,
    154–5, 189, 190, 233

Falkenheim, Frau 126
Fascism 86, 95, 103, 104, 169
FBI
    Childs as informant 75
    Harris family, surveillance of 3, 83,
        225
    and KH 2
    Krivitsky reports 154
    in McCarthy era 221
    possible 'black bag' raid 6
Feklisov, Aleksandr 203
Feldbin, Leiba Lazerevich 147
    see also Orlov, Alexander
Feldel, Lev (alias of Alexander
    Orlov) 147
Feoktistov, Mikhail 242–3
Fermi, Enrico 203
Field, Major Leonard 65–6
FINN 180
'Finnish question' 186–7
First World War 21
Fisher, Nicholas and Maria (née
    Boyko) (CHETA; THE PAIR)
    212–13
Fisher, Vilyam Genrikhovich (later
    known as Rudolf Abel) (MARK) 2,

137–8, 141, 156, 242
Fitin, Pavel 178, 217
Footman, David 150–1
Foster, William Z. *illus*, 44, 82
France
  KH's frontier crossings 101, 104–5,
    118
  proposed military alliance with
    Germany and Poland 104
  suspicion of foreigners 118
Friedmann, Litzi 150
Frinovsky, Mikhail 153
frontier crossings, KH's 56, 101,
  104–5, 118, 140
Fuchs, Klaus 203
  Ruth Kuczynski as Soviet contact
    61

Gennady (intelligence trainer) 134–5,
  177
George, Harrison (Margaret Browder's
  husband) 42, 48, 83
'Gerdy' 97
Germany
  anti-Jewish feeling 50, 106
  Hamburg 48–50
  KH's intelligence reports 104
  loss of Soviet agents after burning
    of Reichstag 106
  proposed military alliance with
    France and Poland 104
  Soviet intelligence on 103–4,
    113–14
  see also Berlin
Gestapo: Soviet agents in 113
GIN (Margaret Browder) 87, 103,
  107
Ginsberg, Samuel 140
  see also Krivitsky, Walter
Giselle, Fraulein (alias of KH) 124
Gitlow, Ben 45, 47, 82, 189–90
  exposure of KH 189
Glading, Percy 162, 179
Goebbels, Dr Josef 4, 128
Goering, Hermann 184, 187
Gorkin, Alexander 225

Gorky (Nizhny Novgorod) 229
  City Prison 226, 228
Gorskaya, Elizaveta 111
  see also Zarubina, Elizaveta
Gorsky, Anatoli 202–3
Gouzenko, Igor 221
Grafpen, Grigory (SAM) *illus*, 142
  background 160
  career 237–8
  contact with KH 161–2
  KH's finances and 174
  and KH's relationship with
    Maclean 177, 181, 182
  report on KH's accommodation
    165–6
Grande, Grigory (alias of Gregorii
  Syroezhkin) 175, 211, 238
Gray, Olga 162
Green Gangs 58
Green, Michael (alias of Itzhak
  Akhmerov) 205
Green, William (President of AFL)
  37
Greinke, William (alias of Itzhak
  Akhmerov) 205
GRU (Soviet military intelligence
  service) operation in Denmark
  130–1
Guderian, General 126
Gursky, Karl Voldemarovich
  (MONGOL) *illus*, 95–7, 99, 100,
  102, 103, 106, 107, 115, 233
  on KH's false passport 105
Gustav (butler) 120–1
GYPSY (KH as) 1, 22–3, 87, 92, 103,
  104, 107, 108, 117, 127, 131, 152,
  153, 206

Hamburg 48–50
Hamburger, Mrs Paul (Ruth
  Kuczynski) 61
Hankey, Lord 203
HANS (Dmitri Bystrolyotov) 139,
  239
Harbin 67, 79
  KH's journey to 68–73

Harold (KH's Hong Kong contact) 63
Harris, Abe (KH's brother) 83, 160,
    175, 210–11
Harris, Esther (KH's mother) 14,
    15–16, 217
  in Canada 19
  meets EB 452
  in New York 43, 82
  pride in British citizenship 82–3
Harris family 9
  and Childs 75
  FBI interview 3, 83, 225
  House of Representatives
    UnAmerican Activities
    Committee and 75
  immigration to the West 6
  importance to KH 6–7, 26, 92,
    225–6, 231
  KH contacts with 82–3, 103, 207,
    214–15, 216, 217
  on KH's birthdate 17
  KH's last letter 230
  move to New York 43
  politics 6
  pride in British citizenship 82–3
  support for KH 3, 25, 48
Harris, Harry ('Bucky') (KH's
    brother) 40, 83
Harris, Isaac (KH's great-uncle) 14,
    15–16
Harris, Jenny (KH's sister) 2, 3, 82–3,
    229
  pride in British citizenship 82–3
Harris, Jessie (KH's sister) 2, 3, 83,
    92, 154, 157, 214, 217, 229, 243
  as KH's confidante 92
Harris, Kitty Natanovna illus, illus,
    illus
  biography: education 4, 19, 38–9;
    social background 4; birthdate
    variations 16–17, 47, 74; moves
    to Winnipeg 18–19; first job 20;
    first protest against unfairness
    20–1; as trade unionist 22, 25,
    27, 31, 35; first intelligence
    assignment 28; happiest night of
    her life 29; moves to Chicago 30;
    as mule 31–3; resists severe
    financial temptation 33; retrained
    as shorthand typist 39; marriage
    to EB 42; in New York 43, 82,
    103, 157, 203; journey to
    Shanghai 48–54; in Moscow
    51–4, 74, 107–9, 131, 133–5,
    140, 153, 199, 200, 220, 226; in
    Shanghai 54–76; journey to
    Harbin 68–73; recruitment by
    Harry Terras 84–6; work in
    Amtorg 84; in Berlin 94–7, 100,
    103, 105–6, 114, 118–19, 122–3;
    first 'active service' assignment
    98; in Paris 100–1, 104, 138–9,
    180–1, 182–3, 185–6, 187–9,
    194–5, 197, 198–9; frustration as
    agent 119; intelligence training
    133–6, 140, 208; in London 140,
    160, 163–6; financial problems
    174, 184; birthday party with
    Maclean 176–7; birthday present
    from Maclean 176, 231; security
    lapse 178, 179; last meeting with
    Maclean 195–6; as teacher
    200–1, 224; in California 201–4;
    distrusted by the Centre 215;
    health 218–20, 226–7; 'isolation'
    226–7; release from prison 227–9;
    funeral 230; diaries destroyed 231
  aliases: Dreyfus, Elizabeth 1, 202,
    207; Harrison, Katherine 1, 47,
    93; Morris, Mrs 1, 73; Read,
    Alice 1, 55, 74; Stein, Elizaveta
    1, 141; Davis, Eleanor 101;
    Giselle, Fraulein 124;
    Trachtenberg, Frau 129
  appearance 1, 3–4
  character 2, 4–5, 26, 61, 207,
    229–30; skills 2; linguistic ability
    4, 19, 136; politics 22, 25, 27,
    35, 41, 133, 183–4, 224; money-
    raising 25; fears 37, 45; as hostess
    60; success at games 75, 108;
    photography skills 119, 137, 151,

164–5, 172–3, 178, 208; memory,
   oral reports from Maclean 173,
   184; limitations as agent 207
code names: ADA 1, 2, 4, 179,
   181, 186, 188, 194, 195, 212,
   213, 215, 216, 217, 220, 229–30,
   231; GYPSY 1, 22–3, 87, 92,
   103, 104, 106, 107, 117, 127,
   131, 152, 153, 206; NORMA 1,
   160, 161, 162, 166, 176
'disappearance' in 1930s 3
identification as Soviet agent 2, 6,
   141, 154, 154–5, 189, 190, 233
KGB files 3, 4, 7–8, 47
language courses as cover 96, 97,
   114–15, 131, 184, 210
nationalities 5–6; applications for
   Soviet citizenship 156–7, 223–4,
   225; American citizenship 206
passports see passports
as radio operator 2, 138, 140, 151,
   156
relationships see Browder, Earl;
   Maclean, Donald; Skonetsky,
   Peter; Toledano, Vicente
safe-houses 100, 121, 127, 149,
   165–6
Harris, Nancy (KH's sister) KNOPKA
   (PUSHBUTTON) 2, 3, 83–4, 217,
   229
Harris, Nathan 14, 15, 16, 92
   as absentee father 26
   in Canada 19
   emigration to London 15–16
   illness 82
   meets EB 452
   moves family to Chicago 30
   political views 17–18, 21, 26
Harris, Tilly (KH's sister) 2, 3, 83,
   217, 229
Harrison, Jack (KH's fictitious uncle)
   (alias of John W. Johnstone) 48
Harrison, Katherine (alias of KH) 1,
   47, 93
Harrison, Mr and Mrs (EB and KH)
   59

Haskell, W.A. (LUND; Shidlov) 74
'Hathaway, Milton' (Thomas Bell) 83
Henderson, Nevile 187
Henri Quatre restaurant, New York
   84–5
Hindenburg, Paul 94, 105
Hitler, Adolf 94, 95–6, 104, 106, 126,
   176, 237, 240
Hong Kong
   EB's involvement 61
   KH's assignment 63
HUNGARIAN (Theodore Mally)
   139
Hutchins, Grace 48

identification of KH as Soviet agent
   2, 6, 141, 154, 154–5, 189, 190,
   233
ILGWU see International Ladies
   Garment Workers
illegal agents
   Berlin 103–4
   finance 102–3
   INO network 80, 81, 82
   radio communications and 120
   restrictions on 118–19
   Shanghai rezidentura 67
'Ilona' 108
Ilyusha (first mate on Komsomol) 107,
   169
Industrial Workers of the World
   (IWW) 24, 36
INO (OGPU foreign department) 67,
   77
   Arturov's report 77–80
   illegal agent network 80, 81, 82;
      finance for 102–3
   and Krivitsky 155
intelligence services: Shanghai 56–7
intelligence training, KH
   for Mexico 208
   in Moscow 133–6, 140
International Ladies Garment
   Workers (ILGWU) 26, 28, 31, 35
International Workers Aid
   Organisation 43

Italy: KH in 125
IWW *see* Industrial Workers of the World

Jakarta
  EB's involvement 61
  KH's assignment 62
'Janos' 99, 100, 106, 107, 115
Japan
  Tanaka Memorial 73
  and US 73
Jena, Frau von 126
Jews
  and Nazi Germany 50, 113
  as Soviet agents 5
  in Tsarist Russia 13–14
Joe *see* Linxin, Joe ('Zhou')
'Johnny' (Chicago contact) 32–3
Johnstone, John W. 48
Juárez, Benito 213

K (woman officer at Moscow Centre) 148–9
Kaminsky, Ivan Nikolayevich 155, 156, 159, 221, 238–9
KARIN 120, 198–9
Karl *see* Gursky, Karl
Karla (Le Carré character) 112
KARP (Yuri Vasilevsky) 188, 210
KGB: KH's files 3, 4, 7–8
KHARON (Grigory Kheifits) 202, 203, 240
Kheifits, Grigory (KHARON) 202, 203, 240
Khrushchev, Nikita 227
King, John 139
Klimov, Lieutenant 231
KMT (Kuomintang) 55, 57, 58, 61
KNOPKA (PUSHBUTTON) (Nancy Bell *née* Harris) 217
Komsomol (ship) 49, 50, 107, 168–9
Konovalets, Colonel 156
Krivitsky, Walter (born Samuel Ginsberg) 140–1
  on counterfeit currency 47
  death 5

debriefing by MI5 197
defection 154–5
exposure of KH 2, 141, 154, 190
FBI information from 154
information on Soviet mole in FO 197
on KH 141, 154
recruitment of agents 113
Kruglov, Sergei 227
Kuczynski, Ruth 61
Kuomintang (KMT) 55, 57, 58, 61
Kvasnikov, Leonid 203

Labour Daily 28
Lamberti (Chicago contact) 31–2, 34–5, 158
Lang, Stefan (alias of Arnold Deutsch) 142, 144, 145
Latvia: KH in 224–6
Le Carré, John: Karla character, real-life equivalents 112
LEGACY (NASLEDTSVO) (Fritz Talbe) 114, 116–18, 241
Lenin, Vladimir Ilyich 27, 80–1, 134
  on Asian strategy 55
Leningrad: KH's first visit 50–1
'Leon' 91–2, 93
LEONID 208, 215–16
LEV (Yuri Vasilevsky) 210
Li (KH's Hong Kong contact) 63
Linxin, Joe ('Zhou') 58–9, 61, 64, 65
LIRIK (LYRIC POET) (Donald Maclean) 161, 162, 163, 166, 168, 178–9, 196
Litvinov, Maxim 156
London
  KH in 2–3, 160, 163–6
  KH posted to 140
  KH's flat 165–6
  KH's parents' emigration to 15–16
  Whitechapel in 1900 *illus*
Los Angeles: KH in 202, 203
Lovestone, Jay *illus*, 44, 45, 82
Lowry, Helen (ELZA) 2, 48, 205
Lozovsky, Solomon 52, 209, 222
Ludwig (co-student in Moscow) 133

Lugonovskaya, Raisa *see* Browder, Raisa
Lukin (alias of Aleksandr Ervin) 127, 129–30, 234–5
LUND 74
Lund (W.A. Haskell) 74
Luriya, Nathan 235

McAlmon, Bob 192
McCarthyism 75, 221, 232
Maclean, Donald *illus*, 146, 147–8, 150
    biography: background 148; recruitment 148–9; Foreign Office appointment 149; access to secret documents 166–9, 170–1; trip to Prague 175, 176; in Paris 182–3; marriage to Melinda 196–7; after marriage 202–3; defection 227; in Moscow 231; death 232
    appearance 193–4
    character 148, 185, 194, 196; indiscretions 178–9, 192–3; lies to Philby 185
    code names: SIROTA 148, 161; WAISE 148, 161; LIRIK (LYRIC POET) 161, 162, 163, 166, 168, 178–9, 196; STUART 179, 181, 186, 194
    and disappearance of *Komsomol* 169
    nuclear weapons information 203
    oral reports to KH 173, 184
    relationship with KH 1–2, 3, 150, 156, 161, 162; changes in relationship 174, 177–8, 186, 191–2, 194, 195–6
    routine on visits to KH 171
    security risk 180
    value of material provided by 167, 171, 176, 186–7, 197
Maclean, Melinda (*née* Marling) 192–4, 196–7
Mafia: KH's involvement 4, 31–2
MAKSIM (Vassily Zarubin) 202, 215, 217

Malenkov, Georgy 227
Mally, Theodore Stepanovich (HUNGARIAN; MALY; MANN; 'Peters') *illus*, 138–40, 141–2, 149, 152, 162, 167–8, 234, 235–6
    death 153
    and disappearance of *Komsomol* 169
    on Maclean 148
    recall to Moscow from UK 153
MALY (Theodore Mally) 139
Manhattan Project 203, 205
Manila
    EB's arrival from 73
    KH's assignment 64–5
MANN (Theodore Mally) 138–9, 234
Mann, Tom *illus*, 54
Marcor, Alejandro Carillo (TEKSAS) 217
MARK (Vilyam Fisher) 242
Marling, Melinda *see* Maclean, Melinda
Meadows, James (probably Abraham Einhorn) 107
Meissner, Otto 122, 123, 233
Menzhinsky, Vyacheslav 77, 80
Mercader, Ramon 210, 238
Mexico 218–19
    KH dissatisfaction with 218–19
    KH in 207, 209–10, 220
    VENONA transcripts on 210
    see also Toledano
MI5: Krivitsky debriefing 197
MI6
    British agent as counterpart to Maclean 168
    information obtained by Maclean 167, 168
    Soviet penetration 150–1
'Michael' (Intourist guide for KH and EB) 50
Mikhoels, Solomon 242
The Mob: KH and 4, 31–2
Molotov, V.M. 80
MONGOL (Karl Gursky) 95–7, 99, 100, 102, 103, 107, 115, 233

Index

Montgomery, Jean (alias of Margaret Browder) 155
MOROZ (FROST) 160
Morris, George (alias of EB) 73–4
Morris, Mrs (alias of KH) 1, 73
Moscow 46, 132–3, 221
  KGB headquarters *illus*
  KH arrested 226
  KH in 51–4, 74, 107–9, 131, 133–5, 140, 153, 199, 200, 220
Moscow Centre (OGPU headquarters) *illus*
  creation of 'communications *rezidenturas*' 127
  lack of trust in KH 215
  and LUND 74
  on Maclean 166, 171
Munzenberg, Willy 106

NASLEDTSVO (LEGACY) (Fritz Talbe) 114, 116–18, 241
Nathan (KH's father) *see* Harris, Nathan
Nazis
  in Berlin 94, 103, 104, 112–13, 128
  in Hamburg 50
  reprisals after Reichstag burning 106
Nazmer, Frau 126
NAZON 188, 199
NELLY (Jane Stowman) 169–70
New York
  CPUSA branch 42–3, 48
  KH in 43, 82, 103, 157, 203
NIKOLAI 160
Nikolayev, Lev (alias of Alexander Orlov) 147
Nizhny Novgorod (Gorky) 226, 228, 229
NKVD
  KH as Maclean's front-line contact 1–2
  on LUND 74
  Margaret Browder as agent 2
  purge of staff 153; KH and

Maclean on 165
Nordwyck (ship) 46, 48–9
NORMA (KH as) 1, 159, 161, 162, 166, 176
'Noulens' (businessman/Comintern spy) 65–6

OBU (One Big Union) 25, 27, 28
  KH and 25, 28
OGPU
  foreign department *see* INO
  headquarters *see* Moscow Centre (OGPU headquarters)
  and OSM 82
  and Shanghai 67
'old-boy' network 7
Oldham, Ernest 139
OLIVER (Antonio Gomez Deans) 229
One Big Union *see* OBU
Operation Barbarossa 113
Oppenheim, E. Phillips: novel used as cipher 66
Oppenheimer, Robert 203, 204, 240
Oriental Literary Society mailbox: Shanghai 66, 74
Orlov, Alexander (born Leiba Lazarevich Feldbin) (SCHWED; 'Lev Nikolayev'; 'Lev Feldel') *illus*, 141–2, 146–7, 183, 242–3
Orlov, Maria 243
Ormsby-Gore, W.G.A. 182
OSM (External Relations Section) 82
Otroshchenko, Colonel Andrei Makarovich 220
OTTO (Arnold Deutsch) 179
Ovakimyan, Gaik 203, 222
Oxford University: suitability for recruitment by Soviet intelligence 144, 146

THE PAIR (Nicholas and Maria Fisher) 212
Papen, Franz von 104, 112
Paris
  KH assignments 100–1, 104,

138–9, 180–1, 182–3, 185–6, 187–9, 194–5, 197, 198–9
Maclean sent to 180, 182–3
Orlov in 147
Soviet Union's unpopularity 187–8
Parparov, Fyodor (YEVGENI) 113, 234, 240
passport blanks: Einhorn's access to 88
passport factories: Roshchin's 100–1
passports, KH's
American 47–8, 74, 92–3, 98, 100–1, 104–5, 115, 156, 157, 159, 160
Canadian 156, 159, 160, 174–5
forgery noticed 104–5
Soviet 141, 199, 222, 224, 229
supplied in Germany 114–15
supplied in Moscow 109, 115
Passy, Rita 126
PATRIOT 213
Pelz, Arthur 152, 158
Pelz, Dorothy 152–3
Perkins (owner of Shanghai ships' chandlers) 59–60, 61, 66–7
'Peters' (alias of Theodore Mally) 162
Philby, Kim (SÖNCHEN; SYNOK) 5, 143–4, 146–8, 149, 150, 151, 175, 185, 195, 227, 235
photography skills: KH 119, 137, 151, 164–5, 172–3, 178, 208
Pitovranov, Evgeny 226, 241–2
Poland
proposed military alliance with France and Germany 104
Soviet intelligence in 79
Pontecorvo, Bruno 238
POP (PRIEST) 88
Powers, Gary 242
Prague
KH in 97–100
Maclean's trip to 175, 176
see also Czech crisis
Pravdin, Vladimir (SERGEI) 217
Profintern 27, 52–3
briefing in Moscow for KH and EB 52

Jakarta and 62
Shanghai posting for KH and EB 45–6, 66

Queen Mary (ship): KH on 89–90

RADIANT (Klaus Behrens) 114
radio communications 120–1
KH as radio operator 2, 138, 140, 151, 156
Raisa see Browder, Raisa
Read, Alice (alias of KH) 1, 55, 73
recognition signals 86, 91, 95, 98, 115–16, 150, 161–2, 204, 211
see also 'Aesop language'
recruitment
of KH 84–6
Krivitsky 113
of Maclean 148–9
Maclean's contacts 167
Stadtler 123–5
suitability of Oxbridge 144
US methods 7
Red Army (Chinese) 66
'Red Milkman' see Childs, Morris
REDAKTOR (Konstantin Umansky) 212, 213–14, 217–18
REDAKTSKIYA (TASS) 214
Reeve, Ella ('Mother Bloor') 36
Reiff, Ignati 146
Reiss, Ignac 154
rendezvous see recognition signals
Riga: KH in 224–6
Roberts, Stanley (OBU chairman) 25–6, 28
Roosevelt, Franklin D. 106, 240
Roshchin, Vasily 60, 73, 100–1, 105
Rotloff, Lieutenant 126
Rozenzweig, Elizaveta 111
see also Zarubina, Elizaveta
Russia
revolution 21–2
Tsarist, Harris family's flight from 6
see also Soviet Union
Russian revolution: influence on KH 22

Index

Ruthenberg, Charles *illus*, 44, 45
Ruthenberg-Pepper-Lovestone group
  (CPUSA faction) 44–5
Ryan, James G. 9, 36
Rybkin, Boris ('Yartsev') 187

safe-houses 100, 121, 122, 127, 149,
  165–6
Sakharovsky, General 238
SAM (Grigory Grafpen) 142, 160,
  237
San Francisco
  KH in 202
  Soviet agents in 203–4, 205
SCHWED (Alexander Orlov) 142,
  146
Secret Intelligence Service *see* MI6
Sedov, Lev 154
Semyonov, Semyon 203
Serebryanskii, Yakov 203–4
SERGEI (Vladimir Pravdin) 217
Serov, Ivan 227
'Sh' (KH's 'rich relation') 184
Shanghai 45, 56–9
  The Bund *illus*, 57, 59
  illegal *rezidentura* 67
  information on KH in 9
  intelligence services 56–7
  International Settlement 68
  KH in 54–76
  police reports on KH 2
  Soviet intelligence in 79
  see also China
Shapiro, Yakov Zakharovich
  (AMBROSIUS) 118, 234, 235
Shidlov (Haskell, W.A.) 74
SHTURMAN (NAVIGATOR)
  (Vicente Toledano) 207, 209, 210,
  214–15, 217–18
Shushkin 239
signals *see* recognition signals
Simon, Sir John 149
Singapore: EB's involvement 61
Singer Sewing Machine Company 67,
  72
SIROTA (Donald Maclean) 148, 161

SIS *see* MI6
Sissmore, Jane 197
Skonetsky, Peter
  KH and 22–3, 24, 28–30, 232
  KH meets again 35, 158–9
  meeting with KH 20
  political activity 21, 24, 27
  in WW1 21
Smedley, Agnes 5, 57, 61, 67–8, 232
Smith, John (alias of Harold
  Stowman) 97, 103, 104, 127–8,
  169–70
Sochi, sanatorium, KH in 108–9
socialism: KH's father and 17–18
Socialist Party of America 26–7
Solovyov 239
SÖNCHEN (Kim Philby) 146
Sorge, Richard 61
Sosnovskaya, Yunona 72, 79, 101,
  232–3
Sosnowski, Jurek 126–7
South-East Asia: EB's involvement 61
Soviet intelligence
  KH and 7
  smuggling of traffic across Atlantic
    93
  training for officers 81
Soviet Union
  first attempt to penetrate British
    intelligence 151
  Harris family's support for 6
  homeless children 132
  interest in China and Far East 55,
    58, 61
  KH and Soviet system 5, 7
  molehunt 168
  proposed military alliance against
    104
  purge of intelligence services 153
  recognition by US 105
  see also INO; OGPU; Russia
Spain: KH in 169, 170
Spiegelglass, Otto (DOUGLAS) 155,
  160
Stadtler: recruitment 123–5
Stalin

anti-Semitism 5
China and 55, 58
and counterfeit currency 47
and CPUSA 43
on INO restructuring 80–1
intelligence chanelled via couriers 3
KH and EB acknowledged by 53
personality cult 134
on training for intelligence officers 81
STEFAN (Arnold Deutsch) 236
Stein, Elizaveta (alias of KH) 1, 141
Stennes, Walter (DRUG) 237
Stevens (cryptographer) 176
Stockholm see Sweden
Stowman, Harold ('John Smith') 170
Stowman, Jane (NELLY) 169–70
STRAHLMANN (Klaus Behrens) 114
STRELA (colleague of Arnold Deutsch) 150
STUART (Donald Maclean) 179, 181, 186, 194
loss of contact in Paris 188
Sudoplatov, Pavel 86, 111, 156, 184, 204–5, 213, 233, 238–9
Sullivan, Thomas 42
Suschitzky, Wolf 150
Sweden
KH in 131
KH's responsibility for 127
Switzerland: Soviet intelligence in 79, 155
SYNOK (Kim Philby) 146
Syroezhkin, Gregorii ('Grigory Grande') 175, 211, 238
Szillard, Leo 203

Tacke, Erich 72, 73, 97, 101, 122–3, 232–3
Talbe, Fritz (NASLEDTSVO (LEGACY)) 114, 116–18, 241
Talbe, Gertrude 114, 116, 117–18
Tanaka Memorial 73
Tao Siang 68

Tarasov (alias of Yuri Vasilevsky) 210
TASS (REDAKTSKIYA) 214, 217
TEKSAS (Alejandro Carillo Marcor) 217
telephone signals see recognition signals
Terras, Harry (alias of Abraham Einhorn) 67–8, 72, 84, 93
identity 87
recruitment of KH 84–6
Thälmann, Ernst 94
THE PAIR (Nicholas and Maria Fisher) 212
Tito: Browder and 222
Toledano, Vicente Lombardo (SHTURMAN [NAVIGATOR]) illus, 207, 209, 211–12, 213–14, 232
KH and 214–15, 216–17, 218
Trachtenberg, Frau (alias of KH) 129
trade unionism
general strike, Winnipeg 24–5
KH and 22, 24
trade unions
Asia, EB and 61
China 58; EB's assignment 53
Pan-Pacific Trades Union Conference, Hankow 54
Trades Union International see Profintern
training for intelligence see intelligence training
Trilliser, Mikhail A. 67, 80, 81–2
Trotsky, Leon 55, 111–12, 209, 210
TUBE ALLOYS project 203
Tudor Hart, Alex 150
Tudor Hart, Edith 150
Tung (first mate of Pearl of the Southern Seas) 62
Turkey: Soviet intelligence in 79

'Ulrike' 108
Umansky, Konstantin (REDAKTOR) 212, 213–14, 217–18
Uncle Isaac see Harris, Isaac
United Kingdom
atomic bomb research 203

domination of Shanghai 56–7
ease of travel to England 140
Foreign Office mole 197
intelligence involvement in China
58, 65–6
KH's intelligence training for 135
Maclean's access to secret docu-
ments 166–9, 170–1, 176
and proposed military alliance
against Soviet Union 104
Secret Intelligence Service *see* MI6
Soviet first attempt to penetrate
British intelligence 151
Soviet intelligence in 79
Soviet Union as model 143–4
Special Branch 57, 65
spying on US 168
see also London
United States
American Communist Party *see*
CPUSA
atomic secrets 203, 204
and Czech crisis, information
provided by Maclean 184
Department of Justice, report on
KH 2
intelligence services and KH 2
involvement in China 58
and Japan 73
McCarthyism 221
Office of Naval Intelligence: report
on KH 2; and KH in Shanghai
66, 73
recognition of Soviet Union 105
State Department, suspicion of KH
92–3
see also California; Chicago; New
York

Van (Harry Terras' friend) 68–73
Vasilevsky, Yuri (KARP; LEV;
'Tarasov') 188, 210–11, 212, 214,
215–16
Veiynshtok (interrogator of Artuzov)
154
VENONA intercepts

exposure of KH 2, 6
information on KH 4, 9
on Mexico 210, 212, 215, 216, 219
Voroshilov, Kliment 53

WAISE (Donald Maclean) 148, 161
Weizsäcker, Ernest von 187
Whitechapel in 1900 *illus*
Wilkinson, Vivian 48
Wilson, Sir Horace 187
Winnipeg 18–19
general strike 24–5
KH's journey as mule 34
Wohltat, Dr Helmut 187
Wohlweber, Ernst (ANTON) 131,
241
Woolwich Arsenal spy ring 162, 179
workers' movements: and Russian
revolution 21–2
Workers' Party (USA) 27

Yartsev (alias of Boris Rybkin) 187
Yatskov, Anatoly 203
YEVGENI (Fyodor Parparov) 113,
234, 240
Yezhov, N.I.: Krivitsky and 154
'Yuri' (Intourist guide for KH and EB
in Moscow) 51

Zarubin, Vassily Mikhailovich
(BETTY, MAKSIM; 'Zubilin') *illus*,
237
appearance 110–11
contact with US nuclear scientists
203
and EB 222
GRU operation 130–1
illegal *rezidenturas* run by 113, 118,
234
and KH 119, 123, 202, 206, 207,
215, 217, 222
marriage to Liza 112
safe-houses 122
and Tacke 123
Zarubina, Anna 111
Zarubina, Elizaveta Yulevna (Liza)

(ERNA; Elizaveta Gorskaya;
Elizaveta Rozenzweig) *illus*, 237
  appearance 111
  Blyumkin assignment 111–12
  character 5, 111
  contact with US nuclear scientists
  203

dentist/agent and 204–5
  on EB 222
  KH and 122–3, 206, 230
  meeting with KH 115
Zarubina, Zoya 112
Zubilin (alias of Vassily Zarubin)
  202